INSIDE TREK

To Kelly this
Please enjoy this
book! Thanks,
nice meeting
you!
Best always,
[signature]
11/14/04

Also by Susan Sackett

Letters to Star Trek

Star Trek Speaks!
with Fred and Stanley Goldstein

The Making of Star Trek the Movie
with Gene Roddenberry

You Can Be a Game Show Conrestant and Win
with Cheryl Blythe

Say Goodnight Gracie! The Story of Burns and Allen
with Cheryl Blythe

The Hollywood Reporter Book of Box Office Hits

Prime-Time Hits

Hollywood Sings!

The Hollywood Reporter Book of Box Office Hits
Second Edition

INSIDE TREK

*My Secret Life with
Star Trek Creator
Gene Roddenberry*

by Susan Sackett

HAWK PUBLISHING : TULSA

Published in the United States by HAWK Publishing Group.

HAWK and colophon are trademarks belonging to the HAWK Publishing Group.

Printed in the United States of America.

Library of Congress Cataloging in Publication Data
Sackett, Susan
Inside Trek/Susan Sackett–HAWK Publishing ed.
   p. cm.
   ISBN 1-930709-42-0

   1.Nonfiction–Television
   2. Nonfiction–Movies
   3. Star Trek
   I. Title
   [PS3563.I42145R4 2000]
   813'.54   80-52413
   CIP

HAWK Publishing web address: www.hawkpub.com

H987654321

To J.B., my best friend,
for teaching me so many things

PROLOG : November 1, 1991.

November 1, 1991. I recall only a series of moments from that day. When I look back, I realize how much of it my mind has blanked out — a survival tactic, most likely. Still, some memories cannot be erased, no matter how I might long for this.

As my friend Mark Hahn and I entered the grounds of Forest Lawn, with its sprawling, green hillside overlooking the 134 Freeway, I had a sense of the surreal — like a dream of being in a movie or play, where everyone knew their part but me. "Go here." Okay. "Stand there." Okay. "Sit there." Okay. Mechanically, I did as I was told.

We entered a large theatre-sized auditorium. Mounted on an easel dominating the stage was a gigantic portrait of Gene Roddenberry. It was a blowup of a familiar photo, one I had mailed out to fans hundreds of times — the sapphire V-neck sweater, the paler blue background, the mischievous, bemused expression. When I saw it, my knees buckled.

Mark and I were led to a section on the left. Seated behind me was Gene's son-in-law, Richard Compton, and alongside him was a pretty, older woman I'd never seen before. She introduced herself as Eileen Roddenberry, Gene's first wife. She was smartly dressed in her tailored knit suit and seemed very refined. All these years I had been hearing about the monster who had been wife number one, but here was a woman who had been divorced from Gene for twenty-two years, yet still cared enough to attend his memorial service.

As people arrived, slides synchronized to an audio track were projected onto a giant overhead screen. Scenes from Gene's life played across the screen — Gene as a child; in his youth; as a young Army Air Corps officer; at work on the Los Angeles Police Force, and then, to the accompaniment of dramatic music welling up in the background, scenes from his marriage to Majel, his second wife, to whom he was wed those final twenty-two years. "Unchained Melody" crescendoed to a photo of Gene and Majel embracing.

Corridor outside our offices, fourth floor, Building G, circa 1980.

The rest of the memorial service was a tear-streaked blur. I remember Nichelle Nichols singing something. Ray Bradbury eulogized Gene, as did Whoopi Goldberg. Patrick Stewart read something. I looked around the audience and spotted Mayor Tom Bradley and Police Chief Daryl Gates and the casts of both *Star Treks*. The family was clustered front row center. Majel sat with their son Rod (his nickname from babyhood — he's really Gene Roddenberry, Jr.). The teenaged boy looked grim. Gene's two daughters, Darleen, the oldest, and Dawn, to whom I had always been closest, were seated side by side, tearfully clutching each other's hands.

The service — I have no idea how long it lasted — ended, and we filed outside into the warmth of the California afternoon, where a squadron of private airplanes buzzed the courtyard in the "missing man" formation. I wondered what Gene would have made of it all.

I spotted a wheelchair with Gene's eighty-seven-year-old mother, Caroline "Glen" Roddenberry. She was only seventeen years old when she gave birth to Gene, and I knew she must be feeling terrible pain at losing her firstborn child and only son.

"Glen, I'm so sorry," was all I could say. I bent over and hugged her.

She smiled up at me. "I hope you won't forget me," she said through her tears.

"Oh, of course not! How could I ever forget you?" I wanted to add, How could I ever forget the mother of the man I'd been in love with for seventeen years?[1]

I longed to tell her, to tell the world. But I knew it had been Gene's wish to keep silent. We had sworn our love for each other, and I had always held fast to his desire of maintaining silence about our relationship. I had planned to do this for the rest of my life.

But the time seems right now. I've kept the genie imprisoned too long. At last I'm ready to uncork this bottle and let my story spill out. I'm sure Gene would understand. Just as he had understood everything from the start . . .

---

[1] Gene's mother died in 1998, at the age of ninety-four.

LOG ENTRY 1:

It was 1966. The Supremes' "You Can't Hurry Love" was at the top of the charts, and mini-skirts were giving people their first post-war peek at female thighs. Lyndon Baines Johnson was serving his first full term as President of the United States to the accompaniment of escalating protests about the war in Vietnam. And I was preparing for my own first full term, as a teacher at Miami's Coconut Grove Elementary School.

School began right after Labor Day. I usually didn't have much time for television, but for some reason, Thursday September 15th found me turning the knob absently through the local TV channels (no remote controls in those days!). Something caught my eye: What was this? People in strange costumes, working at desks that were not quite desks, lots of strange sound effects, blinking lights — could this be a science fiction program? I loved science fiction! But what really got my attention — and the attention of many people the world over — was a man with pointed ears. Here were all these people working together on some problem or other, cooperating, and there was a man with pointed ears in their midst who seemed to go unnoticed. I wanted to shout, "Look, you people! Don't you see that man over there? He's got pointed ears! Why don't you see that?" I soon realized that they were aware of his ears, but it just didn't matter to them. Wow! Something was happening here, and I had to know more.

Gene signs a copy of The Making of Star Trek for some fans.

Had I known that this was going to be the turning point in my life, I might have made a note of it on paper — "Dear Diary, Today I saw my first episode of *Star Trek*."[2] I had failed to recognize this as an epiphany, but I was hooked.

In 1968, I fulfilled a lifelong dream to live in Los Angeles, California. Since I was a child, I had dreamed about working in television. I quit teaching and went to work for NBC, the network that aired my favorite show, *Star Trek*. Unfortunately, my job as secretary in a publicity office did not take me anywhere near *Star Trek*. And not long after I landed my job, I learned the sad news that *Star Trek* had just been canceled. Talk about timing. Here I was, meeting people who actually worked on that show, interviewed its cast members, reviewed its scripts, had contact with that wonderful series, who might at any moment find a way to invite me to the set to visit . . . and now the show had been given the ax.

My NBC years were great, but eventually I moved on. Then, one rainy January day in 1974 as I drove to work, the car behind me slammed into my ancient Rambler. Unable to continue at my job due to a sprained neck and back, I spent the next five months on disability insurance, and three more collecting unemployment. To make ends meet, I held garage sale after garage sale, wondering if I would ever work again.

And then, with one phone call, my whole life changed.

The call was from Fred Bronson. I'd met Fred several years before, when he was a publicity intern at NBC. We had subsequently worked together at several science fiction conventions and had developed a close friendship.

Fred knew I was job-hunting and told me he had a hot lead on an opening: Majel Roddenberry was looking for someone to work as a clerk in her Lincoln Enterprises mail order business. "Who's Majel Roddenberry?" I asked, aware of the name Gene Roddenberry, and wondering if there was some connection. Then I remembered she was the *Star Trek* actress Majel Barrett, who had married Gene Roddenberry in 1969.

I had actually met the Roddenberrys a couple of years earlier, in 1972, when I had acted as celebrity coordinator for a science fiction convention produced by Bjo Trimble (whom I had met through Fred). I had no connection to fandom then and had never done anything like that before, but Bjo promised I would have a chance to meet two of my heroes — Ray Bradbury, my favorite science fiction author, and Gene Roddenberry, the creator of *Star Trek*, so I'd jumped at the celebrity coordinator offer.

The event was held over the long Thanksgiving weekend. On Friday after the holiday, I was looking over my program notes in the pressroom when an almost inaudible voice greeted me. "Hi, I'm Gene Roddenberry. I'm supposed to check in here."

From my seated position, my eyes scanned upward searching for the top of this 6' 3" tree of a man. I was rewarded with a smiling, expectant face and green-gray eyes that beamed from beneath a sandy, unruly thatch of hair. The tree was dressed in a blue jeans leisure suit, the popular attire of the day. I jumped to a standing position, although at 5'1", from his perspective, it most likely didn't appear that anything had changed.

He handed me the famous *Star Trek* "Blooper Reel" as I escorted him to the auditori-

---

[2] *Star Trek* premiered Sept. 8, 1966, but I missed out on that episode; I was a late bloomer, becoming a fan only after the second episode aired on Sept. 15.

um of the Ambassador Hotel (the same hotel in which Robert Kennedy had been assassi-
nated three years before). We chitchatted as we walked, and I remember thinking what a
remarkably soft, gentle voice he had for a person of such imposing stature. He immediately made me feel at ease with a smile that reached clear to my heart.

One of my assignments was to assemble the guests of honor for the banquet that
evening. I noticed a very tall, dark-haired woman accompanying Gene and recognized her
as his wife, Majel Barrett, who had played Nurse Chapel on *Star Trek*. Even without her
blonde Nurse Chapel hairdo, there was no mistaking that familiar face. She and Gene
were to be seated together at a table with ten paying fans, but there was an overflow of
guests, so it was decided to add another table, which then needed a celebrity at its head.
I asked Majel if she would mind being separated from her husband so the other guests
could have a celebrity, too. I felt a bit guilty about this, since the pair had already settled
into their chairs, but Majel agreed to make the move. Gene indicated her vacated seat by
his side, and after a moment's hesitation, I took my place next to my hero as reward for
my convention chores. The conversation wasn't particularly memorable, but just being in
the presence of this man was more than I had ever hoped for. I was in heaven.

So when Fred called, memories of that encounter with Gene and his wife stirred a
vague feeling of déjà vu. Still, my first reaction was, "No, I don't want to work in mail
order." But after two more weeks of Tuna à la Mode, Tuna au Gratin and Tureen of Tuna,
I turned in my can opener and picked up the telephone.

When I rang Majel, she asked me how fast I could type; I said 80 words a minute,
apparently an astounding speed for those days. "You know, my husband Gene is looking
for a secretary," she said. I learned that Gene, who had been producing movies and pilots
for television since *Star Trek*'s cancellation, had just completed a film at Warner Bros. studios. He was now between projects (Hollywoodese for unemployed), and he'd moved his
office to his home, taking with him his studio-assigned secretary Ralph Naveda. Ralph
was anxious to return to Warner's because he had accrued pension benefits and a health
plan. He was a company man. I thought he was nuts. Who cared about benefits when
you could work for Gene Roddenberry?

I had once been in Gene's office on the Warner lot, where I was dispatched to pick up
some film for another Bjo-run convention, Equicon '73. It was a Saturday, and Gene was-
n't in, but his art director Matt Jefferies was there, hard at work on plans for the sets of
Gene's upcoming TV pilot, *Planet Earth*. I recognized Matt as the man responsible for
designing the Starship *Enterprise* and was delighted to be in his presence. Matt was most
charming and gave me a tour of the offices and the futuristic designs on his drawing
boards. While I waited for him to locate the film reels, he told me to be seated at Gene
Roddenberry's secretary's desk. I didn't want to appear star struck in front of Matt, but
my heart was racing just being there. At the same time, I had the oddest, slightly precog-
nitive feeling as I sat in that chair, but I quickly dismissed it.

And now I was going to be interviewed for the job of Gene Roddenberry's secretary. I
began to wonder if there really was such a thing as predestination. Had I known, deep
down inside, that this would occur? It just seemed that everything that was happening
was somehow being orchestrated for me — and who was I to fight fate?

LOG ENTRY 2 :

The directions Gene had given me over the phone were simple — up Coldwater Canyon, left on Cherokee, left on Evelyn, left again on Leander Place. I was nervous and excited as I drove for the first time through the Trousdale section of Los Angeles, where it meets the city limits of Beverly Hills. Several times within the short distance of a few blocks, I crisscrossed from L.A. to Beverly Hills and back again into L.A. At last I arrived at the address and parked in the cul-de-sac by his home, a rather large sand-colored house in a very well-to-do neighborhood. I expected to be greeted by a servant, but after a few seconds the door opened and Gene was standing there, clad in brown corduroy Bermuda shorts, pink polo shirt, and sandals, grinning and pumping my hand enthusiastically. There I was, Dorothy at the gate to Oz, and the Wizard was home! The familiar green-gray eyes squinted with merriment at some unknown inner joke as he ushered me in.

I followed him up the stairs to his office where he conducted the interview. Some interview. His first question to me was, "Are you related to [producer] Bill Sackheim?" I politely replied that no, my last name was Sackett. Oh God, I thought, does that mean I won't get the job? He kept smiling with amusement and bade me sit. He had a way of putting people at ease, a Gene Roddenberry trademark, I later learned, and I immediately took to him. It was *like* at first sight.

It was lunchtime, and as we talked, from time to time he absently scooped up mouthfuls of blueberry yogurt from a paper container. "Today is my 53rd birthday, and I'm cele-

From his bedroom balcony, Gene looks out over his swimming pool and all of Beverly Hills. This was the home in which I first worked with Gene.

brating it with — yogurt!" I glanced at the calendar on his desk. It read August 19, 1974. Before I could wish him happy birthday, he continued, "Majel and I just returned from La Costa." I smiled. I had never heard of La Costa, but it seemed to have some significance. "We worked out at the spa and ate all our meals there. I took off ten pounds." He indicated the yogurt cup. "We were both practically alcoholics before we checked in." Again I smiled and nodded. He seemed especially pleased at this last remark. I hadn't a clue as to how I should respond.

We talked about our mutual friend, Fred Bronson. Gene told me what he was working on, now that he was away from a studio. Finally, he began talking about the job and my qualifications. I reached into my briefcase and, being careful not to extract my writing, assistant publicist or TV commercial coordinator resumés, I located the one designated "secretary." He immediately placed this one-page summary of my life as an ace secretary in his center desk drawer. I had expected him to study it thoroughly and was a little disappointed when he didn't even glance at it. "I'll read it in a bit," he said. (Many years later, I found that resume still shoved in the back of his center drawer, as unread as on the day I first handed it to him. "Why didn't you ever read my resume?" I asked him when I found it. "Because I knew you could do the job just from your interview.")

One of the first things he asked me was if I was a fan. I wasn't prepared for this and wasn't quite sure how to answer. It was obvious he didn't recall our first encounter at Bjo's convention. "Well, I'm familiar with the show . . ." I began. "Good! I wouldn't want to hire a big fan. It could get in the way of work." I kept my mouth shut and nodded agreement.

He told me the basics about the job, like where my office would be, where the supplies were kept, etc. He introduced me to Ralph and asked if I could start tomorrow. Was he serious? Of course I could!

I phoned my mother that night to give her the good news. "He writes science fiction books, right?" she asked. She thought I was working for Ray Bradbury, a not uncommon confusion shared by these two science fiction giants.

The next day I arrived at 8:30 — thirty minutes ahead of schedule in order to make a good impression. Ralph answered the door, and I was told that Gene was already up in his den, as he referred to his home office, hard at work. Ralph gave me a guided tour of the house. The library, which was Ralph's (and now my) office, was off the hallway/balcony overlooking the two-story-high living room. The centerpiece of the living room was a hot-pink conversation-pit sectional facing around an enormous inch-thick glass coffee table. A fireplace soared through both stories, to a height of about twenty-five feet. A stuffed and mounted swordfish had found its final resting place on the wall opposite the fireplace.

Gene had taken over one of the four upstairs bedrooms for his office. The room had once belonged to his daughter, Dawn, who had lived several years with her father and stepmother as a teenager. It had the best view in the house. On a clear day you could see all twenty-six miles across the sea to Santa Catalina Island. The rest of the upstairs consisted of a guestroom, the master bedroom (complete with walk-in closets but a surprisingly small bathroom), and the baby's nursery.

Ralph continued my guided tour with a visit to the nursery, where we tiptoed up to an infant's crib. There, fast asleep on his stomach, was a tiny, black-haired five-month-old infant — Gene Roddenberry, Jr. Gene later told me that all young Roddenberry males are called Rod; it had been his own nickname until he was well into adulthood. Little Rod, completely oblivious to his ancestry, slumbered on as we retraced our tiptoes out into the hall and closed the door.

Back downstairs, Ralph showed me the kitchen and introduced me to the live-in housekeeper. I was also introduced to the microwave at this time — the "funny oven," as the Roddenberrys called it. It was the first microwave I'd ever seen, and I was enchanted by this new toy. He also indicated the well-stocked refrigerator, from which I could help myself at any time. The remainder of the downstairs consisted of a maid's room and bath, a long, narrow dining room, a front terrace which was later enclosed and made into a playroom for Rod, and a rec room with pool table and myriad games, including Pachinko and "Pong," the forerunner of modern video games.

While I was trying to take all this in, Ralph walked me back upstairs to his/my office and gave me a quick ten-minute lesson in how to use the Dictaphone and where things were kept. The next thing I knew, he was saying good-bye and wishing me luck! It was barely 9:30 in the morning, and I was on my own.

Gene wasted no time in making me feel at home. He told me to get some coffee from the kitchen. "What should I say when the phone rings?" I asked. "How about, '4474?'" he suggested. (These were the last four digits of his phone number at the time.) And so it went. At lunchtime, the housekeeper fixed us both sandwiches and oversized brandy snifters of Lipton instant iced tea, which we enjoyed at an umbrella table by the pool. Gene brought the rolodex to the table, and as we ate, he explained the names with which I needed to become familiar — his accountants, Singer, Lewak, Greenbaum & Goldstein, his attorney Leonard Maizlish, and other important contacts. I jotted everything down, striving for the instant recall I prided myself on, but finding this all so overwhelming. I was riddled with insecurities in those days, especially after eight months of not working; yet sometime that first week, Gene said to me, "I predict you will go far." I was puzzled by this remark coming so early in our working relationship. Had he seen something in me of which I was unaware? I was mindful of the fact that Dorothy (D.C.) Fontana, who had been one of his secretaries during the first series, had become a story editor and a successful television writer. So I certainly wasn't about to argue.

Gene introduced me to Majel that evening when she returned home from her office in Hollywood. She didn't recall our brief encounter at Bjo's con any more than Gene did. With so many people crossing paths with these celebrities, I wasn't really surprised. It was a highlight in *my* life, not theirs.

On the first evening of my new job, Majel told me she had spent the day at her mail order company, Lincoln Enterprises. A few years earlier, Gene had developed this business to answer fans' requests for *Star Trek* souvenirs. After their marriage, Gene turned the business over to Majel. With few acting parts coming her way following the demise of *Star Trek*, Majel filled much of her leisure time with golf each Tuesday and Friday, but she was also grateful for the opportunity to occupy herself several hours a week by supervising a staff at the Hollywood warehouse where the orders were processed. *Star Trek*, which had failed so miserably during its three-year network run, had become a runaway hit in syndication, and there was a growing demand for Lincoln's newly developed line of Paramount-licensed products.

Majel and I shook hands and smiled pleasantly at each other. She insisted on pouring me a drink, which surprised me because Gene had made such an issue about the recent drying out they had done in La Costa. I asked for a Diet Coke, but she encouraged me to have something stronger, which I accepted reluctantly — after all, this was my first day on a new job. As she handed me a glass of champagne, I noticed how tall she was — nearly as tall as Gene. I also noticed that her hair was black, not the blonde it had been in the TV series.

"I'm lucky I have any hair at all," she exclaimed. She explained that when she had been pregnant with Rod, her body had undergone numerous physical changes, including the considerable thinning of her hair. I gathered her pregnancy difficulties were attributable to her age — she was less then three weeks shy of her forty-second birthday when Rod had been born the previous February. Still, if the pregnancy had taken its toll six months earlier, its effects seemed to have worn off. She looked good for her age. There was a rough beauty about her, one that had an angular edge to it. Her face looked almost sculpted, with symmetrical dimpling on either side of her narrow mouth which, when she smiled, displayed a set of perfect-for-the-camera teeth. Her dark hair flowing over a long neck brought out the bright blue of her eyes.

The couple planned an early dinner, and they both insisted I come along. So with Rod in tow, we headed for Eddie's Little Shanghai on the Sunset Strip. At our table in this popular Chinese eatery (no longer in existence), Rod, now fully awake and smiling, gazed worshipfully up from his infant carrier as Gene tickled and cooed to his son. "Those two have a special relationship," Majel confided. And so the evening went. Just the three-and-a-half of us Hollywood folks, out for a nice early dinner. I could get used to this, I told myself, as I pretended I'd been doing this all my life.

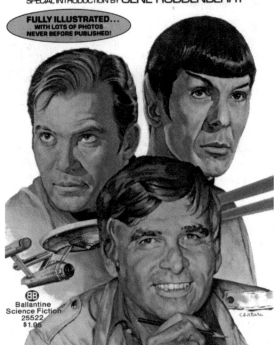

LETTERS
to
STAR TREK

SUSAN SACKETT

SPECIAL INTRODUCTION BY GENE RODDENBERRY

FULLY ILLUSTRATED...
WITH LOTS OF PHOTOS
NEVER BEFORE PUBLISHED!

Ballantine
Science Fiction
25522
$1.95

LOG ENTRY 3 :

The next day, it was business as usual. I settled into my routine of getting tea (I've never liked the taste of coffee), then checking Gene's out box for any dictation tapes to transcribe. Gene did practically all of his initial writing by speaking into a stenorette. He seldom sat down to work at the typewriter; he liked to speak out loud, as if he were reading from some draft he saw in his head, inserting every punctuation mark as he spoke. He did this with everything he wrote — letters, scripts, speeches, novels. When he finished a session, he'd remove the tape from his machine, replace it with a fresh one and give the recording to me to transcribe. I'd bring him the freshly typed pages and pick up a new tape, and he'd begin marking up the hard copy. He'd write his first twenty pages of a project, then rewrite it at least a dozen times before moving on. This would drive me crazy, because I'd be waiting to see the outcome, and he'd be busily perfecting the early part. But it was a good lesson in writing, from a master.

Cover art from my first book, **Letters to Star Trek.**

I loved hearing his dictation. He had excellent diction, although he didn't put much drama into his speaking. It was hard to believe that I was privileged to be the first person ever to hear his creations as his gentle voice whispered directly (via my twin stenorette and earpiece) into my ear. Whenever he reached the end of a tape, he invariably would say, "And that's all there is on this tape, Susan. Thank you very much." In seventeen years and thousands of tapes, he never once failed to do this. His traditional Southern mother must have been a stickler for manners when she was rearing him. Gene was the most polite person I ever worked with. For nearly all the years I was with him, he thanked me each night before I'd leave the office "for all your help today."

In the middle of my first week of employment, Gene gave me a book. "Here's your first gift," he said, handing me a copy of The Gulag Archipelago, by Aleksandr Solzhenitsyn. It was six hundred pages of tiny type with hardly any paragraph breaks! Was I expected to read this and report on it? "Like all Russian books, this one is too wordy," he informed me. I thanked him, excited to be receiving a present, and began reading it that night. I got as far as page 24 and threw in the towel. Gene left for a speaking trip the next day and forgot all about the book, so I never had to discuss it with him. (I still own this enormous paperback and hope to read it someday when I'm retired.)

About a week after I had begun working at the Roddenberry home, I got the chance to see Gene and Majel strut their stuff as "Mr. and Mrs. Star Trek." Just before noon, as I glanced out my second-floor office window to the street below, a stretch limo pulled up to their driveway. Soon Gene and Majel emerged from their bedroom, oozing casual Hollywood elegance — he in a denim leisure suit, she in a chic knit outfit. "We're off to the Wax Museum opening," Gene announced as they hurried out the door. So while they were whisked away to the Movieland Wax Museum in Buena Park to help launch the new Star Trek exhibit, I was entrusted to hold down the fort, my first time alone in their huge house. Although I felt a bit wistful watching them drive off, I was pleased that they had this much confidence in my ability to manage things.

A couple of hours later when they returned, Gene told me how much fun it was for him to be together again with some of the cast members — Leonard, Bill, De, Nichelle — the names dropped, and so did my jaw. They had all been chatting about a possible new Star Trek series. Could this happen? I could hardly contain my excitement.

Gene really went out of his way to see that I was made a member of the household, and his family soon became my surrogate family. About three times a week, Majel and Gene invited me to stay for potluck. Although Majel had household help, she insisted on doing the cooking, and she fixed most of the nightly meals. My tuna casserole days were still fresh in my memory, so I jumped at the chance to have home cooking.

The free dinners were my only perks. I had neither health plan nor pension in those early days, but I did get a raise by my third week. Gene was out on a speaking tour and telephoned from the road to see how things were going at home. I told him all was going "swimmingly," one of his favorite terms. "Splendid!" he replied, using another favorite word. "Oh, and by the way. I've decided to give you a raise." I held my breath. I was earning $150 a week, $50 less than at my last job, but so what? I loved what I was doing. Still, who doesn't appreciate a raise? Then he apologized, and said it would be only $5.00 a week more, all he could afford. And I realized this must be true. He was not being reimbursed by anybody for my salary — it came out of his own pocket. And Paramount hadn't paid him a dime in profits yet. (Gene said they claimed *Star Trek* was still $1,000,000 in the red — an oft-quoted figure at the time.) So I was thrilled with the idea of the raise, not the amount. To think — I had pleased him enough to want to offer this. I thanked him profusely.

On afternoons when we didn't have much work to do, Gene would suggest that we take a swim break. He kept the pool heated to a bathtub-like ninety-two degrees, telling me that Majel froze if it was any cooler. Also, the prescribed dress code for swimming was — nothing. Nada. In the buff. This custom began innocently enough with infant Rod's swimming instructor, Lynne, of the famous Crystal Scarborough Swim School. Infants as young as four and five months old were taught to hold their breath and blow bubbles underwater while supervised by parents and instructor. Lynne would implore the baby to "Kick kick, paddle, paddle" and "Blow bubbles," while offering a demonstration. At that age, so the theory goes, the child still retains a natural instinct to hold its breath and has not developed any fears of the water (although this should never be attempted without a professional instructor). Lynne also insisted that the baby should be in as close to a natural state as possible, i.e., without a tiny swimsuit, which she felt would inhibit Rod. Somehow, Gene had been able to persuade her that this rule should apply to everyone (as if Rod, at the age of five months, really cared). His motivation, no doubt, was to see this curvaceous blonde instructor as naked as the day *she* was born. So Lynne, Gene, Majel, and all invited guests including myself were encouraged to swim in the nude. I was terribly embarrassed at first, but figured this was the Hollywood thing to do, and I certainly didn't want to be classified a prude.

Gene saw my hesitation and teasingly labeled me a "Puritan." At first, I was bewildered by this allusion. I'd always confused Puritans with Pilgrims — history wasn't my favorite subject in school — so I pictured myself in a huge white-collared and long-sleeved dress, fixing turkey for the Indians. No way was I going to be thought of as a Pilgrim or a Puritan. I admired this man greatly, and I didn't want him to think I wasn't just as hip as he was. And so I shed my clothes, although not all my inhibitions, and took the plunge into what I was certain was Hollywood decadence.

Little did I realize that as I stripped off my clothing, I was also about to uncover a whole new aspect of my life.

LOG ENTRY 4 :

My early days working for Gene were filled with typing endless rewrites of a novel he called *Starship*. On my first day of employment, Gene needed a fresh typing of a chapter about the hero, whose name I've long forgotten, standing in line at the grocery store. In a stream of consciousness, this character prattles on about a cockroach in the razor blades by the checkout stand. The book seemed promising, but it wasn't paying any bills, and there was no ticking clock, no deadline connected to it. Several weeks later, with only a few chapters to show for the effort, the story was abandoned when Gene received a more lucrative offer.

One of his former secretaries, Anita Doohan (Jimmy "Scotty" Doohan's ex-wife), was working as a producer for Sandy Howard Productions. She had suggested Gene for a badly needed rewrite of a script called *Magna One*, which they were readying for filming by 20th Century Fox. Gene was, at that time, in dire need of an income and not too proud to be a writer for hire. He jumped at the offer.

Set in the year 2111, the story concerned an underwater mining city. The eponymous "Magna One" (were there to be others?) was a Stephen Kingesque sub-oceanic bulldozer gone amok. It was busily chomping the divers and denizens of the deep instead of

Gene gives a talk at one of his college lectures. These sustained him financially throughout most of the '70s, the years in which Star Trek was not being produced.

doing the mining job for which it was intended. Most of the project, including Gene's pol- ish, was forgettable. It wasn't his fault; it was the material he was saddled with in this rewrite. Nevertheless, he took it as seriously as he could, turning something hokey into what could have been an entertaining bit of B-drama.

Two things about the *Magna One* script still stand out in my mind. One was Gene's fascination with the word "maw." In long descriptive passages never intended to be read by any audience Gene took great care in describing the machine's giant maw — this thing was half a mile wide! He seemed to take a delight in the sheer size of this maw, or of any- thing of gargantuan size. Years later he would find a way for this to metamorphose into the giant cloud of V'Ger (*Star Trek: The Motion Picture*), and yet again in the new, improved *Star Trek: The Next Generation* Starship Enterprise NCC-1701D, which was described as being as huge as the Paramount lot! The other thing I noticed was his cre- ativity when it came to coining words. The man who brought us "phaser," "tricorder" and "tritanium" decided that "submersible" was too much of a mouthful. He quickly referred to the two-person vessels in the story as "submersiles." By dropping the "b," (and an extra syllable) he gave it a touch all his own. I grew to recognize this coining of words and phrases as a Roddenberrian trademark.

One evening, less than a month after I started my new job, I was enjoying dinner at home in front of the TV set as usual, when I bit down on a hamburger and a sliver of a bone chip wedged in a tooth filling, cleaving the tooth neatly in two. I saw the dentist early the next morning, but I still showed up at the Leander house for work as usual. I did- n't mention my aching tooth, but I did take the medication the dentist had prescribed — Tylenol with codeine. I had no appetite, which meant that I was taking these tablets on an empty stomach. Around two o'clock, I suddenly had the urge to barf, excused myself from dictation and stuck my head in a toilet bowl in the guest bathroom. Not feeling a whole lot better, I returned to the task at hand. Gene took one look at my face and guessed that something was wrong. I was about to protest when another wave of nausea hit; I barely made it to the john in time. Gene insisted that I lie down in the guestroom, and I didn't argue; the world had begun to swirl around me. I fell into a heavy sleep, not awakening until about 6:00 p.m., when I felt a hand on my forehead. I opened my eyes to see Gene, a concerned look on his face, smiling over me. I have never forgotten that moment and the genuine concern he showed for me. I was embarrassed about missing the afternoon's work, but he said to forget it. Did I want to spend the night in the guest- room? I assured him I was okay to drive and needed to get home to feed my dog. He helped me up, making sure I was really all right as he walked me safely to my car.

During the first few years or so, when we were working out of the house, Gene always saw to it that I was included in Roddenberry family outings. One Saturday not long after I had begun working for him, Gene invited me to come along for a day at Dis- neyland. I adore Disneyland and couldn't wait to see Gene's reaction to it. I thought he would be very childlike and enjoy all the rides, but it was really Majel who was more into the Mickey Mouse spirit. I was surprised how easily Gene grew tired of the park, appearing almost bored. Majel, however, was completely oblivious to this, totally unconcerned about her husband's lack of enthusiasm at spending the day surrounded by squealing children. She was having the time of her life and so were Rod (still an infant in a stroller), the nanny and myself. We visited all the major rides with time out for lunch at the invitation-only Club 33, a secret oasis for VIPs and the only place in the park that served liquor. Leave it to Gene to know about this restaurant. By mid-afternoon, Gene had had his fill of "The Happiest Place on Earth," finally persuading Majel it was time to leave. We took the monorail to the Disneyland Hotel, where he and Majel ordered drinks in one of the bars, while Rod happily crawled around under the tables. Much revived, Gene treated us all to a nice dinner in the hotel. But as far as the park was concerned, he'd had enough. I don't remember him ever visiting Disneyland again, although many years later he took Rod and grandson Steve to Walt Disney World in Orlando.

By now I was starting to notice the importance drinking seemed to play in the Roddenberrys' lives. Before coming to work for Gene, I had never been around heavy drinkers. Most Jewish homes have little emphasis on drinking alcohol. Aside from wine at Passover, and an occasional scotch and something at a party, I had never seen my father take a drink. My mother once had a couple of whisky sours at a party given by the next-door neighbors. She then excused herself, started walking home, and promptly threw up on the front lawn. In college I drank beer a couple of times but hated the taste. In my twenties, I tried to cultivate a palate for good wine, but Chablis or Chardonnay was always something to have with a meal or at a party. I was unused to the afternoon cocktail ritual.

I adapted easily to my twin roles of secretary and honorary Roddenberry family member. I was having dinner there at least three times a week; I adored being around Gene during non-working hours, so at his insistence I never refused an offer of a home-cooked meal. Soon I became accustomed to the routine of drinking that always seemed to precede and follow dinner. (The La Costa week he spoke of on my first day seemed completely forgotten.) Wine or cocktails at the end of the workday (around 6:00 p.m.) was followed by homemade tacos or stew or lima beans and ham or spaghetti carbonara. During dinner, wine flowed freely from personally labeled bottles from the Windsor Vineyards, northern California vintners from whom Gene purchased wine by the caseload. And following dinner, there would be more rounds of drinks.

They saw to it that my glass was never empty, and I tried to show that I was a good guest and accepted graciously. I could never match their capacity, however. After a glass or two of wine, I'd either get sleepy, silly, or sleepy and silly. Once or twice, I got downright drunk, an experience I hated. Unable to drive, I'd spend the night in the guestroom, only to awake with the world's worst hangover the next morning, yet I was expected to be at my desk by 9:00 a.m.

The Roddenberrys seemed to take this sort of thing in stride. If they awoke with hangovers, Majel would prepare the "hair of the dog," a concoction usually of Bloody Mary mixer and some sort of alcohol, designed to ease their symptoms. I never could face this morning-after ritual; my stomach wouldn't allow much except water, which I craved by the gallon.

About this time I became friendly with both of Gene's daughters, Dawn, the youngest, who was working in the mailroom at Warner Bros., and Darleen. Both daughters were drop-dead movie-star attractive. Dawn had long, ringletted strawberry blonde hair and was thin as angel hair pasta (I learned later that, unbeknownst to anyone, she had been struggling at the time with anorexia). Darleen, with her white-blonde hair and equally pale skin seemed more delicate. She had two children — Gene's grandchildren, Trasey and Steven — and she had recently gone through a divorce when I met her.

Darleen began a stay at her father's house for several weeks soon after I'd started working there, and I got to know her quite well. She was recovering from a hysterectomy, and we'd spend afternoons chatting or opening Lincoln's mail. One day when I arrived, I noticed she looked paler than usual. "I've been hemorrhaging heavily," she said, and I sensed she was close to panicking. We phoned the doctor's office, and since everyone else was away from the house, I rushed her there in my car, where she was properly attended. I must admit, I was terrified, afraid she might bleed to death before we were able to get to the doctor's. Darleen recovered, but over the years she had many physical hardships, including frequent surgeries, causing her father (and me, too) many hours of concern.[3]

In those early days, Gene was frequently out of town doing college lectures, his main source of income. While he was away, I was assigned to help Majel with mail at Lincoln Enterprises or whatever else she needed. In time, I became her reluctant buddy. We had little in common, but I felt sorry for her. She didn't seem to have many friends to pal around with when Gene was away, and she insisted I join her when she needed someone to keep her company for bar-hopping or shopping expeditions. One time she decided she wanted to buy a weapon to defend herself, since Gene was away so frequently. He owned a gun, which he kept holstered in a tall bureau in the walk-in bedroom closet. I think he had owned it since his police days. Gene told me that one night when he was rip-roaring drunk, he took the pistol, stood out on the balcony of their bedroom, aimed, and *shot the lawn* because it refused to grow properly! I never knew if this was meant as a joke or if it was true, but they both told the story so often I had to believe there was some truth in it.

Majel didn't want to use Gene's gun for self-defense. She had heard about something that had just come on the market called a TASER. Maybe she chose this because it sounded like the *Star Trek* weapon, the phaser, or maybe because it was supposedly non-lethal and didn't require a license for ownership. We drove out to Burbank and the only store in the county that sold these weapons. There, before she could purchase the item, we were obliged to watch a film about how this stun gun worked. It disabled an attacker by shooting immobilizing darts connected to wires into the target, delivering a high voltage charge and knocking him down. She bought the device, but as far as I know, she never had to use it.

[3] Darleen Roddenberry-Bacha died as the result of head injuries sustained in an automobile accident on October 29, 1995. She was 48 years old at the time of her death. News reports erroneously listed her as the daughter of Gene and Majel Roddenberry. Her mother was actually Eileen Roddenberry, Gene's first wife.

Majel's concern about intruders continued for years. After the news stories about the Chowchilla, California kidnapping in 1976 (when some jerks hijacked a school bus full of kids and forced them, along with their heroic bus driver who eventually rescued them, into an underground pit), she worried for years that someone would grab Rod, the Son of a Famous Producer, and demand ransom money. The security system installed in their home by the Bel-Air Patrol was always being beefed up. And once she decided to turn her fears into a screenplay, and even hired writer Jon Povill to co-author a treatment with her, about the kidnapping of a busload of children.

● TELSTAR ● TELSTAR ● TELSTAR ● TELSTAR ● TELSTAR ● TELSTAR

WHY STAR TREK STILL HAS MILLIONS IN ITS POWER

By GENE RODENBERRY, Star Trek's creator

THE question most often asked about Star Trek is: Why?

WHY the incredible support of its fans? WHY is it playing to larger audiences than ever, even though the series is on its twelfth rerun in some cities?

WHY the conventions, attracting thousands of fans?

WHY has it spawned what seems to be almost a cult? Since Star Trek went off the air in 1969, all three networks and a half a dozen major studios have spent many millions of dollars trying to repeat the same kind of science fiction phenomenon.

The formula seems simple enough. Some strange gadgets, lots of blinking lights, toss in a few strange-looking creatures . . . and stir.

But their problem was that in searching for a magic formula, they overlooked the one thing that was obvious to every Star Trek fan.

Star Trek was not basically about space ships and planets and gadgets and aliens — it was about US. Humanity. The problems and challenges facing us now.

As a writer, I saw an opportunity to design that series into a vehicle for my comments and personal philosophy.

Fear

Star Trek came on the air at a time in which we were shipping our first combat troops to Vietnam and it made the immediate statement that we never have the right to interfere in the natural evolvement of other peoples.

It covered the years when our fear of Red China was reaching an hysterical peak; when Martin Luther King was still making marches in the south — during which time Star Trek was making the statement that we must learn to value the differences we find in other people.

If we cannot handle the small variations between our own kind here on Earth, God help us if we ever get into space and meet the variation that is almost certainly to exist out there.

Star Trek offered another opportunity, too. Most past motion picture and television science fiction had treated the subject carelessly, acting as if the rules of believability, characterization and story did not apply.

As a non-science fiction writer for years, I knew that the audience responded best to

BEST-LOVED flying saucer with creator Gene Rodenberry

The magic formula was humanity

stories of believable people in believable circumstances and saw no reason why the same rule shouldn't apply to science fiction.

As a result, one of the first people on our Star Trek staff was Harvey Lynn, a physicist from the prestigious government "think tank," the Rand Corporation in Santa Monica, Calif.

We also obtained technical advice from Cal Tech, Jet Propulsion Laboratories in Pasadena, and from N.A.S.A.

We established the rule that we would show nothing on Star Trek that was not rooted in some science fact or theory, and we encouraged our technical advisors to carefully scrutinize every line of every script. We insisted on

stories and characters which would be entertaining not just to sci-fi fans, but also to those whose normal television fare was medical shows, westerns, cops, private eyes, etc.

Humanity

I tried to say two things in Star Trek: First, that humanity will reach maturity and wisdom on the day it learns to value diversity in life and in ideas, that the worst thing that could happen to

us is for everyone to look and talk and act and think alike.

Second, Star Trek was our statement of affection and optimism about living things in general, and humanity in particular.

Although man is still in his childhood, there is out there a great reservoir of intelligence and good will and good lives waiting and wanting to flower.

It pleases me to see signs that Star Trek has and will continue to be part of all that.

The article I wrote for the National Star, along with its infamous headline. I also took this classic photo of Gene with the three-foot model of the Enterprise. The model went missing during production of the first Star Trek movie and was never found.

LOG ENTRY 5 :

Gene encouraged my own writing from the moment he learned that I was interested in being more than a secretary. The first writing I did was to update his four-page biography, which had last been revised by Dorothy Fontana. Pleased with that job, he gave me more opportunities to use my abilities. *The National Star* (known today as simply *Star* magazine) called and asked Gene for a byline piece. When he said he was much too busy, they told him it was all right to have it "ghosted," and Gene asked me to write the story, which we then scrutinized together in order to perfect it. I was paid the whopping sum of $100 and thought I'd died and gone to writers' heaven. When the article appeared, both of us were stunned by what the Star had done to our headline. Instead of calling it by Gene's suggested title, "WHY THE STAR TREK PHENOMENON?", the caption read, "WHY STAR TREK STILL HAS MILLIONS IN ITS POWER" — by Gene Roddenberry. I was flabbergasted! They made it sound like Gene was a power-happy, money-grubbing Hollywood megalomaniac. The story, at least, was intact, and they used the photograph I had taken of him seated at his desk with the three-foot model of the *Enterprise*.

Other writing opportunities soon arose. When a magazine called *TV Showpeople* decided they wanted to do a feature on Gene, I asked the editor to give me a chance to write it. The article turned out well, although a bit gushy, even with Gene's guidance. I opened by comparing the creator of *Star Trek*, whom most fans knew by the nickname "The Great Bird of the Galaxy," to another Creator:

> *In the beginning, all television was waste and void. And darkness was upon the face of the screen. And The Great Bird of the Galaxy said, "Let there be light, and starships, and other wondrous things." And he saw that it was good, and he called the good* **Star Trek** . . .

"I've got a healthy ego," Gene said at one point in the article, "but my ego is certainly not strong enough to stand people treating me like God." (It wasn't difficult to tell that I was a bit taken with my new boss, although he did let the opening paragraph stand.) Somehow, I managed to come back down to Earth and write a coherent piece which summed up Gene's feelings about a possible new movie based on *Star Trek*, as well as tidbits of the Roddenberry philosophy gleaned from his speeches: "It isn't all over; everything has not been invented; the human adventure is just beginning." (That last phrase would make its way into the advertising copy of *Star Trek: The Motion Picture* four years later.) I concluded the feature with Gene's mid-'70s speech closing, which quoted William Faulkner's Nobel Prize acceptance speech in 1949: "'I believe that man will not merely endure, he will prevail . . . it is our privilege to help man endure by lifting his heart, by reminding him of his courage and honor and hope and pride and compassion and pity and sacrifice which have been the glory of man's past.'" Believe it or not, I ended the article with the word "Amen."

Gene and his healthy ego applauded my efforts loudly. He wrote me a note, which I treasure to this day: "Good job. Well written with a feeling of zest and humor. I think you're going to make it as a writer!" My editor was so pleased with it, he published the story uncut. Later, I did another story for them about a stuntwoman named Paula Crist, who was a friend of the Roddenberry family. *TV Showpeople* folded after only a few issues (I like to think that it wasn't my fault), but by then the publishers had created another, more lucrative and much more exciting magazine. It was named *Starlog*, and by the sixth issue, I had landed a position as columnist.

Over the course of the next four years, I became what I called a *Star Trek* cheerleader — reporting on the always-upcoming production of the exciting new *Star Trek* movie: isn't it fantastic, any day now cameras will start rolling, blah, blah, blah. The film didn't start production until nearly three years after my first column touting the imminent commencement of production. I felt like a trained seal, balancing the *Star Trek* ball on my nose all those years, never letting it drop. However, it was a wonderful opportunity to hone my writing skills and earn a few (very few) dollars, to boot. After the picture premiered, the publishers and I parted our separate, friendly ways.

Sometime near the end of that first year working at Gene's home, Gene made his first intimate advance toward me. We had taken a break from work and gone for a dip — a skinny dip — in the pool. By now, I had gotten over my inhibitions about bathing in the nude and was really starting to enjoy the freedom of being outdoors *au naturelle*. I was still tense, but I tried to get into the spirit of the moment by attempting to see us as two mature adults enjoying the California sunshine and chlorine together. Suddenly Gene reached over and kissed me. I sprang back, startled. Puritanical, I thought, but I just wasn't prepared for this. I was baffled and confused. I quickly searched my mind to see if I had somehow been sending him flirtatious signals. I knew I hadn't. It would never have entered my mind to do so. I was relieved when he didn't pursue it, but later, after we'd dried and dressed and returned to the office upstairs, he teased me again about being a Puritan. I insisted I was not. His next words nearly knocked me out of the chair. Teasingly he asked if I would engage in a certain sex act — delicately put, it's the one Monica and Bill enjoyed so much in the 1990s. Today this would be grounds for a harassment suit, but in those days this sort of thing generally went unchallenged. I blushed and quickly changed the subject, trying to ignore him. Yet the thought persisted: had I misjudged him? Was he a Hollywood producer-type after all?

He tried the same line on me a few more times, usually late in the afternoons, when he'd be relaxing with a drink after working all day. My reaction was always to giggle, or quickly move to another topic. I couldn't understand his attitude. I had assumed Gene and Majel were a happy couple after five years of marriage. But I began to take a closer look at their relationship, an opportunity afforded me as their frequent dinner guest.

Looking back on it now, I'd have to say that these evenings were the beginning of our real friendship. After Majel headed upstairs, Gene and I would sometimes smoke marijuana (Majel had no interest in pot), and we'd laugh and talk for several hours before he would head up to their room, while I'd find my way to the guest room I sometimes occupied.

I had had some limited experience with pot as a survivor of the '60s counterculture. When I began working for Gene, I was only 30; Gene was 53 years old, a senior-citizen hippie, so I thought. How cool! I found his young-thinking attitude attractive, and his passes were becoming harder to ignore. Yet I was terribly confused by these feelings. He was a married man, and my sense of propriety told me this was wrong. But I also saw him as slightly more than an average human being. He was my hero, a man I considered a genius. More and more I was finding myself uncontrollably drawn to my new friend and mentor, not just because of his strikingly handsome appearance, but because of the way he touched my mind — and I know I touched his.

My mind thus "expanded" and buzzing one lazy winter's afternoon as we sat chatting and smoking pot in his office, I allowed Gene to kiss me again, this time a deep and serious kiss from which there was no backtracking. I saw him differently now, a man who was not as happy as he appeared, who needed comforting and understanding. I adored him, and although I felt overwhelming pangs of guilt, they were outweighed by the even more enormous empathy I was now feeling. He was still a god to me, but he was a god in pain.

I could resist him no longer.

LOG ENTRY 6 :

Early in January of 1975, Gene began another round of college speaking engagements while I assisted Majel at the house with the mail at Lincoln Enterprises. On one visit to a college town, he took a nasty tumble on some black ice and suffered a disc injury to his back. When he returned to Beverly Hills, he sought treatment from his regular doctor and an orthopedist, who ordered up a hospital bed and prescribed complete bed rest. Poor Gene had great difficulty moving about. He told me that when the accident first happened, he was in so much pain, "it brought tears to my eyes. And I haven't cried in many years."

Actor Greg Morris, star of the original TV series *Mission: Impossible* and a good friend of Gene's (both *Star Trek* and *Mission* had been filmed simultaneously on the Desilu lot in Hollywood), recommended a chiropractor in the San Fernando Valley. This doctor had a reputation for helping when all else failed. So one afternoon, we loaded the rented wheelchair into the trunk of my car, and I drove Gene to an appointment with this miracle worker in Van Nuys. I had my doubts about the doctor; his office didn't even have a parking lot and we had to park on the opposite side of Van Nuys Boulevard. Braving California

Gene speaks to a large crowd during an early '70s Star Trek convention.

traffic and the frantically blinking *Don't Walk* sign, I pushed Gene and said chair across six lanes of this major thoroughfare. Fortunately, the doctor was able to give Gene some relief after only a few visits.

Unknown to me, this visit to the Valley back-cracker was a turning point in our relationship. A few years later, Gene confided that he'd fallen in love with me that afternoon on Van Nuys Boulevard. "You showed such concern, such caring," he told me.

At the end of January, Gene and Majel went to a convention in New York City, where they were the guests of honor. It was my second awareness of them as *Star Trek's* first couple (the first time having been their publicity shoot at the Hollywood Wax Museum).

During the trip, Gene's back was still giving him problems, so the wheelchair had to be airfreighted back East for him (I have no idea why they couldn't have rented one there). While they were off wowing the East Coast fans, Gene asked if I would baby-sit young Rod because their Salvadoran housekeeper was recently hired, and they weren't completely confident in trusting her to look after an infant. Since I would have no one to watch my dog, Gene suggested I bring "Phaser" to the house to stay the two nights. This proved to be a disaster.

Phaser, a Shepherd-Labrador mix, was overwhelmed by Majel's three miniature poodles, Fang, Bump and Climax. He had never been socialized as a pup, and didn't know what to make of this canine pack. He barked at them as if he owned the place, rather than vice versa. I had to isolate poor Phaser the whole time, which made him miserable. He spent most of the weekend with his nose pressed against the giant sliding glass doors trying to get out to the back yard and the terrified poodles, leaving

My first dog, Phaser (1973-1986). He terrorized the Roddenberrys' poodles when we baby-sat during their trip to a New York convention.

great globs of doggie slobber in his wake. I was greatly relieved when the Roddenberrys returned, and I was able to take my own traumatized pooch home.

Gene's back was healing nicely when he returned to the college circuit in February. I was constantly amazed by his recuperative powers. I'd never seen anyone recover so quickly, not just from this back injury, but anything he might suffer — a cold, a cut, a sprain. His body seemed to have a remarkable resiliency.

One rainy afternoon when Gene was on the road, Majel had been to the post office box to collect the huge sacks of Lincoln Enterprises' mail. Typically, Majel would press into service anyone who was around the house, including guests, visitors, maids and yours truly. On this particular day, the bags were spread around the living room while all of us — Majel, myself, and a young couple, Barry and Nancy McMartin — were hard at work opening and sorting the mail. It was good to see the McMartins again, these neighbors of Gene's elderly mother, Glen, who frequently drove her to Beverly Hills from her home in the San Gabriel Valley.

The McMartins had brought Glen to the house on this particular afternoon and had been immediately drafted by Majel to help with the mail. Soon Barry noticed that the interesting letters weren't being saved, just tossed out in favor of the more profitable requests for catalogs and merchandise. The writers' addresses were the only things being kept for the all-important mailing list. "Someone ought to save some of these; they're so funny!" he remarked, then proceeded to read several out loud. I agreed. "There are enough interesting letters to put together some sort of book," he suggested. Wheels, cogs and such began turning in my brain. By the end of the day, I had a fistful of cute, funny letters.

The more I thought about the idea, the more interesting it sounded. Instead of tossing these letters, I began saving them. After several weeks, I had enough to approach Ballantine Books, the *Star Trek* licensed publisher at the time, with the idea of doing a book of one-liners with cute little illustrations. Gene heard of my newest venture and, unbeknownst to me, put in a good word with Judy-Lynn Del Rey, the editor at Ballantine. "Susan's a good writer," he told her. "She won't let you down." I was thrilled at the idea of doing a book, and Gene's extra push clenched it for me. My first book deal! Then I learned about editors. They are the people who take your brilliant, sacred concept and change it (generally for the better, but I didn't know this).

"We love the idea of a book of fan mail," Judy-Lynn told me, "but I think it should go a little bit further than just funny letters; bring us some of the intelligent letters, ones from doctors, scientists and business executives." So I sat down with several years' worth of files, combed through these and came up with what I considered to be the best of the letters to Gene and the show. In order to use them, I had to contact every individual to obtain written permission. This was time-consuming, but nearly everyone was cooperative. The only person who did not give me permission was Carl Sagan, who maintained that his letter to Gene was private, and I respected that. And besides, it was just a friendly note to Gene saying how much he admired Gene and appreciated hearing from him. I was also unable to obtain a letter from then-President Ford, which was the only correspondence I tried to solicit, but I did get a nice polite note on White House stationery saying that he was involved in this and that and was unable to comply.

Although begun in 1975, my first book, *Letters to Star Trek*, wasn't published until 1977. The cover bore a picture of Gene, with the characters Kirk and Spock, and the Enterprise, which appeared to be firing its phasers right through Gene's head. Nevertheless, it was a beautiful illustration, and thanks to this artwork and an introduction by Gene himself, the book sold a respectable eighty-five thousand copies.

And I owed it all to an idea by Barry McMartin. We were shocked and saddened a few years later when Barry's beautiful wife, Nancy, lost a hard-fought battle with kidney disease. Gene and I drove together to Rose Hills Cemetery in Whittier, where this young woman was laid to rest. After that, Barry faded from our lives. But I'll always be grateful to him — Barry's suggestion that winter afternoon was a turning point in my life. Without his encouragement, I might never have begun writing books.

LOG ENTRY 7 :

Despite his popularity as a public speaker, Gene was beginning to have financial difficulties. The college lectures paid between twelve and fifteen hundred dollars a pop, hardly enough to maintain his Beverly Hills home and accustomed lifestyle, which included live-in help, a nanny for the baby, and a membership in the famed Bel-Air Country Club. In Hollywood's golden age, this club had boasted such members as Bing Crosby, Clark Gable, Katharine Hepburn and Jimmy Stewart, and now Gene and Majel Roddenberry. Gene usually played golf on weekends, while Majel played on "ladies' days" — Tuesday and Friday mornings — religiously worshipping at the Church of the 18 Holes. I never knew her to miss a game unless she was deathly ill, and even that didn't stop her most of the time.

Once or twice I was invited along. On one of these occasions, I was riding on the back of Gene's electric golf cart when he took a turn too quickly. I went bouncing out onto the soft green grass. Gene, completely oblivious, kept right on going. People were hollering and pointing, and he didn't even realize why! My dignity was the only thing hurt, as I ran to catch up with the speed demon of the links.

On another occasion, we were having lunch in the clubhouse with some of their friends. I remarked off-handedly that it was chilly in the room, and someone offered me his cardigan. I gratefully accepted it, and as I wrapped the soft, blue cashmere around my shoulders, Majel whispered the name of my benefactor. "That's Ray Bolger," she said, seemingly in awe. Yikes! The Scarecrow from *The Wizard of Oz* himself had offered me his very own sweater. I was speechless, but managed to mutter my appreciation.

Gig Young and Gene go over dialogue for Spectre, 1977.

As impressed as I was with this club, its kind people, and the fantastic view of West-wood and UCLA from the dining room, I also chided Gene for holding membership in an all-white, all-WASP and practically all-Republican institution. "Gene," I pointed out, "you're not like that. You haven't got any of these hang-ups, and I know you're a dyed-in-the-wool liberal Democrat. How can you belong to such an exclusive club?" He told me it was simply a question of business. "Many of these people are producers, studio heads and so on. It's a good place to entertain." And it was hard to argue the point.

Gene struggled to earn enough to maintain these aspects of his life. But one afternoon in early 1975, he confided in me that it might all come crashing down soon; he needed twenty-five thousand dollars within three days or he would lose the house. I didn't under-stand, but I hadn't been working with him that long and didn't ask questions about his personal finances. I'm sure it was true, and he appeared more worried than I'd ever seen him before.

And then, an amazing thing happened.

On that very same afternoon, the phone rang with a call from an old friend who knew of someone who needed to hire a writer to present his ideas to the public. This benefactor was willing to pay the sum of — you guessed it — twenty-five thousand dollars for a script, plus all expenses.

The gentleman's name was John Whitmore. *Sir* John Whitmore. A gentleman by title, he had a home in Ossining, New York, as well as a country manor outside of London. He also had money, lots of money. When you have that kind of money people sometimes take advantage of you. I believe this is what happened to Sir John.

By all appearances, John was a normal man — middle-aged, balding, great English accent. He seemed very intelligent and articulate when he arrived the next day to meet with Gene about his project. They talked behind closed doors for several hours. When he left, Gene looked bemused. I asked him what was going on, would he be taking on the project? Maybe, was all he would say.

Over the next few days, I learned what the mystery was all about. Sir John Whitmore had been convinced by a group of people that the Earth was about to be greeted with the arrival of aliens from a star cluster in space called the Pleiades. Apparently John had sur-rounded himself with a bunch of cuckoos. Or gold diggers. Or both. Gene had agreed to meet with people in John's entourage, several of whom by themselves were quite rep-utable in the field of paranormal investigation. Others were of questionable validity. Gene promised to meet with them all, and told John that he would only write what he believed. That was good enough for John, and the deal was set.

Gene began by interviewing all sorts of "experts." One was the "psychic"/spoon-bender Uri Geller. Gene met with Geller on a flight from New York to L.A. On the airplane, Geller asked the flight attendant for a spoon from the galley and, to Gene's amazement, bent it before his eyes. Gene brought the spoon back to the office and showed it to me. It was indeed bent, as was one of Gene's own keys. Although many have attempted to debunk this handsome Israeli as a nothing more than a clever magi-cian, Gene had difficulty believing that Geller was a charlatan, since nothing could have been prearranged. (Years later, a Humanist friend of mine, Ferd Goldsmith, showed me how easily spoons can be bent while giving the appearance of being done "psychically." He learned this simple trick from renowned magician/skeptic James "The Amazing"

Randi, who frequently demonstrates how easily anyone can perform spoon-bending.)

Another aspect of this venture included the imminent re-emergence of Atlantis from the seabed. (Yes, Atlantis. Why does belief in Atlantis always seem to go hand-in-hand with belief in extraterrestrial beings?) Sir John paid for Gene to pop down to the island of Bimini in the Bahamas, where believers claimed to have discovered that fabled continent lying just offshore. Indeed, there were submerged blocks of what looked like a paved road just a few meters below the surface of the sea.

Did Gene scuba dive? his escorts asked. "Of course," he replied, although he didn't know a regulator from an air hose. "Just refresh my memory if you would. "It's been a while." As a certified diver myself, I know that Gene could have had a serious accident by faking it, but he had a great sense of adventure and was never afraid to take chances. He took the plunge and survived. The neat rows of stone blocks that he saw below amazed him. But was this Atlantis? He wasn't convinced.

In San Diego, Gene visited with Clive Baxter, a renowned scientist who was experimenting with the "emotional reactions" of plants. Baxter wired up some plants with a device similar to a lie detector, one that measured galvanic skin responses. The little green things twittered gently, steadily, unremarkably. In another room, a pot of water was boiling rapidly. Poised above the water was a dump dish loaded with living shrimp. At given intervals, the mechanical arm of the dump dish would toss a few shrimp into their scalding watery grave below. Baxter simultaneously took a reading from the plants' lie detectors. Invariably, the needles shot off the scale at the moment of shrimp dumping. His point was that life — even plants, with no brain and no sensory organs — can sense the loss of another life form. This didn't seem to have much to do with aliens from the Pleiades, but since Gene was being paid for his time, it made for some extremely interesting research. I always looked forward to his reports back to me after each encounter.

Thelma Moss and her experiments at UCLA into Kirlian photography were another aspect of this research. She photographed the "auras" around living things — a plant, a hand, a person. The most amazing part of this was the "phantom leaf effect." When photographed with this form of photography, a leaf with its tip amputated still showed the pattern of its full outline, including the missing part.

These experiments continued for several months, with Gene frequently flying between the West Coast and John Whitmore's New York headquarters. Throughout his investigations, which lasted nearly a year, Gene continued to maintain an attitude of curious skepticism. At times, he found the data and experiments compelling; frequently, he thought the whole thing a fraud. One person who did reach him, however, was someone he interviewed on a research trip to Manhattan sometime during the first few months of this project. There, Gene met with a psychic whose reading shocked him. He played the tape for me, and I, too, was astounded. This person whom Gene had never met, and who had never met me, said he saw trouble ahead for Gene in his marriage. He predicted complications from an outside interest — "a secretary, perhaps." Gene and I were indeed physically interested in each other, but it was so strange hearing about it from a third, unknown, party. After playing the tape for me, Gene hid it so that Majel would not find it.

The psychic was right. Our physical relationship, although still one-sided, was an undeniable reality. Gene and I were necking and petting several times on those afternoons when we were alone at the house. He would call me into his den, lock the door and motion me toward the couch. I invariably became flustered, nervous and giggly. I was beginning to have feelings for him, and I knew this was a strange and hopeless situation. Eventually, I'd take a seat on the couch; he would get up from his desk and join me there, talking and joking and trying to put me at ease. He was so charming and boyish then, kissing me like a schoolboy stealing a forbidden kiss. It was impossible to resist. We'd kiss until we'd both be aroused. Then he'd beg for oral sex and I'd reluctantly comply, while remaining completely frustrated. Then he'd hug me and kiss me and we'd chat. That was the best part. Although I felt somewhat used and left out, I was convinced that I was really a very lucky girl, to be here in this time and place. It was almost as if I felt a responsibility to the fans, to keep our hero happy. I was still in awe of this great man, falling in love with him, and I would have done anything to please him.

And so, to paraphrase Queen Victoria's suggestion to young English brides, I closed my eyes and thought of *Star Trek*.

LOG ENTRY 8 :
In March 1975, we learned that Paramount had given the green-light to a Star Trek feature film. It would have a budget of three to five million dollars, big bucks compared to the original episode costs of one hundred eighty-six thousand dollars each, but modest by movie standards. Nevertheless, Gene was thrilled, and in May the two of us set out for our first trip to the Paramount lot to check out available space for our offices.

Six years had passed since Gene had been headquartered at Paramount, and as we drove to the studio, he pointed out all the sights so familiar to him on his former daily drives. We passed through neighborhoods that had seen better times in Hollywood's glory days of the '30s and '40s. Our route east along Willoughby Avenue was lined with small stuccoed, tile-roofed bungalows with the ubiquitous bird-of-paradise flowers gleaming orange and blue in the brilliant California sunshine. We reached Gower Street and turned right for one block, then left on Melrose Avenue, where the main gate to Paramount was located. Before entering the studio, Gene pointed out two of his favorite

The Paramount water tower. Originally painted with the Desilu logo, it is the same water tower an executive showed Gene as the potential "rocket ship" to use as the Enterprise.

restaurants that I would get to know so well in the coming years — Nickodell's and Lucy's El Adobe. Both were major studio hangouts (Nickodell's, which closed its doors in the early 1990s, was even referred to in the movie *Sunset Boulevard*), and Gene knew the owners of these establishments. In weeks to come, they would be united like long lost friends.

After driving up to the entrance known as the Windsor Gate (because Windsor Blvd. dead-ended into the studio at Melrose), Gene met with a representative in charge of facilities on the Paramount lot, who gave Gene a choice of several available office suites. He wasted no time in selecting the suite that was to be our home for the next five years. It turned out that he had a sentimental reason for choosing these offices on the ground floor of Building E. This was the same space he had occupied during the making of the original *Star Trek* series. At first, we had only half of the first floor, whereas during the production of the TV show, the entire floor had been given over to *Star Trek*. We looked forward to the day when production would be in full swing and we could once again take over the first floor of the building.

We began moving in almost at once, setting up the offices with our personal touches. My outer office, which was to be Gene's reception area and the first impression for arriving visitors, was originally decorated in what I called "early Chamber of Commerce." Gene had received a number of awards and plaques over the years; now he decided he had the perfect place to hang them: my office! Shortly after our arrival, I called the studio Executive in Charge of Hammering, and his assistant, the Vice President in Charge of Holding the Nail to Be Hit (those unions are really something), and we created what amounted to an "ego wall" with literally dozens of awards to Gene and *Star Trek*. After many hours of positioning and leveling and shifting various plaques around, I was finally satisfied that everything looked perfect. I invited Gene to inspect our handiwork.

He hated it.

"Take it all down," he insisted. "It's really tacky." I was immensely relieved to clear out all those wooden prizes. Instead, we chose some framed artwork of various antique magazine covers. Gene selected some interesting artwork for his walls too — a framed graphic of Laurel and Hardy, his favorite comedy team, plus a poster of Albert Einstein. He delighted in the contrast of the two, and visitors never failed to comment on it.

From his home library, Gene brought numerous books to line the abundant shelves in his office. He selected the complete Science and Nature libraries from Time-Life Books, along with Will and Ariel Durant's magnum opus, *The Story of Civilization*. These were among the books Gene treasured most in his life, so I was thrilled when, years later, he paid me his supreme compliment when he said, "I want you to be Ariel to my Will Durant." I don't know if that ever happened, but we did co-author two books together, and I was so flattered that I've never forgotten the moment he said that.

Gene's office consisted of the main room, with his desk, bookshelves, sofa and large conference area. Behind this was a smaller room with brown leather sofa, refrigerator, cabinets and bar area. To the right of that was a bathroom and tub/shower combination. Gene said he had stayed overnight there many times during the production of the first *Star Trek* series. He stocked the fridge with bottles of soda and mixers for the liquor with which he had filled the cabinets. There was an abundance of scotch, vodka, bourbon, wine, etc., along with an array of glassware and drinking paraphernalia such as

Gene and Matt Jefferies pour over blueprints for the sets of **Star Trek: The Motion Picture**. Matt worked with Gene on the original series and drew up the original plans for the Enterprise.

Gene with a toy plastic model of the original Enterprise from the TV series. This was taken shortly after we moved into our first office at Paramount Pictures. Note the print of Laurel and Hardy on the wall. This was Gene's favorite comedy team.

corkscrews, stirrers, an ice bucket and so on. With the hectic hours Gene intended to put in working on the new production, he didn't want to be caught short during the evening cocktail hour.

Not long after our arrival on the lot, we were escorted on a walking tour around the studio, where we were shown the various sound stages that we might be using for our production. Gene pointed out highlights of the backlot where he had spent some of the happiest moments in his life. We stopped at the water tower, whose lettering still faintly bore the logo of Desilu (although that studio had been acquired by Paramount in a 1967 takeover). Suddenly Gene burst into laughter. I asked him what was so funny.

Then he told me a story I never forgot.

In 1964, when Gene was finally able to get backing for his original *Star Trek* television pilot, one of the executives at Desilu (the studio which was to film the story), brought Gene over to the water tower and told him they had found a way to save a great deal of money. "Gene," this executive announced proudly, "we've found your spaceship!" Gene looked up at the pointy water tower looming overhead on its stilt-like pilings and said, "You've got to be kidding." No, the executive was serious. Didn't Gene notice the rocket-ship-like appearance of the skyward-aimed water tower? Wasn't it perfect? Fortunately, Gene did not agree, or the Starship *Enterprise* might have looked just a tad different from the one he and Matt Jefferies eventually designed. For years after that, every time Gene and I would see a water tower, we'd point and laugh at the resemblance to a starship.

Once I asked Gene what exactly water towers did. I had always assumed they were for storage of water in case of an emergency. Gene immediately launched into a discus-

Gene on the phone discussing Star Trek's return shortly after we moved into our first office on the Paramount lot in 1975.

sion of how water towers work. "They certainly couldn't hold enough water for an entire city," he said, looking at me as if my IQ had just dropped to that of a chimpanzee. "They are used mainly to supply water pressure. The water is pumped up into the water tower, then released, and the force of gravity helps distribute the water through the pipes." Now it was my turn to look at him like he was from Mars. "What!" I exclaimed. "That's the most ridiculous story you've ever invented. Why on Earth would they waste all that energy pumping water up so it can fall down? Surely they'd just pump it to where it has to go." I truly believed that, and for years we had a running argument and joke about the real purpose of water towers. I never gave in, never bought into his explanation. Well, Gene was right, of course; that's exactly how water towers do work, but I didn't learn this until recently. It always seemed far-fetched to me.

We had lots of running "arguments," really discussions of science and other things that we chuckled over for hours. For instance, upon sighting a portion of the moon still visible in the daytime, Gene would ask me, "How come the moon is out in the day?" I'm sure he understood the concept of the Earth's rotation and the position of the sun and moon and how light strikes the moon. But he never admitted he was pulling my leg. He would insist I go into a lengthy explanation, which I did with gusto, as if I were back teaching the fourth grade. I'd get paperweights, or coffee mugs — anything handy, and position them on the desk. He'd still profess not to understand. Then I'd have him stand in the center of the room and be the sun, and I'd be the Earth, and someone handy would be the moon, and we'd all rotate until I was sure he would understand the concept. Then, the next day, we'd be out driving somewhere, and he'd look up at the sky at lunchtime and say, "I still don't get it. How can we see the moon in the daytime?"

Another running gag had to do with my love of paleoanthropology, begun in my college days. He encouraged and delighted in my ever-expanding search for our humanness, something he too spent his life pursuing. But he teased me when I would recite the human primatial lineage — *Pithecanthropus, Australopithecus, Homo habilis, Homo erectus, Homo sapiens* . . . When I'd get to "*Homo erectus*" he'd always stop me. "That's your favorite, huh?" he'd say. The pun always made me blush, and he continued to tease me. He even managed to work the concept into his speeches while describing the ascent of humankind with some vague references to "every college coed's favorite subject." Gene loved joking about sexual references and double entendres.

Sex was one of Gene's favorite preoccupations. After moving to Paramount, he continued to request (he never demanded) that I join him on the couch for a drink after the day's work. He'd draw the blinds, pour us a drink, and we'd talk. I loved talking with him. It was always a mental high for me, and the fact that he enjoyed my thoughts and ideas was a great turn-on. When the inevitable advances happened, I was actually disappointed, as I'd much rather have continued talking. Our relationship was still very much a one-sided thing as to who was pleasuring whom.

I continued to suffer guilt from this arrangement. If his marriage was in trouble (and he continued to insist to me that it was), I didn't want to add to his problems. Complicating this was the fact that I was still having dinner with the Roddenberrys at their home a few times a week, at Gene's insistence. Admittedly, it didn't take much for him to persuade me to join them for dinner. I was falling in love with him and couldn't turn him down — for anything.

LOG ENTRY 9 :

Although Gene was expected to begin drafting a script for the movie version of *Star Trek*, he was still under obligation to complete his work on the script for Sir John Whitmore, now titled *The Nine*. So the paranormal research and experiments continued. Whitmore sent Gene to meet with two researchers at Stanford — Hal Puthoff and Russell Targ. Their work was probably the most acceptable to the scientific community, which generally considered the whole field of parapsychology a crock. Puthoff and Targ, however, provided us with one of our most convincing experiments, utilizing a technique they called "remote viewing."

Gene, myself, and several of the people who were working with us or in our building — about eight of us altogether — were to divide ourselves into two groups. One group would remain in Gene's office. The other group was to take a stroll around the Paramount lot and select a site at random. They would then focus on this site and try to project an image of what they saw to the people in the group remaining in Gene's office,

Gene and I were in the wedding of a close friend, held on my patio; he gave the bride away and I was the Maid of Honor.

about a half a mile away. These people were to try to receive a mental impression of what those in the remote group were viewing, and then draw it on a sheet of paper. When the remote group returned to the office, they would look at the drawings and decide how accurate they were. And they were uncannily accurate. If I hadn't been there and hadn't participated in this experiment, I never would have believed it. There were no tricks, no gimmicks. After the first experiment, the groups switched positions, and the office group went out into the field, while the others now took up pen and paper. Again, people seemed to be receiving visual imagery from the group. One person, however, appeared to have failed, when he drew something that wasn't the image the group was supposed to be projecting. But a quick walk to the site brought a shocking answer — the person who made the drawing had actually sketched something that was visible beyond the studio wall, across the street! The one doing the sending hadn't realized that he was projecting an image seen only peripherally, but that's just what had happened. It matched the drawing exactly.

Gene was soon having to spend most of his time working on his script for the film, so he turned *The Nine* script over to Jon Povill. I had met Jon when I first began working with Gene at the house on Leander Place. Tall, balding, and pensive, Jon gave the impression that every word he spoke was carefully thought out before it left his mouth. Somewhat of a '60's hippie holdover, Jon had been assisting Gene before I had begun working at the house. He was a struggling young writer whom Gene felt he had "discovered" and had decided to take under his wing. Unfortunately, there weren't many writing opportunities at the time, so Gene paid Jon to do some chores around the house, such as babyproofing the swimming pool and electrical wiring. When we moved to the studio, Gene brought Jon in as "assistant to the producer," although eventually he functioned as story editor when the film and proposed TV series progressed. By the time *Star Trek: The Motion Picture* was actually produced, Jon had made it all to the way to associate producer.

At first Gene had intended for Jon to polish *The Nine* script, but his involvement became so integral that he eventually gave him co-credit for the writing. The script became a "slice of life" story about a science fiction guru, not unlike Gene Roddenberry, who begins investigating various psychic phenomena — not the most imaginative of concepts. Yet Gene was remarkably unabashed in his depiction of himself, right down to his ever-increasing bouts of impotence, a dysfunction he imparted to the script's central character. Sir John seemed pleased with the script, although it was never produced. After Gene's death, Jon Povill attempted to revive the project, since he had co-writing credit, and there was the possibility that it might someday be produced.

Gene didn't hear much from Sir John Whitmore after completion of the script. He did give Gene one bit of information before he flew off to his home abroad. In 1975, John handed Gene a sealed envelope, with instructions typed on it reading "Do not open until 1980." Gene made me solemnly swear to uphold the integrity of this secret envelope, which was locked away for many years. It resurfaced while I was cleaning out some files shortly after the due date. I begged Gene to open it, and we discovered that its message was just as weird as the rest of the Whitmore project. In effect, it said that the people from the Pleiades were going to land in Australia, and by the time we read this letter, the event would already have taken place, or would shortly become a reality.

It wasn't that Gene was vehemently opposed to the idea of extraterrestrials. Indeed, he agreed with Carl Sagan — that with billions and billions of stars, there had to be life out there, and it would be foolish to think that this is the only place where life had ever happened in all of creation — just us, all alone in the universe on this little planet. But he also didn't think that Earth was so wonderfully special that aliens from all over the galaxy were converging on our world in their saucers to check us out. Ironically, however, he wrote several scenarios using that very premise!

For the first *Star Trek* movie script, Gene chose a premise that had intrigued him all his life. Always an iconoclast, Gene delighted in challenging traditional beliefs, and his script for what he called *Star Trek II* (*Star Trek I* being the TV series) would be no exception. The story concerned no less a concept than "Captain Kirk meets God," only the God of the Old Testament turned out to be a damaged computer whose programming had run amok. Unfortunately, the studio execs did not sing hosannas to this script, and Gene received what was to be the first in a long series of painful rejections from the studio. I thought it was an excellent script, one of the best examples of Gene's writing I'd ever seen. We were never told exactly why they didn't go for it; Gene's feeling was that the subject matter was probably too controversial, and the studio didn't want to offend *Star Trek*'s millions of paying customers.

For the next several years, many rejections and setbacks would take their toll on his self-confidence. At one point during 1976, following months of giving it everything he had, the project seemed about to be canceled. Gene hung up the phone after talking to an executive, and I knew immediately from the look on his face that it was bad news. "Oh, Susan," he sighed dejectedly. He seemed on the verge of tears. In fact, I don't remember ever seeing him more despondent. I could almost hear his heart fracturing. All I could do was go to him and hug him and tell him it would turn out all right, maybe there was still hope.

At times it seemed as if Paramount was jerking him around. The studio couldn't make up its collective executive mind. Was *Star Trek* simply a television concept after all? Or should it be a movie for television? Maybe it could launch a fourth network (a pet project of then-studio head Barry Diller, who eventually did just that at Fox). A perpetual optimist, Gene never was one to throw in the towel, but this project seemed to have a pall of doom over it.

It was a saga that would be played out, at times painfully, over the next four years.

LOG ENTRY 10 :

Gene leaned over and whispered in my ear: "Someday you'll be doing that."

I looked at him as if he were crazy and shot back a forceful, "No way!" I was seated beside Gene, his mother, and Majel as we watched Dorothy Fontana, so poised on the stage, addressing the Filmcon 3/Equicon '75 audience. Dorothy, who had begun back in the '60s as Gene's secretary, had gone on to greater things, as every Star Trek fan was well aware. She had climbed her way up the professional ladder, and as "D.C." Fontana, she'd written some of the best stories and scripts to come out of the series. Now she was addressing fans from all over the world as they gazed worshipfully at her. Whatever gave Gene the idea that I would do anything like that? I had taken only one speech course in college, a prerequisite for teaching, and to me, my knees knocking together always sounded louder than my voice. I had planned never to get up in front of a group again. But Gene refused to accept my timidity, nodding knowingly, "That's what Dorothy used to say."

It was an exciting summer weekend, being with Gene as his guest at a Star Trek con, rather than having to work for the committee as I had done in the past. He had invited me to stay with the family in their rented condo in La Costa (about 20 miles north of San Diego), my first visit to the resort I had been hearing about from day one. The drawback was lack of sleep; Rod, now a year old, didn't understand the meaning of the words "sleep in" and was wide awake at six a.m. sharp each morning. And so were we all. Apart from that, it was great fun.

The Roddenberrys were members of the La Costa Country Club and Spa, and we took full advantage of the facilities. They played golf, of course. In those days Gene was nearly as avid a golfer as Majel. Between rounds, Gene went to the men's spa, while Majel had the complete spa treatment on the woman's side of the complex — head to toe whirlpool baths, massages, pampering and pummeling. Gene saw to it that I was treated to a facial massage and whirlpool bath that was extremely relaxing. I felt like a queen! Later I was their guest for drinks and dinner in one of the country club's elegant restaurants.

The only wrinkle in the whole thing was Gene's constant flirtation with me, which unnerved me, since Majel and Gene's mother were usually within earshot. Gene, however, seemed to thrive on the thrill of possible discovery. He would kiss me or fondle me when they'd be on the verge of entering a room, and I found myself constantly having to dodge his advances. The worst moment for me was on a drive back from San Diego one night after the day's convention activities.

It had been a wonderful day, meeting fans and celebrities alike. I was thrilled to finally meet another of my heroes, writer Ted Sturgeon. I also met his wife Wina for the first time that weekend. Ted pointed her out to us as "the woman over there with the squirrel in her hair." Sure enough, she came over to greet us, and nesting in her highly teased blonde hair was a baby squirrel. Even Gene, used to the Hollywood scene, thought this a bit bizarre, but we all smiled politely. Wina eventually settled down and became one of our good friends, but for years Gene still talked about the moment when he first met Wina, "the cuckoo with the squirrel in her hair."

Late that evening, we drove back from the convention to the La Costa condo. Everyone was exhausted from the long day. Majel drove, as she usually did whenever she and

Gene went somewhere, and Gene's mother was seated in the front next to her. Gene and I were in the back seat of Majel's huge Lincoln Continental. While still engaging them in conversation, Gene casually reached his hand over and began fondling my breast. I froze. Then he took my hand and placed it in his lap. What could I do? I couldn't very well say, "Gene, would you mind removing your dick from my hand? Thank you so much." So I sat in petrified silence, except to respond when spoken to. Meanwhile, he continued to carry on a casual conversation with Majel and his mom throughout the drive home. If he enjoyed the danger of being caught in the act, then this was his ultimate thrill. For years he gleefully reminded me of the night we "did it" with his mother and wife sitting just inches away from us in the front seat.

Our first time in a hotel together came that January, shortly after the New Year. I was dispatched to my first convention, at the New York Hilton Hotel on January 23–25, 1976. The temperature was a brisk zero degrees, with an added wind chill factor that had meteorologists frantically scurrying for their record books. I still hadn't gotten over my stage fright. The only reason I went was because the producers of the con wanted to show the famous *Star Trek* Blooper reel, a compilation of hilarious outtakes which was in Gene's (and no one else's) personal possession at that time, and no one else was available to bring it to them. They agreed to pay all my expenses if I flew there with this reel, so Gene entrusted it to me.

I was assured that all I would have to do was to drop off the reel; after that I planned to go hide out in a corner somewhere. No such luck. They had set aside a room and a time for me to speak. So I bravely got up and began to talk about where I worked, what we did there, how plans were being formulated for a new movie — when a buzz began circulating around the room. I continued speaking, and as I did, people began to leave. I must be really awful, I thought, looking for that corner to crawl into. By the time I was finished with my talk a mere fifteen minutes later, the room was virtually empty. I meekly stepped down from the platform, vowing never to do that ever again. Then, off in the distance, I heard this ear-shattering applause. Well, I thought, at least someone is appreciated. Curious, I moved toward the sound of the happy crowd and discovered who was on stage in this other room. And then it all became clear. Even without his pointed ears, I knew it was Mr. Spock. So, they had scheduled me opposite Leonard Nimoy! Relieved, I caught the tail end of his speech and decided that I would someday try again as a convention guest.

Today, with close to a hundred appearances under my belt, I truly enjoy getting up in front of a room filled with people, joking and just having a good time. The key, I've found, is not to take it all too seriously. So, Gene was right after all.

Although Gene did not appear at the convention, he had arranged to be in New York City for a few days immediately afterwards to visit his lecture agent at the Leigh Bureau. Before leaving Los Angeles, we made plans to meet at the Warwick Hotel, where he had reservations. An older hotel without much of a lobby, it was quite a comedown from the plush Hilton where I had been staying.

I arrived before he did and announced myself to the concierge, who never batted an eye when I introduced myself as Mr. Roddenberry's assistant, here with some papers and some of his luggage. He gave me the room key, and I proceeded there to wait for Gene. This was to be our first time out of town together, alone, away from his home and the studio. Our lovemaking would not be a quickie, with the fear of imminent intrusion. I'd never done anything like this, and I was at once excited and extremely apprehensive, pacing while I waited for him in the room.

Gene arrived that evening after his transcontinental flight. The first thing I noticed was that he was drunk. Then he started acting slightly crazy. He began to

Souvenir napkin from our night on the town in New York, 1976

order me around. "I expect you to unpack for me," he said, tossing his suitcase on the bed. I was confused and a little scared. I'd never seen him act this way. I thought about leaving and returning to the Hilton. As I started unpacking, I began to run different escape scenarios in my head, crying softly. When Gene saw my tears, he became angry. Through sobs now, I told him this was not how I expected him to behave, and I was thinking about leaving. Then he began to calm down. He was just as nervous about the situation as I was, compensating for his feelings by trying to sound in control, barking orders and demanding things. He could see it wasn't working, and he started to relax a little. He came over to me and kissed me; I was tense but slowly relaxed.

It was an awkward beginning for what turned out to be an incredible weekend. The only drawback was that Gene was totally impotent the whole time. I was really disappointed, as this was to be our first time for intercourse. Try as he might, it just didn't happen. I assumed it was his nervousness, his drinking, our eagerness — who knows? Perhaps it was all of those things, plus his guilt at having an extramarital relationship. We spent the weekend petting and caressing, finding alternative ways to satisfy each other until the wee hours, then holding each other through the night.

We did some New York things, like visiting the Museum of Natural History and the Hayden Planetarium, but we were so sleepy from our previous all-nighter that we could hardly keep our eyes open, and we dozed off under the planetarium's stars. When the lights came on, we stumbled outside and grabbed a taxi and returned to our room for a quick nap. That night Gene treated me to dinner at the Four Seasons, the most elegant restaurant I had ever seen. Its opulent interior sparkled like a faceted jewel, and the staff cooed and fawned over us as if we were royalty. I felt like a fairy princess in a fancy black evening dress I had bought just in case he took me out someplace special. The Four Seasons fit that bill nicely.

After dinner we taxied over to Dangerfield's (owned by comedian Rodney Dangerfield), a nightclub that Gene had wanted very much to see. By this time I had begun to cough quite a bit, but I wrote it off to being tired. We watched the comedy show, had some more drinks, and arrived back in our room around 3:00 a.m., exhausted and barely able to collapse into each other's arms. By now we were thoroughly in love, unable to keep our hands off each other even as we drove together to the airport the next day. We had separate destinations — Gene was heading for a speech in Pittsburgh, while I was homeward bound. Neither one of us wanted to leave. The taxi driver practically had to pry our mouths apart. We said world-record good-byes, and I headed home, happy, yet feeling like I had the worst hangover in the world.

Six hours later I arrived at LAX and picked up my car, which I'd parked at the airport. I nearly fell asleep on the freeway while driving myself home. I was surprised I was having so much trouble shaking off a hangover. The next day, Friday, I awoke with a 104° fever, the highest in my life.

I forced myself to get to the doctor, who pronounced me ill with bronchitis and the flu, and gave me a shot. I spent the rest of the weekend in bed. On Monday morning, since Gene was away, I was supposed to work at Leander Place, not the Paramount office, so I dutifully dragged myself to the house. Majel met me at the door and told me to help her get Gene's bag out of the car. Huh? Why was his bag in the car if he was in Pittsburgh? No, she told me, he was upstairs — sick in bed with the flu! He had come home over the weekend, having become ill in Pittsburgh. There he'd been hospitalized with flu, pneumonia, and a 105° fever. It had taken him a couple of days to recover enough to fly home. Although I had been on the verge of announcing my own illness, I decided it would be best to keep quiet. The shot had given me enough of a fighting chance, so I continued with the day's work. Poor Gene. My thank-you gift to him for the best weekend of my life had been a horrible case of flu. (I later learned that nearly everyone at the Hilton convention that weekend had developed the same illness.)

I went up to see him. Would he be angry with me for making him ill? We hadn't been in touch since we parted in New York, so he didn't know I had come down with the flu also. I knocked at the door, and a weak voice bade me enter. He was in bed, shivering, although it was incredibly hot in the bedroom, with the heat pushed up high and the fireplace blazing. By now, Majel had left the house to run an errand, and Gene immediately asked me for a sexual massage. He said, "It makes me feel good to be fooled with when I'm sick." What a shock! Here I thought he was practically dying, and he had sex on his mind. I never quite understood this constant preoccupation he seemed to have with sex and things sexual. He just seemed to love it so much.

LOG ENTRY 11 :

While attending the convention in New York, I met Ed Naha, an A&R (artists and repertory) person for Columbia Records. I had had an idea tucked away in the back of my mind for some time, and I suggested to Ed that it might be fun for Gene to do a "spoken word" record. He was very enthusiastic about the idea, and we set up a meeting with Gene, who seemed intrigued with the opportunity to branch out into a different area of entertainment.

Gene and Ed spent long hours on the telephone planning the album's contents. They decided to include other luminaries in the *Star Trek* and science fiction world, rather than just an hour of Gene's discoursing on a record. Gene would be the album's centerpiece, sharing inside anecdotes about the creation of *Star Trek* and the Mr. Spock character; there would also be a chance for him to expound on the *Star Trek* philosophy, which just happened to be Gene's own point of view. Guest artists would include William Shatner, DeForest Kelley, Mark Lenard, Ray Bradbury and Isaac Asimov. Gene would write his own musings as well as the dialogue for the two-person sessions, and some of the original *Star Trek* music would be tossed in for flavoring.

Most of the recording sessions took place at the United Western Studios in Los Angeles, and I was privileged to be present. What great fun it was to watch all these people I had long admired, working on this album!

I had met Ray Bradbury a few years before, at Bjo's convention, and was still in awe, thrilled to be in his presence. I had long admired his writing, and here was a chance to watch him do something few people would ever witness: make a recording. Just prior to the recording session, Ray and Gene discussed and rewrote some of his lines. And even

The cover and sleeve from the spoken word album Gene made.

Ray Bradbury records his segment for Gene's spoken word album. (The segment never made it onto the album.)

William Shatner, during the recording session for his segment on Gene's record album.

though Ray recorded his portion of the album with great enthusiasm, there was some uncertainty about his payment; at the last minute it was decided to drop his track.

William Shatner dropped by our offices a week before the recording session to talk over the details with Gene. Our office walls had been decorated with pictures of the cast from the original series, so their faces were in front of me every day. But when Bill walked in for the first time, I did a double take. I glanced from Bill, to his photo, and back to Bill. I couldn't believe it — Captain Kirk had just beamed up to our office! All I could blurt out was, "You're him!" as I pointed toward his photo. He nodded that he was indeed *he*, and ignoring what he knew was an embarrassing moment for me, headed into Gene's office.

No mention was made of this encounter when I saw Bill at the recording studio. He appeared, as he usually did, calm, cool and self-assured, dressed in white shorts and T-shirt, this time apparently having beamed in directly from the tennis court.

DeForest Kelley impressed me as a gentleman—kind, friendly and outgoing, with a warm Southern smile. He made everyone around him feel comfortable. Over the years, I would always look forward to having moments to chat with De at fan conventions or on the set. He recorded his cut, "McCoy's Rx for Life," with total profession-alism, perhaps the smoothest of all the people who were taped for this album.

I didn't have an opportunity to meet Mark Lenard at his session since he recorded his portion from New York, where he lived part of the time. Later, I would get to know Mark better as I attended fan conventions and had time to visit with him. His cut on the album was in character, as Spock's father, Sarek. The piece Gene had written for him had to do with how Spock was born from the union of people from two species, Human and Vulcan.

Isaac Asimov, who had a dread of flying, also recorded his part about the world of science fiction from a studio in New York, so I didn't get to meet him this time (I would later have that pleasure at another New York convention).

Gene also taped a few of his college lectures, which were added to the record. One of my favorite cuts was "Letter from a Network Censor," a piece he often used as part of his college talks. It pokes fun at both religion ("God creates faulty humans, then blames them for their mistakes"; Noah's ark is too expensive — couldn't just a few strong swimmers be saved instead of all those animals? and so on) and what Gene saw as the unjust system of network interference in the writer's creative process.

"Inside *Star Trek*," as the album came to be called, never made any top ten lists, which disappointed me a little because I was hoping it would be a huge hit and maybe even win Gene a spoken word Grammy. It may have had to do with the marketing of the album. While it did appear in record stores for a brief time, it was eventually sold only through Lincoln Enterprises in their mail order catalog. If you were fortunate enough to latch on to a copy of the 33 1/3 vinyl disc, hang on to it; no doubt it's worth a considerable amount today as a collector's item. The album's producer, our friend Ed Naha, later left CBS Records and went on to a successful writing career, including a popular book called *The Science Fictionary*. Even more noteworthy was his co-writing credit many years later on the smash Disney film, *Honey, I Shrunk the Kids*.

Candid shot of Gene demonstrating the Vulcan salute, "Live Long and Prosper."

< < <   > > >

In the early days of working for Gene, Majel offered me a job at Lincoln Enterprises. I considered it briefly; my biggest concern was that if he went to a studio, Gene wouldn't be able to take me with him, as the studio union might assign him a secretary. I asked Gene about this, and he said I was free to accept a position at Lincoln if I wanted to, but he certainly *did* plan on taking me with him. And, of course, we eventually did go to the Paramount lot. Fortunately, Gene had me on his own production company's payroll, so the studio had no objections. He was even able to arrange for Paramount to reimburse most of my salary, which helped him financially.

While Gene was waiting for Paramount to proceed with the next phase of the *Star Trek* movie project, he continued to spend several weeks at a stretch on the road giving lectures. During the time he was out of town on these lecture trips and there was little work to do, he asked me to pitch in at Lincoln Enterprises. Usually Majel assigned me routine tasks like filling orders and sorting merchandise, but early in 1976, she invited me to create a newsletter for Lincoln. Since that year was America's Bicentennial, I coined the term "*Star Trek*tennial." Lincoln had been selling a newsletter called "*Inside Star Trek*" for years, but *Star Trektennial News*, as I renamed it, would be a whole new, top quality publication. As editor and sole writer, I was given free rein to do whatever I wanted, supplying camera-ready material containing photos, contests, interviews, and especially updates on the progress of the potential new *Star Trek* movie. Altogether, I did twelve issues, through the end of 1977, by which time Majel was aware of my relationship with Gene and decided to pull me off the project, substituting a friend of hers as editor.

To further capitalize on our nation's and *Star Trek*'s anniversaries, Majel brought out a whole line of *Trek*tennial merchandise that year — belt buckles, commemorative coins, buttons, patches, etc. Then in order to promote these items, she decided to make a commercial to run in local TV markets. I helped her write it and went with her to KTLA-Channel 5 in L.A, where she planned to tape the spot. When we arrived at the KTLA lot, they had booked a studio and arranged for a technical crew to tape her spot. Unfortunately, no one had thought to assign a director to oversee the taping. Somehow, I was pressed into service as the director. I'd never done this in my life, but managed to fake my way through the session, encouraging Majel to speak faster, or slower as those of us in the booth timed and taped the thirty- and sixty-second spots. It was the first time I ever directed anything. What a kick! Now I knew why everyone in Hollywood is always saying, "What I really want to do is direct!"

LOG ENTRY 12 :

In April, Gene was out of town on a speaking tour. One night he called, sounding desperately lonely. Would I get on a plane and rendezvous with him at his next stop? Would I! The sound he heard in the background was my suitcase slamming shut. Gene had been joking with me ever since I had begun working for him that someday I might actually get to travel with him on his lecture circuit. I had always thought I might go to some exciting U.S. cities like New Orleans, Boston, or Nashville, but Gene used to joke that he would take me to Pocatello, Idaho just as soon as he was booked into that town (which I would have been okay with). So now I was off to a place I'd never even heard of — Midland, Michigan. I couldn't have been more thrilled if it had been Paris, France!

We rendezvoused at O'Hare Airport in Chicago and boarded a plane for Bay City, the closest airport to Midland, where he was to speak at Northwood Institute. A nervous young man from the college met us at the Bay City airport. We drove through fifteen miles of lush green rolling hills and neatly plowed farmland, which was just beginning to show signs of a spring thaw. Our destination was the Holiday Inn, the finest motel in this town of about 30,000. I was nervous that someone would think it inappropriate for me to be with him, especially Gene's agency people, who were there to coordinate the event. But no one acted as if this were out of the ordinary. Celebrities travel all the time with their secretaries, and it seemed reasonable that I would be along. Or so I reassured myself.

Gene being interviewed at a Star Trek convention. The press was constantly astounded by the Star Trek phenomenon. When asked why so many people were fans, Gene always said he thought it was the optimistic future the show portrayed.

As would later become customary whenever we traveled together, Gene requested two rooms, one for each of us. It seemed a waste of money to me since I never used mine except for storing my luggage and to be seen exiting it in the morning. When others were present, we would head off to our respective rooms. The minute the coast was clear, my phone would ring, I would pop my head out in the corridor to be certain there were no spies in the hallway, then make a beeline for his room.

I remember Midland so clearly, as this was our first romantic tryst since New York, and the first spur-of-the-moment encounter. We made love with the fury of two convicts just released from prison, and although Gene was still unable to become fully aroused, we were by now becoming quite good at satisfying each other. I knew I really wasn't that good yet, but I was learning what pleased him, having committed whole passages of *The Sensuous Woman* by "J" to memory, and I added enthusiasm to what I knew he liked. Despite "J's" (and Gene's) conclusions, pleasuring a man orally is not always that satisfying for a woman, but when it is done for the man you love, it somehow becomes important to give it your all because the reward is to have the happiest person on Earth lying next to you, singing your praises. I delighted in that, and he knew it. I could also tell he was falling deeply in love with me at this time, which frightened me a little, because I still didn't feel comfortable about being involved with a married man, no matter how unhappy his marriage might have been.

After Midland we went to Albion, Michigan for a similar college visit. I was not crazy about flying in those days, and when we hit sudden turbulence, I grabbed on to Gene's arm and clung to him for dear life, as if he could keep the plane from falling out of the sky. It was absurd, but he didn't laugh, and he reassured me that, as a pilot, he knew everything was okay and we would be fine. I calmed down and, indeed everything was okay and we were fine. Only afterwards did I begin to question my blind faith in him.

I knew that this man, my hero, had survived a serious plane crash during his days as a pilot for Pan American Airways. When his aircraft lost power over the Syrian desert and crashed and burned, he was among a handful of survivors. Gene had told me once that this was the most humiliating incident of his life, not because the plane had met with a horrible accident (which was not his fault), but because at the moment just before impact, he had cried out for his mother and lost control of his bodily functions, soiling his shorts. He claimed he had never told a soul this before. I explained that this was natural, given the kind of stress he was facing — imminent death — but he had gotten the notion into his head that he should have been in control under any circumstances and wouldn't hear otherwise. Nevertheless, he managed to think calmly after the crash when, although injured with broken bones, he helped organize the rescue party. I was touched that he felt comfortable enough with me to tell me this embarrassing story, and it brought me even closer to him.

Despite this tragic mishap, he never lost his love of flying, which had begun when he was a very young boy. As a child, he said, his father had taken him to the local airstrip. There, a barnstorming pilot was selling rides to anyone brave enough to join him for a few moments of thrills aloft. "I'll give you a dollar if you go up," Gene's father offered his seven-year-old son, enticing the future flying ace with a bribe and unknowingly setting him on his life's path. "Sure!" the little boy cried excitedly. According to Gene, his mother was so scared that she begged him not to do it. Gene said he wasn't a bit frightened, and quickly returned to Earth to collect his reward.

His other aerial mishap had occurred during World War II. He enlisted in the Army Air Corps on December 18 (my birthday, as Gene liked to reminisce when we celebrated it), 1941 (not my birth year, however — I came along two years later). He trained to be a bomber pilot, was awarded his wings and shipped out for the South Pacific. There he was assigned his own B-17 bomber. He loved his plane, and once wrote poetry to her. When I asked him if he would share that poetry with me, he recited "My Love Has Wings," which I immediately typed up. For many years I kept a copy of this on my office bulletin board. Part of this poem appeared in a 1966 *Star Trek* episode called "Where No Man Has Gone Before." In it, the newly deified Gary Mitchell (Gary Lockwood) reads from "one of the greatest love poems of our time," referring to "My Love Has Wings" as poetry about some alien creature from another planet — but it was actually a revamped version of Gene's original ode to his World War II fighter plane.

After our visit to Albion and another night of intense lovemaking before and after his speech, Gene continued on to Holland, Michigan, while I was put on a homeward-bound jet to L.A. I'm not sure if it was because his passion was spent after two nights, or he thought it would look best not to be with me in too many places. I had guessed it was a combination of the two. To me, it was always like going through withdrawal whenever we parted. I played back the past two days (and especially the nights) over and over in my mind on the flight home, like a Moebius tape that somehow had no end, because I didn't want it to ever end.

That same year we also rendezvoused in Greensboro, North Carolina, and there would be many other towns and cities across America in years to follow. It was always a thrill to fly in and be welcomed into Gene's arms. And of course, I also enjoyed watching this man as a lecturer.

During all the years I knew him, he constantly strove to improve and contemporize his speech. Generally, he spoke about the topics that were ongoing in his life — his battles with the networks during the making of the original series, the preparation for the new *Star Trek* movie, his interest in his and humanity's future, his philosophy of life, his fascination with the computer age. His speeches, like the man himself, were in a constant state of flux and evolution. In the early days, he (understandably) grumbled about his harsh treatment at the hands of the networks. He had little use for those in authority and made no bones about how television's true purpose was to sell toothpaste and hemorrhoid ointment — an observation he credited to his colleague Harlan Ellison. He always closed his speeches in those early years with a passage from playwright Christopher Fry's *A Sleep of Prisoners*:

> [This] Is no winter now. The frozen misery
> Of centuries breaks, cracks, begins to move,
> The thunder is the thunder of the floes,
> The thaw, the flood, the upstart Spring.
> Thank God our time is now when wrong
> Comes up to face us everywhere,
> Never to leave us till we take
> The longest stride of soul men ever took.

After this, he would always take questions and answers from the audience, and only then could I see him visibly begin to relax. He'd leave the stage as the projectionist began to roll the seventy-minute black-and-white film of "The Cage," the original *Star Trek* pilot. Then a small group of us, usually Gene and I, the sponsors and his agent, would go off and have dinner. Gene wouldn't eat anything before going on stage, although he always fortified himself with a scotch. I believe it was actually in his contract, or at least verbally agreed upon, that he had to have a bottle backstage in his dressing room.

LOG ENTRY 13 :

At all of Gene's speeches, his showing of the Bloopers was always the icing on the cake. These were the outtakes from the original *Star Trek* series, mistakes made by cast and crew, saved by thoughtful directors and editors to be shown as a gag reel at the yearly Christmas parties. Kirk walking into doors, Spock laughing and sucking on a Tootsie Pop, people blowing their lines — these things were very inside, never intended to be shown to an outside audience. But somehow, their notoriety spread, and since Gene had the only copy in existence at the time, he took them with him on all his public appearances, and their reputation soon grew to legendary proportions.

One day he got a phone call from Hugh Hefner, the *Playboy* mogul. His son was in town and would love to view the famous Blooper reel. Could Gene send it over? So Gene asked me to drive to Hef's manse (yeah, sure, I always talked "Hollywood" like this). I was told I'd even be invited to dinner. I'd seen pictures of his Playboy Mansion West but was totally unprepared for what I saw there.

My '74 Plymouth Duster coughed and sputtered up Charing Cross Road, a steep, winding street in the exclusive Holmby Hills area of Los Angeles, adjacent to Bel-Air and Beverly Hills. I found the address and spotted the electronically controlled entrance gate. After I announced myself at the McDonald's-like box by the road ("I'll have a big Mac, an order of fries, and three Playmates, please"), the huge wrought iron gate magically swung open and I urged my trusty Duster up the long driveway to the house I couldn't even see. When I did arrive, there was a large parking lot in what I presumed was the

This photo of the space shuttle Enterprise was given to Gene by NASA after he attended the rollout ceremonies. It decorated his office wall, along with posters of Laurel and Hardy, and Albert Einstein.

front of this grand stone residence, a stately mansion that appeared more suited to the English countryside than smoggy L.A. I parked and was greeted at the door by Hefner's secretary.

We entered the cavernous central hallway where I was soon introduced to the lord of the manor, Mr. Hefner himself. He was wearing his trademark pj's and silk robe, and showed me into the screening room, where someone relieved me of the reel and assured me it would be well taken care of. A few people were seated expectantly around the room, and I assumed one was his son. There were a few ladies present as well, but they were all completely clad. I think Gene was expecting me to come back with reports on the decadence I was sure to witness there; I knew I would have to disappoint him. His secretary escorted me out of this room, and I never saw Hef again. But I did get a lovely, private tour of the majestic grounds, including the aviary, private swimming grotto, and expansive lawns dotted with strutting peacocks. To this day, it remains the largest, most impressive private residence I've ever seen. Yet for all its splendor, it was extremely livable, welcoming, and somehow intimate. An oasis of peace in the big city.

I really was invited to stay for dinner, but it was just the two of us secretaries, seated at a vast dining table especially set up for us, while the chief playboy and his son and guests, having sent for their dinner on TV trays, were still holed up in the projection room watching Kirk bumping into doors and Spock taking pratfalls and breaking up with laughter.

*Star Trek*tennial being the year of America's Bicentennial, some fans planned a special *Star Trek* convention in our nation's capital to tie the two events together. Unfortunately, *Star Trek* Expo, as it was called, didn't begin until July 9, so we missed out on the major Fourth of July festivities and fireworks. Still, it was exciting to be in Washington, D.C. during this historic time. As an invited convention guest, I got to fly first class with Gene, Majel, Rod and the nanny. It was a unique experience for me; I'd always been content to fly coach, but the convention sponsors insisted on giving me the VIP treatment. During the flight, one of the cabin attendants performed magic tricks with cards and ropes, mainly to impress Rod, but I found myself fascinated by this. Gene always got off on watching my enthusiasm for anything new. Impressed by the attendant's performance, I asked Gene if this was routine for first class flights since I hadn't sat in the front of the plane before. He assured me it was indeed part of the service. At first, I was naïve enough to believe him, which gave him yet another thing to tease me about for years to come — first water towers, then *Homo erectus*, and now "magic or non-magic."

Back at Paramount, the progress on the *Star Trek* movie was causing Gene no end of frustration. The studio shifted the project from the motion picture department to the television division, and back again to the movie division. Gene's script, "The God Thing," was resoundingly rejected, but Gene kept up a good front. He was the producer, and he busied himself assembling writers (two guys from Britain, Chris Bryant and Allen Scott), an executive producer (Jerry Isenberg) and a director (Phil Kaufman, who, although he would eventually lose out on *Star Trek*, went on to direct such fine films as *The Right Stuff*, *The Unbearable Lightness of Being*, and *Quills*). My own responsibilities had increased so that in addition to assisting Gene with all his personal secretarial needs, I was also now a fan liaison, coordinating information to various clubs in the form of press releases, as we did not yet have a studio publicist. Since things were incredibly busy from an office standpoint — the volume of mail and phone calls had at least quintupled since preproduction on the film began — Gene promoted me to administrative assistant, and I hired my own secretary/assistant.

If Gene wasn't a hero to the studio executives, there were many people in the scientific community who did recognize his contributions to twentieth century literature and lore. *Star Trek* fans were to be found everywhere, from the lowliest floor-sweeper at the Greyhound Bus depot to the highest echelons of government. Among Gene's biggest fans were those employed in the aerospace industry, many of whom were inspired to pursue science careers after becoming hooked on *Star Trek* as youngsters. He counted astronauts among his acquaintances, and the walls of his home were decorated with autographed photos of some of their space exploits.

Quite often, when there were exciting events happening in the NASA space program, Gene was invited to be present. One such event was the July 20, 1976 landing of the first unmanned spaceship on Mars. Gene, Ray Bradbury and others were among the honored guests at Cal Tech's Jet Propulsion Laboratory as the Mars Viking lander began sending back signals from the Red Planet. America, too, watched on its home TV sets as pictures of a surprisingly Earthlike desert scene were beamed into our living rooms. Oddly though, the scientists seemed to forget the planet's "red" moniker, and they immediately color-corrected the images to show a pale blue sky in the Martian background. Eventually someone pointed out that Mars was Mars, not Earth, and pink was perfectly okay for the sky color.

On his way home from Pasadena, Gene stopped by my place in Burbank, and told me of the wonders he had just seen. His excitement over what he had witnessed was such that he couldn't wait to share it with me — he knew I would be a receptive audience. I was disappointed at not having been invited, as I would have so loved to have been present at this event.[4]

Happily, I *was* included in something that happened out of the blue in the summer of 1976. Gene received a phone call from an agent representing Paul McCartney — yes, *that* Paul McCartney, the ex-Beatle. He was a huge *Star Trek* fan and he wanted to hire Gene to write a screenplay that would star his rock band, Wings. Gene was impressed, and also grateful for the opportunity to do some writing, since Paramount hadn't approved his script for the *Star Trek* movie. When Paul and the group came to town, he provided tickets for Gene, Majel and myself to attend the concert. We had great seats a few rows from the stage. I enjoyed myself tremendously, clapping along, jumping up and down, really getting into the music, lasers, and so on, while Majel, in her mid-forties, and Gene, well into his fifties, looked a bit bewildered by it all.

[4] A few years later I got my chance. On November 12, 1980, our mutual friend Richard Hoagland saw to it that I was invited along with Gene to view the Saturn flyby in the Cal Tech pressroom. It was awesome.

But the best part was after the concert, when we were invited backstage to meet Paul and his wife Linda. We all sat around a giant table, sipping drinks and chatting like we were old friends. I was introduced to Paul, who shook my hand warmly and seemed genuinely glad to meet me. But it was Linda who took me by surprise, when she said upon being introduced to me, "So *you're* Susan! I've been hearing so much about Susan from Gene." I was slightly embarrassed. Just what had she been hearing? Then I realized she was probably just being polite, to make me feel at ease. It worked. I felt like I had known these people for years. Unfortunately, I never met them again after that evening. And I was terribly saddened when Linda died in 1998 from cancer. I cherish the memory of these two special people.

Gene worked on and off with the McCartneys for about a year on their project. He even took his notes with him on the road. In the fall, for example, we were in a hotel room in Jacksonville, where he was to give a talk, when he turned to me and said, "Let me dream now." I thought he meant he wanted to take a nap, but I soon realized this was how he did his creating. He lay down on the bed and stared at the ceiling, seeming to enter another dimension entirely. I doubt if he even realized I was still there in the room with him. I tiptoed into another part of the suite to let him dream.

Months passed, and still Gene hadn't come up with a concept that seemed to satisfy Paul, who went so far as to send his own scenario to Gene, hoping to put him on the right path. Paul's story was about two bands (one from Earth, one from another planet) entering into a competition. Gene continued working on the project for about a year, but eventually, as with a lot of projects Gene started, it fell by the wayside.

One of Gene's biggest thrills was to be present at the rollout ceremony for the very first NASA space shuttle, named Enterprise following a massive letter-writing campaign by **Star Trek** fans. Most of the cast was present, including (l. to r.): unknown NASA official, DeForest Kelley, George Takei, James Doohan, Nichelle Nichols, Leonard Nimoy, Gene Roddenberry, unknown official, and Walter Koenig.

< < <   > > >

On September 17, 1976, Gene and the entire original cast (minus William Shatner, Majel Barrett and Grace Lee Whitney) headed up to the Rockwell International orbital assembly plant in Palmdale, Calif. to witness an historic event. The first of NASA's orbiter space shuttles was about to be rolled out. Only a few weeks before, this shuttle had been slated to be commissioned *Constitution* in honor of the day of its unveiling (Sept. 17 is Constitution Day, a holiday nobody in the United States has ever heard of). But under a barrage of an estimated four hundred thousand protest letters from *Star Trek* fans demanding that the new shuttle be named *Enterprise* after their beloved starship, President Gerald Ford finally relented. His comment to NASA: "I'm a little partial to the name *Enterprise*," adding that he had served in the Pacific aboard a Navy ship that serviced an earlier aircraft carrier of that name. Poor Gerry Ford. He just didn't get it, or wouldn't own up to the influence the fans of a "minor" television show could have on the U.S. government!

At the roll-out ceremony that crisp autumn morning, Gene, Leonard Nimoy, DeForest Kelley, George Takei, Jimmy Doohan, Nichelle Nichols and Walter Koenig received the royal treatment from the NASA folks. Gene later confessed to me that it was one of the most emotional moments in his life. "I expected the band to play something patriotic, like *The Star-Spangled Banner*," he told me. "I just couldn't believe my ears when they struck up the theme from *Star Trek*. It gave me chills!"

Paramount Pictures wasted no time in taking advantage of the publicity opportunity to promote its future movie, still in the scripting stages. They took out a full-page ad in *The New York Times* on Sept. 21:

WELCOME ABOARD . . . SPACE SHUTTLE ENTERPRISE

Paramount Pictures and the thousands of loyal fans of *Star Trek* are happy that the United States of America's new space shuttle has been named after *Star Trek's* starship, the *Enterprise*. (It's nice to know that sometimes science fiction becomes science fact.) Starship *Enterprise* will be joining Space Shuttle *Enterprise* in its space travels very soon[5]. Early next year, Paramount Pictures begins filming an extraordinary motion picture adventure — *Star Trek*. Now we can look forward to two great space adventures.

Well, yes, but not quite that soon. There were many delays in launching Paramount's version of the *Enterprise*, and as Gene went through numerous disappointments, he turned his attention to other possible projects.

[5] Although the fans succeeded in having the shuttle renamed *Enterprise*, the vessel never actually flew a mission into space. After much ballyhoo and a piggyback trip to the Kennedy Space Center, the ship was eventually returned to its point of origin, where it was cannibalized for parts for other orbiters.

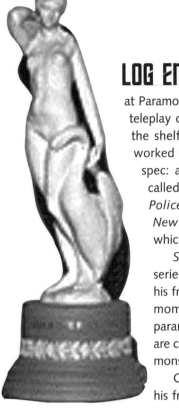

LOG ENTRY 14 : Because of the continuing delays at Paramount, later that fall Gene began to work on *Spectre*, a teleplay co-written with Samuel Peeples that he had kept on the shelf for several years. During leaner times, Gene had worked up a portfolio of scripts which he hoped to sell on spec: an updated and decidedly adult *Tarzan*; a TV pilot called *Police Story* (written prior to the actual TV series *Police Story*, which was scripted by someone else); *The New Tribunes* (another story about police), and *Spectre*, which Gene called his "spook show."

Spectre had been written as a pilot for a weekly TV series. The main characters were a top criminologist and his friend, an alcoholic doctor, who is cured in the opening moments of the story. The men team up to investigate paranormal cases, a kind of early *X-Files*. In *Spectre*, they are called to England to check out a religious cult that summons the devil himself.

Gene dusted off the script, punched it up, and sent it to his friend, the late Sy Salkowitz, then a top 20th Century-Fox TV executive. Gene was delighted when the studio showed interest in filming *Spectre* as a pilot for a possible new series. He was given an office at the Fox studios on Pico Boulevard and a studio secretary to hold down the fort (since I couldn't be in two places at once). Fox decided to film on location in England, where costs were reasonably inexpensive.

Gene made several trips overseas to begin preproduction, staying at the trendy Athenaeum Hotel in London. His longest visit there lasted three lonely weeks, but after this extended stay, he returned with a special gift for me. I had been collecting Wedgwood jasperware for many years, but I really hadn't thought Gene was the type to take notice — he rarely paid much attention to decorations or knick-knacks. So I was very surprised when he presented me with one of the finest pieces in my collection.

Mention Wedgwood and most people think of those blue and white ashtrays Aunt Martha displays on her Victorian end table. But Wedgwood comes in many styles, shapes and colors. I had amassed numerous plates, candlesticks, trays, cups and vases, but I had never seen anything like the gift Gene brought me. It was a 10-inch high sculpture of the mythological characters of Leda and the Swan, crafted in smooth, pure white jasper on a Wedgwood-blue base. It took my breath away! The image was inspired by a classic Greek story — one with which I had no familiarity, but Gene educated me. It seems that Leda was a Greek goddess who was enchanted by Zeus, the king of the gods. He appeared to her in the form of a swan. My beautiful sculpture was a classic portrayal of these lovers, the nude Leda posed with her Swan draped suggestively across her body. It didn't take much imagination to realize that Gene was comparing us to this mythological couple —

The "Leida and the Swan" Wedgwood statue Gene brought me from England when he was in preproduction on Spectre.

but just in case I missed the point, he told me anyway. And a few years later, he surprised me with a crystal version of the same two characters. Clearly, Gene had a very romantic streak in him.

< < <   > > >

Shortly after the Roddenberrys had left for England for the *Spectre* production, I got a call from Gene's daughter, Dawn. She was the younger of the two daughters, and from the moment I met her, I could see how devoted she was to her dad. Each year we'd discuss his Christmas and birthday gifts for hours, trying to decide on just the right present for her to get him. So when she phoned me around the end of the year, I assumed she wanted to talk about his gift. I was wrong.

"I've just been to my psychic," Dawn told me. I could hear the agitation in her voice. Okay, I thought, she goes to a psychic. Lots of people do. I had been once or twice myself, strictly for the entertainment value.

"Yes?" I said, trying to sound interested.

"What she told me was very upsetting. She told me she saw death surrounding a loved one, possibly my father." Of course, I didn't believe this, but cold adrenaline began pumping through my veins.

"Go on." She had my attention now.

"Well, my psychic says that it might mean the death of love in his life, a big loss of love."

I wanted to pour my heart out to her — to relate to Dawn that, yes, I believed there was that loss in his life, but not to worry, because he would never lack for love — I loved him with all my being. But I could only tell her I was sure he was all right — I'd just spoken with him from London and everything was fine.

I felt it my duty to lend my moral support to Gene's kids, as I knew he would want me to. But something was gnawing at the back of my mind. I mentioned the subject of psychics to one of my friends. "Oh," she exclaimed with more enthusiasm than I'd ever seen before, "I have the best psychic! She's always very accurate; she's an eighty-year-old Russian woman, nearly blind. She uses cards, but she can't really see them . . ." My God, I thought, people are so gullible. However, out of curiosity I agreed to see her psychic.

Elizabeth, the nearsighted octogenarian psychic, lived in a modest apartment in Beverly Hills. When she greeted me at the door, I sensed something charismatic about her. She bade me enter what appeared to be a normal home in every respect — no tables covered in black cloth, no crystal balls, no bat's wings flapping in the background. We sat and sipped tea on the sofa, and I was very careful not to divulge anything about who I was or why I was there. Then we moved to the coffee table.

"Papers! Letters! I see writing everywhere," she exclaimed as she turned over enormous cards. "You are writer," she pronounced in her thickly accented voice. I told her I had done some writing, but it wasn't my full-time work. "You will be wery busy writer," she insisted. (Walter "Chekov" Koenig could have taken Russian dialect lessons from her.) Okay, I could buy that. "But you are here because of man." How astute. Who didn't go to psychics because of their love life?

"This man — he loves you wery much. But there isss problem."

She was doing all the talking, I was listening, trying hard not to give clues. I knew my friend, who was really more of an acquaintance, had no knowledge of my personal life, so this woman was tossing out this stuff on her own. "There isss someone else. I see . . . another woman. It isss vife. But there isss no love there. He loves you."

This came pouring out of her, and I was totally unprepared to hear this. I told her I wasn't there about love, that I was only concerned with his health.

"He drinks too much," she told me. "I vould never let my late husband touch me if he drank. I vanted to know that he vas one who vanted me, not drink." I didn't say anything, but what she said made sense. She continued, "You are thinking of leaving him."

This was true, but I had never told anyone about this. I wasn't sure if I could continue working for and loving the same person. My life was getting too complicated and I wasn't mature enough to deal with it, so I'd been toying with the idea of bailing. She shook her head. "This vould be mistake, terrible mistake. If you leave him, he vill die."

And there it was. The death thing Dawn had talked about. Without me, he would die? This was too hokey, this whole scene. I was getting ready to leave when she grabbed my arm. "You must believe me. There isss something blocking his love for you. He isss not free to leave. I see . . . child, yes, that isss it." She seemed self-satisfied at this pronouncement. I thanked her and paid her for her time. "Please call me again if you need anything."

What I needed was a less complicated life, but unfortunately there was no way she could give me that. If anything, she had just dealt me some extremely large cards which, in her blindness, she saw much more clearly than I did.

I never mentioned any of this to Gene. I wasn't sure I believed the old woman's predictions. I knew Gene was having an unhappy homelife, and that Majel was constantly bugging him about her career, and quite a bit about me. She was very aware of our involvement, although Gene was in denial about her awareness. "I think she suspects something," was all he would allow.

I had decided very early in our relationship never to push Gene into leaving Majel. One, I knew it was a good way to lose somebody, and two, I wasn't sure it was what I wanted. Also, Gene seemed determined to make his second marriage work, at least at this stage of our involvement. The failure of his first one had left such tremendous scars; I was not about to become a leech on those old wounds.

LOG ENTRY 15 :

In February, Gene invited me to fly to London, ostensibly to work on *Spectre*, but he admitted it was because he missed me. I arrived on February 19 and headed for a bed and breakfast, which at that time cost around eleven dollars a night. The room was huge, and the bathroom was even larger. There was also a bidet, the first one I had ever seen. I leaned over this curious looking toilet-sink thing and turned on the taps. Water shot straight into my face and eyes. Clearly, this was not for washing one's socks at night!

The next morning Gene and his driver, Rupert Evans, picked me up for the long ride to EMI Elstree studios north of London, where *Spectre* (which starred Robert Culp, Gig Young and John Hurt) had just completed principal photography. The *Movie of the Week*, as it was now designated, was in post production. I was disappointed I was unable to have been there sooner, especially because there had been some interesting moments. For example, during production, Gene had called me one night from London, depressed about a big blow-up with Robert Culp over some dialogue Culp wanted to change. The production had nearly shut down. Gene did not take kindly to having others rewrite his dialogue. This incident gave Gene unnecessary stress, but eventually a compromise was reached.

I was also disappointed that I had missed the big wrap party two nights before I arrived. It was attended by hundreds of *Star Trek* fans from all over the U.K., many of

Clive Donner, British director of Spectre

whom were penpals I had hoped to meet in person one day.

At the studio I was introduced to the various secretaries and personnel in the offices, including the director, Clive Donner. Since I was supposedly there to work, Gene had seen to it that I was provided with my own office, typewriter and stenorette, and he dictated some correspondence just to keep up appearances.

EMI Elstree was a much friendlier, warmer studio than the cavernous Hollywood lots I was used to. The commissary, for instance, was more pub-like than our American counterparts, with all sorts of wine, beer and spirits served at lunch time. The crews there had to be kept happy while playing the traditional darts that were very much a part of this facility. The mere presence of this time-honored British sport made for a feeling of camaraderie among the workers that is totally unknown in the U.S. Every day at lunch, I would admire the British chaps as they went about their dart games, longing to join in. Gene's driver Rupert once challenged me to a toss of the darts, but I wasn't much competition for him.

Rupert was the brother of Mark Evans, a Fox studio executive back in the States, and it was Mark who had recommended Rupert as Gene's full-time driver. Rupert and I became good friends, spending many hours talking in my office. And Gene and Rupert really hit it off (which had been Mark's intention), sharing long hours in the car discussing Rupert's long film career as a stuntman, plus their mutual interest in British naval history and other such topics. Theirs turned into a lifelong friendship, with Rupert eventually making several trips to La Costa and Los Angeles as Gene's guest.

We had many exciting afternoons during my stay in London. I got to watch the music scoring and dubbing sessions and learned a lot about post production. When there wasn't much to do at the studio, Rupert would find interesting pubs for us all to have leisurely lunches. There we discovered such time-honored British fare as "bangers and mash" and "plowman's lunches." In the evening, we would all go out to dinner, or to private gambling clubs recommended by Gene's attorney, Leonard Maizlish, who was in town briefly and introduced me to the pleasures (since Gene was staking me) of gaming in these clubs. One night, we went to dinner at Mirabelle Restaurant in Mayfair, the poshest area of London. The restaurant featured dance music, and Gene danced with Majel, and then with me. I couldn't believe it! He did it on the pretense of being polite, but it was our first dance together and I was tingling from head to toe. I learned later that Gene didn't go in for dancing much. The only other time we danced together was at a hotel on the road a few years later. When he finished his speech, we returned to the hotel for a nightcap, and there was a dance band. After a bit of prodding on my part, he did a couple of twirls with me around the dance floor. I must admit we made an awkward pair, my Jeff to his Mutt, and we never tripped the light fantastic again.

These London days were idyllic times; it would never be like that again. Sometime during my stay over there, Majel learned that Fox had not paid my way, but rather Gene had bought my ticket out of his pocket. I believe it was then that she began to realize that I was perhaps more than a family friend.

< < <   > > >

That June, I attended the 1977 *Star Trek* con at the Los Angeles Convention Center, where sixteen thousand *Star Trek* devotees paid $7.50 to hear William Shatner speak and watch reruns of old episodes on a big screen. I had also been signed as a speaking guest by the convention organizers. My little talk was supposed to have been about what it was like working with Gene Roddenberry; then I would take a few questions from the audience and beat a hasty retreat. But Paramount Pictures, on learning that I would be appearing there, decided to have me read a press release aloud to the fans. Still, I thought this would be no big deal.

Imagine my surprise, then, when I entered one of the main rooms at 11:00 on a Saturday morning to find thirty-five hundred bright-eyed Trekkers awaiting me! I barely had time to steady my quivering legs when I noticed the lights. And the cameras. Lots of them. It looked like a sound stage. Not only had the press been notified, but Paramount had chosen to record this moment for their archives and for future publicity purposes. Actually, I was glad no one had warned me in advance that this would be a Big Production, or I probably would have pleaded a case of Rigellian fever that morning. So there I was, holding up a press release for all the cameras, smiling and nodding after reading the announcement that work would begin in the fall on a new series of *Star Trek* episodes to be released for syndication. I answered questions and posed for pictures, my head swirling. I had brains enough to realize that the thunderous applause was for what I had just told the audience, rather than for the fabulous personality now standing before them, but I allowed myself to be swept along in the tide.

By this time, the thermostat on our relationship was turned all the way up. Not only was Gene seeing me for dinner whenever he could, but he frequently invited me down to the condo in La Costa, where he went for some down time away from the studio. The first time I drove the eighty-six miles to spend two nights with him, I was highly nervous. Did my hair look all right? Was my makeup on straight? Did he really miss me as much as he said he did or was I just imagining it? I was so insecure, I stopped at two gas stations along the way to check myself in the mirror.

I couldn't believe what I saw when I arrived. There was Gene, vacuuming the rug! It was a small, two-level apartment, so it wasn't a massive chore for him to sweep the carpets, but I was shocked. Here was this gifted (and rather spoiled) man in cutoffs, cleaning — and for me! Not only that, he had just made up the bed, spread and all, and even picked up his clothes — and he never picked up his clothes; they landed wherever they landed and lived there until someone else removed them to be laundered. I was impressed. This had to be true love.

During that weekend we became really close, not just sexually but emotionally. We spent practically the whole time in the condo, either talking or making love. We'd known each other for years, and yet there was so much to learn about each other. When Gene suggested that we pick a place to have dinner out the first night, I mentioned that it might be fun to eat in. He agreed — it meant more time alone together. So we shopped for steaks at a nearby market and grilled them on the common area barbecue instead of going out. It also meant we wouldn't have to be far from the sofa or bed, which made it even more perfect.

Over the years and months to follow, I would get to know La Costa and Gene's various residences there quite well. We eventually did have dinners out, at the La Costa Country Club, in nearby Oceanside, at the Quail's Inn overlooking the lake in San Marcos and even down in trendy La Jolla. For one of my birthdays he took me to the Sky Room at La Jolla's La Valencia Hotel, where we dined on Wedgwood china (yes, I turned over the plates and checked) while overlooking the Pacific. This intimate restaurant contained only twelve tables, more reminiscent of a private club with its ornate fabric-covered walls and matching French antique chairs. I learned that it was once a favorite spot of William Randolph Hearst and Marion Davies. The Sky Room was elegantly romantic, and once again I felt like royalty. With each "ooh" and "aah" as the servers brought our classic French cuisine, Gene's smile grew broader. He was always so happy when he saw me enjoying the finer things that life with him offered. He'd grin at me and I'd grin back. Then he'd reach out across the table for my hand, and we'd stare romantically into each other's eyes, just like in a corny movie.

Sometimes when we'd be dining together, he'd joke that he liked my "rabbit teeth," saying it was the part of my smile he liked best. That became a nickname he had for me — "Rabbit Teeth," and while I thought this didn't sound like an attractive feature for a person to have (and which I certainly didn't think I had), coming from Gene it somehow seemed like the most desirable trait a person could ever hope for. It was just one more way he expressed his love, and I adored him for it.

On other occasions, we would dine at one of the many seafood houses along the beach. Afterwards we'd roll up our pant legs, stroll hand in hand along the beach and let the icy cold waves play tag with our toes. He was delighted to find someone who enjoyed the sea as much as he did. Sailing and the ocean were passions of his. His secret longing had always been to live in a house by the water, but he told me he had never been able to convince either of his wives to do this. Although when I knew him he no longer owned his boat, the *Star Trek II*, he never lost his love of the water. It seemed to calm and inspire him.

Once or twice, we rented little two-person sailboats and sailed around the lakes and inland waterways near Oceanside, Carlsbad and San Diego. At the helm of those little boats, he seemed transformed from an intensely creative, passionate twentieth-century icon admired by millions to an old salt, at one with the sea and the sails, a reincarnated ancient mariner from centuries past.

LOG ENTRY 16 :

Gene was once again by himself down in La Costa when *Spectre* had its premiere on *NBC Saturday Night at the Movies*, May 21, 1977. He asked me down that weekend to be with him. Meanwhile, a well-meaning friend, thinking that he would be alone, had invited Gene over to view the two-hour show with him. We had an early dinner, and then Gene went to his buddy's house to see the movie. Naturally, he couldn't take me with him, so I stayed in the condo and watched it on his TV there. I felt weird, watching Gene Roddenberry's production on Gene Roddenberry's television in Gene Roddenberry's condominium, without Gene Roddenberry. Gene returned immediately to my side as soon as *Spectre* ended, but his mood had shifted. He was palpably glum. I couldn't imagine why, nor did he offer any explanation. The movie looked terrific: well-acted, fine production values such as music and makeup, and, as we later learned, it did well in the ratings. I think Gene's moodiness was a kind of postpartum depression. I had expected jubilation; instead, he barely spoke to me and was inconsolable. The next day, his depression had lifted slightly, although not entirely. We went to SeaWorld, and I drove back to L.A. that evening, while he stayed on a day or two longer.

As wonderful as these times together were, he always seemed to enjoy his solitude. It

My autographed photo of Leonard Nimoy, given to me by a friend at NBC in 1970, just after the first series was cancelled.

was as if the excitement of our being together had wound down and now I had become an overstaying guest. Was he bored with me? Had he stopped loving me now that he was sexually satisfied? I realized none of this was true. He was just being himself. He needed some alone time.

When he got into these moods, it was almost a relief to escape to my own home. Never having lived with someone, I wasn't sure how to act when I became a "weekend wife." This wasn't my home, and without him to chat with, there wasn't anything for me to do there. I felt like I was playing house — we did all the things couples do, but, of course, we weren't a couple at all. I would fantasize about what life with him would be like. But in the end, fortunately, it was just a fantasy. I liked my life the way it was, with all of my freedom.

Generally, after a loved-filled couple of days at La Costa, I, too, would feel down. Gene may have enjoyed the constant rounds of reunion/separation, but an inner loneliness always remained with me as I drove back north on the San Diego Freeway. I'd leave after breakfast and very often would return straight to the office to finish out the workday. Once, I was pulled out of line at a routine border patrol checkpoint, an official station set up to catch illegal immigrants being smuggled into the country. Of course, nothing happened and I was soon on my way. I told Gene about this later, and he said it must have been my dark hair and dark eyes that made me look suspicious. I knew he was teasing, but I was pretty uptight in those days and only half-jokingly confided to him that I thought I might have ended up being returned to "my own people, in Mexico." "Just smile, and when they ask you if you're an American, say 'Si!'" he grinned at me. This became a running joke for years during my trips down there; every time he'd kiss me good-bye, he'd remind me to "Say si!"

Occasionally, following a weekend in La Costa, Gene would leave his car there and ride with me to Paramount, so I'd have company for the two-hour drive. I loved having him along for the trip, but it was even more difficult emotionally, because once we reached the office, it would become imperative that we immediately return to our secretary/boss roles. This would create even stronger feelings of separation blues in me than if he had stayed in La Costa. One time when he rode with me to the studio, he had a meeting with Chris Bryant and Allen Scott, our two English writers. My low mood was apparently noticeable to Gene during the meeting, and although he didn't have the opportunity to tell me verbally, he managed to slip me a note typed on his "from the desk of" memo pad:

> Love,
> You are a bit down today. Please, especially with our writers (very important to me) be the charming, smiling person I love. I want them to feel that way about you too.
> (signed)
> Gene

Of course, this made me even more stressed, to know I was inadvertently doing something to hurt him. I smiled bravely, then had a good cry in the ladies' room.

< < <   > > >

Late in the year, Leonard Nimoy filed a request for arbitration with SAG (the Screen Actors Guild) over the use of the Bloopers. As I recall, he found the footage of himself as Mr. Spock laughing and missing cues in these outtakes (which had never been intended for a general audience), highly embarrassing. I was told Nimoy wanted their showing stopped, and an arbitration was sought. Gene told me he was very hurt that Leonard would feel this way about something that he thought Leonard had been aware of for quite some time, since Gene had been using the Bloopers in his college talks for almost five years when this hearing was convened, and Leonard had apparently attended conventions where the Bloopers had been shown.

We met in a room on neutral ground somewhere downtown. There was a large table, around which the contenders positioned themselves like pieces on a chessboard. Nimoy was flanked by his allies — his lawyer, his assistant Teresa and others. Gene had Leonard Maizlish by his side. Majel was there also, and surprisingly, I was asked by Gene and his attorney to attend.

By lunchtime, virtually no progress had been made. The subject matter of the hearings — Gene's continuing use of the Bloopers at events — wasn't even discussed. Instead, both sides had tried to decide who would be the arbiters of this case, and they couldn't agree. Representatives of SAG would proffer a name, and one attorney would reject it; another name, a rejection from the opposing side. This was boring, to say the least, and it continued right on up until 5:00 p.m., when the two sides still hadn't decided who was going to hear the case. The session was adjourned, to be reconvened at some future date. As far as I know, the dispute was never arbitrated, and Gene continued using the Bloopers in all his future talks. Some fans eventually got hold of the film and had copies made illegally. A few years after that, the VCR revolution began, and these tapes were cloned and sold everywhere. No fan ever again had to be without his or her very own copy of the infamous Bloopers.

Leonard Nimoy almost didn't appear in the first *Star Trek* movie. When the first film was in the planning stages, he was unavailable, due to his starring in the Broadway production of *Equus*. In order not to disappoint the fans, who were expecting a Vulcan on the bridge of the *Enterprise*, Gene had the role recast with a handsome and talented young actor named David Gautreaux. David was thrilled at winning the part, and immediately threw himself into the newly created character of a full-blooded Vulcan named "Xon." He took up vegetarianism; he went on long fasts; he meditated. (Fortunately, he didn't have an ear job.) David was screen-tested in full Vulcan make-up right down to the ears. He would have made a splendid Vulcan.

But it was not to be. At the last minute, Leonard Nimoy became available. How could there be *Star Trek* without Mr. Spock? Impossible! Exit David. (He later won a small role in *Star Trek: The Motion Picture* as the station commander who is blown up by V'Ger in the first five minutes of the film.)

Getting the *Star Trek* movie into pre-production took more than three years, with Paramount Studios uncertain of which genre was the best for this latest incarnation. At first *Star Trek* was to be a remake of the original TV series. The studio purchased a num-

ber of worthy scripts, which were eventually put on the shelf when the concept was changed to a small motion picture.[6] During those years, a *Who's Who* of science fiction writers paraded through our office doors (Harlan Ellison, Ray Bradbury and many others), all of whom were eventually rejected by the studio brass.

At last it happened; Gene's dreams were about to come true. On March 28, 1978, Paramount Pictures held a press conference announcing the forthcoming production of *Star Trek: The Motion Picture*. For the first time since 1969, all the original cast were present in the same location — on the Paramount lot at a Chasen's-catered brunch for the media. Robert Wise, the Academy Award®-winning director was introduced; he would helm the new film, now budgeted at fifteen million dollars. Gene received a standing ovation from the entire cast when his name was announced, and with a tear in his eye proclaimed, "I have never been so touched and moved in my entire life."

Too bad there still was no shooting script on the horizon. Gene had his work cut out for him, and the days to come would be some of the most trying of his life.

---

[6] At least two of these scripts were later salvaged and turned into episodes of *Star Trek: The Motion Picture.* More information on the saga of the first *Star Trek* movie can be found in *The Making of Star Trek: The Motion Picture*, by Susan Sackett and Gene Roddenberry.

During the preproduction of Star Trek: The Motion Picture, Gene and I took time out to enjoy the sets under construction.

LOG ENTRY 17 :

Preproduction for the *Star Trek* movie began that spring and continued through the summer of '78, with filming set to begin in August. It had taken over three years to reach this stage; the late Charles Bluhdorn, who guided the goings-on of Paramount from his towering New York Gulf+Western offices, had a daughter who was a big *Star Trek* fan. When the film was foundering, it was daughter Dominique's pleading that became the catalyst for mobilization of the production. Historically, this was one of the most creative periods in recent Paramount history — the "killer Diller era" (as the late Hollywood producer Dawn Steel — then a fledgling Paramount executive, one of many assigned to supervise production on *Star Trek* — once referred to it), characterized by the rise to power of Paramount moguls Barry Diller, Michael Eisner, Jeffrey Katzenberg and Don Simpson, all of whom had a hand in supervising *Star Trek: The Motion Picture*. (Simpson, who died in 1996, became an independent producer; the rest became big-time heads of studios.)

Filming began on Monday, August 7. I celebrated one day earlier by signing papers for my first home purchase. It wasn't that I would now be getting a huge salary, or that Gene was backing me (he wasn't, my parents and life savings were); it was simply a wonderful coincidence. It certainly seemed like a good omen. This was a great house in a not-too-great neighborhood of North Hollywood. I loved it, and Gene and I wasted no time creating new memories there. My new home had an enormous fireplace nearly large enough to stand in, three small bedrooms — ample area for a home office and a guest bedroom, and plenty of room for my queen-size bed without it touching both walls.

Unfortunately, our time together was considerably less than it had been when he wasn't producing a multi-million dollar film. We weren't getting together there as often as we had in my previous, rented, homes. My house was at least twenty minutes away; another twenty minutes for the return trip left little time for us to be together, and no time at all for lunch. One afternoon at the studio Gene took me aside and said, "I have an idea. Why don't you see if you can rent us a small apartment near here? That way, we can get away at lunch time!" I realized that there was a certain logic in this, and I was beginning to miss the chance to cuddle with him without feeling rushed. I combed the neighborhood near Paramount studios and found something that seemed safe yet inexpensive — around two hundred dollars a month. It was a single, a one-room apartment with a fridge and countertop but no stove. The olive drab carpet had chew marks where either a dog or some hapless individual had vented its frustration. The landlord confirmed that the previous tenant had kept a large German Shepherd. I assured him I did not plan to bring in any pets. The one luxury the place had was air-conditioning, a necessity in the brutal Los Angeles summer. There was also a closet where Gene and I could hang up our robes, and a bathroom for our toothbrushes and a quick shower before returning to the office.

I was in seventh heaven, outfitting this place like a newlywed. Although I didn't harbor any ideas about our ever living together, I enjoyed indulging myself in harmless fantasy as I decorated in "early garage sale": cheap plates, should we want to order in some lunch and not eat out of cartons; a throw rug to cover the doggie hole, and some sheets for the convertible sofa that doubled as a bed, the main object of our furniture interest. We soon discovered that this bed must have been subjected to some frantic sessions before us. It sagged almost to the floor under our combined weight. At first, we dragged the mattress onto the ground, but eventually I bought a satiny coverlet and we simply placed this directly on the floor.

Gene brought over the eight-track cassette player he had been using in the office, and he went out and bought a bunch of easy-listening tapes featuring Jackie Gleason and his Orchestra. Eight-tracks were just beginning to decline then, and so was Gleason, but his elevator-zombie music was good background for lovemaking. It took some educating on my part to get Gene to admit that ambiance was important. He was a very focused person, perfectly content to have the news or a talk show blaring away on the tiny TV I had found at a swap meet. I told him how important soft music was in helping me relax, so he bought those Gleason tapes. His choice in music made me painfully aware of our generation gap. Fortunately, Gene was very musical and enjoyed a wide range of genres. Eventually, I was able to sneak in a few tapes of the British rock group Queen during our car rides together. We both appreciated the use of harmonics in their albums *A Day at the Races* and *A Night at the Opera*.

Our lovemaking at that time usually began with our sharing a joint. There was always a steady flow of pot in our office, and we enjoyed the heightened sexual awareness it gave us. Yes, we inhaled! But by the time our ninety-minute lunch was over, we'd be reasonably clear-headed and able to return to work.

Pot was just a natural extension of our lives in those declining days of the '70s. To us, it was as routine as having a glass of wine in the evening might be to someone from an earlier generation — and although this included Gene, he always surrounded himself with young, freethinking people. Virtually everyone in our offices was into it. Every Friday evening, the whole gang would gather around Gene in his office or one of the other rooms for a glass of wine and/or some pot. Smoking marijuana on the studio lot was fairly commonplace. At any given time, you could smell the odor wafting from myriad office windows around Paramount, and could almost get high just walking through the studio streets and alleys. We'd sip our wine, toke up, and discuss the week's efforts, the world in general, or whatever nonsense seemed substantial in our hazy states of consciousness. Always, Gene was the axis around which our little group revolved. Part of his charm was the way he made everyone feel that they or their project were special and important. He could never say no to anyone, even when common sense demanded it.

About the only one who didn't participate in these weekly gatherings was the film's director, Robert Wise, who seemed far too dignified (although not censuring). He would merely shake his head or cluck his tongue. I think he looked upon us all (Gene included) as silly children. We simply accepted and respected him for the dignified gentleman he was.

Our relationship was in full swing, but with the pressures of making the film, not to mention the double life we were leading, it was also a terrible strain on both of us. Eventually, we both found it necessary to turn to outside help. Gene began seeing a Beverly Hills therapist. He told me he knew it was "going Hollywood," but I was pleased that he was trying to cope with his obvious stress and mounting depression over the difficulty he was having trying to balance his marriage and his profound feelings for me.

At this time, I was often feeling depressed because I was uncomfortable being the other woman. I had had these guilt feelings right from the start of our relationship. This was not part of the All-American girl's dream I had grown up with in the '50s. I had always thought I'd work until finding the right man, then settle down to a life of kids and kitchen floors (dressed, of course, in high heels and pearls). Now I was revising my goals. Perhaps a career was really what I wanted after all. I certainly didn't want to be saddled with babies when I could be working in film and sharing my days (and many evenings) with a man with whom I was joyfully in love. So, at the same time Gene was seeing a shrink, I was trying to reassess my own life. I had never been to a therapist before, and I wasn't sure if I wanted to get into that scene. Then a friend recommended something that sounded so far out it intrigued me, and I knew I wouldn't be satisfied unless I went to see this person.

Jennie Elford was also an old friend. I'd met her through Cheryl Blythe, a secretary who worked across the hall from Gene and me when we first came on the lot (and who would later become my friend and writing partner on several books and script projects). Jennie had been an executive at ABC Television, but had left that field to pursue a variety of interests, including owning her own wall upholstery business and a career as a massage therapist. But it was her training in a technique called "past lives therapy" that intrigued me. Cheryl sang Jennie's praises, and although this seemed to be on the cutting edge of weird, I decided it might be fun.

It was more than fun. It was totally releasing. I went into this program a complete skeptic and emerged convinced that there was much to be gained from the experience (although still skeptical of actual past lives). The methodology didn't set out to reveal whether or not I had been Cleopatra in another life, or who else I might have been; it didn't matter that I might not even believe in past lives. The point was, through a self-induced relaxation state, I was able to let my mind roam into *what might have been* a traumatic past life. It could just as easily have been my overworked imagination conjuring up such events. It didn't matter. I relived some strange experiences, felt all the emotions of these events, and then released them in order to move on. Research has since shown that this can be an effective form of therapy that frees the mind, removes blocks, and allows the patient to begin to relate to the struggles of daily life with a much greater sense of control. After several weeks of seeing Jennie, and learning that I either had some very strange past lives (a pioneer who starved to death crossing the Great Plains; a child trapped down a well) or an overworked imagination, I began to feel much more centered and less stressed about my relationship with Gene.

LOG ENTRY 18 :

When Gene was able to fabricate an evening meeting so that we had a chance to spend time together, it would usually begin with a trip to my North Hollywood home in the Valley, followed by a dinner in some fine restaurant. I had purchased a Betamax VCR, one of the earliest introduced for the consumer market, and we would watch a tape I'd recorded from a Public Television special. One of our greatest pleasures was the viewing of all sorts of PBS documentaries and special programming. Together we enjoyed such now-classic series as *The Body in Question, Cosmos, The Making of Mankind, The Brain, Life on Earth, The Heart of the Dragon, The Day the Universe Changed*, and *The Story of English*. Gene said he had very little opportunity to watch these at home, as Majel's tastes ran more to game shows than documentaries. Gene called game shows "greed" shows, but I really couldn't go along with him on that, having appeared on several of these myself! And I was pleased that my eclectic viewing habits made it possible for me to be the one with whom he could share more erudite programming.

When he came over to my house, we'd settle down to a tape of some documentary that I'd recorded. Inevitably during the first fifteen minutes of the program, Gene would make his move. Sometimes we'd make it to the bedroom, although frequently we made love on the sofa to the accompaniment of Public TV's documentaries. Fortunately, we were both members of this viewer supported alternative television. I thought it was a bit strange, but since we'd paid for these programs, I reasoned it justified using them as a background for anything we wanted to do. Gene certainly wasn't very discriminating when it came to lovemaking background sounds. TV, radio, those Gleason tapes — and probably the entire USC Trojan Marching Band wouldn't distract him once he decided to tune them out. I never quite learned this art, and frequently had to interrupt him to request a change of venue or at least of auditory ambiance.

One of our favorite PBS series was Bronowski's *The Ascent of Man*. The late British scientist/philosopher Jacob Bronowski presented his point of view on the emergence of Western civilization and humanity with a unique perspective on art, literature and the sciences. Gene, who loved repeating satisfying literary experiences, such as rereading his favorite Hornblower or World War II history books, insisted we rewatch the Bronowski tapes on countless occasions, until the magnetic particles had nearly worn away. I had recorded the episodes in 1977 as best I could on my original Betamax, and spent the next fourteen years searching for a professional copy as a gift for him, but to this day I have never located a set of these tapes. I suppose the producers declined to release this series on the basis of its being dated, since much of the science has been superseded by more current findings.

For a person who made his living in television, Gene cared for very few of its offerings. He loved to laugh and always enjoyed a good comedy, but he could be very critical. I always hesitated to introduce him to some new comedy series I thought was funny, for inevitably it would be a bad episode and I'd end up being apologetic. His favorite program was *Barney Miller*. He was intrigued with the idea of a funny police precinct, since he could relate to this through his experiences in the early 1950s, when he was still a flatfoot by day, a struggling writer by night. If reruns of this show came on during an afternoon or evening when he was visiting my home, his eyes would shine with a contented light.

Gene and I usually preferred to dine in some elegant restaurant (as in the popular joke, "What does a Jewish woman make for dinner? Reservations!"), but I also enjoyed fixing dinner for him. I seldom cook for myself. If I can't nuke it in the microwave or slip it on the barbie, I seldom bother preparing elaborate meals. But having Gene as my very appreciative guest gave me an opportunity to trot out my heirloom china, best crystal and functional stainless steel flatware. I was delighted to have someone to fuss over, and I tried out all my mother's best homestyle recipes on him. Pot roast and baked beans, noodle kugel (pudding), stuffed cabbage, stuffed peppers with gingersnaps — Gene liked his food Old World-ish and hearty. His favorite soup, for example, was Chasen's (the world-famous Beverly Hills restaurant) version of cream of tomato. I experimented until I came up with a reasonable facsimile (by adding beef bouillon, heavy cream and a touch of sherry). And he adored Mexican food. His family had migrated to Los Angeles from El Paso, Texas when Gene was only two, but his mom brought all her best Tex-Mex recipes with her. Gene had cut his teeth on his mother's enchiladas. I didn't try to compete with this, but once I managed to whip up an old-fashioned tamale pie that completely blew him away. Another time he volunteered to cook meat loaf for the two of us, and to my surprise, it turned out to be the very same recipe my own mother had been using for years.

My remaining bottle of the infamous Foaming Milk Bath.

One afternoon, a couple of years after he'd written the rejected *Star Trek* script, "The God Thing," Gene popped over to my house with a surprise. I was expecting him for dinner, and he showed up with a sheepish grin on his face and an enormous box under his arm. He was also toting several huge plastic shopping bags full of some unseen treasure. He glanced around and finally settled on the living room for the scene of the presentation he was about to make. From the box he produced an eight-foot-diameter child's plastic-lined swimming pool, the kind you set up in the back yard in the summer and kids wade in, knee deep. Uh oh, I thought. Better put the dogs in the back.

After unrolling the kiddie pool, he showed me what was in the shopping bags. He'd been to Thrifty's (the local pharmacy), and had bought twelve pints of generic baby oil, and also three bottles of something labeled "Foaming Milk Bath." I had no trouble guessing what was coming next. In his script and partially completed novelization of "The God Thing," there was a scene in which several female sirens tantalized Captain Kirk while they engaged in a weightless free-for-all, rolling in oil, their bodies glistening in what began as a sensual gymnastic event for Kirk and turned into a deadly contest for his life. I knew immediately when I saw the baby oil that Gene wanted to enact this fantasy (minus the fight to the death, I assumed).

"Let's get naked and just see what happens," he suggested, uncapping one of the bottles of oil and pouring it into the plastic pool now sitting in the middle of my formal living room. I pulled the blinds. Good grief, what would the neighbors think? I brought out all the old towels I could find and readied them by the pool. Six bottles of oil and some Foaming Milk Bath later, we tentatively touched our toes into the mixture. He hopped in, sitting dead center in the pool. "Come on, be brave!" he implored. Jeez, I thought, I really don't want to do this. Then again, why not? I was happy to indulge him in this harmless game. At worst, it would be good for our skin. But there was hardly enough oil to cover the bottom of the pool, and it didn't mix well with the Foaming Milk Bath. We tried to slide around in it and pretend we were weightless, writhing space cadets or something, but it was really quite messy. Also, the floor was hard, so it wasn't very comfortable. The showers afterward were the best things about this experience. That, and the lifetime supply of baby oil and Foaming Milk Bath. I still have some of the oil left after twenty some-odd years (I use it to remove eye makeup, not to play slip-'n'-slide), and a pint of Foaming Milk Bath — which works much better in a bathtub, with water, the way Nature intended it.

Don't get the wrong idea; even though Gene could be extremely creative, it wasn't always the surprise *du jour* whenever he came over. Generally, we'd just talk for hours on end. His favorite topics of conversation were history, literature, and the development of civilization and of humankind. He was always a student of humanity, constantly amazed at what made this animal tick. He had a particular interest in that aspect of the mind called "consciousness." Many of the original *Star Trek* episodes dealt with his exploration into consciousness versus physical bodies; the theme was explored over and over again. In the science fiction arena, characters' consciousnesses could be transferred from body to body, body to container, or body to space with frequency and ease. Yet when I discussed Gene's beliefs with him during the '70s, he was uncertain as to whether or not our consciousness could actually survive the body upon death, although at times he seemed convinced this was possible.

Once when the subject of consciousness came up, I asked him if he'd ever had an out-of-body experience.

"Yes," came his unexpected reply. I supposed I should not have been so shocked at his belief in this esoteric notion, given his history of consciousness-themed episodes. But it still caught me by surprise. "When I was a child I was very sickly," he continued. "I had every possible allergy as well as severe asthma. One day I was just so fed up with being sick, I wished I could be out of this miserable body. And suddenly I was! I found myself in the corner across the room, looking back at my body. I know this happened; it was not a dream." He told me this had never occurred again, and he had practically forgotten about it until I had asked him about out-of-body experiences. We never chatted about this again; I merely filed it away in my mind under "one more interesting aspect of Gene Roddenberry."

His spiritual beliefs were extant, although they were revised frequently. When I first discussed this with him, he believed in what he called the "All," the life force of the universe. Occasionally he referred to this concept as "God," although it was clear that his was not the Judeo-Christian god concept in any shape or form.

It was this fascination with religion that had formed the basis of Gene's rejected sequel script for Paramount. In that story, Captain Kirk and company encounter a seemingly omnipotent being who claims to be the God of the Old Testament. After a few parlor tricks, such as restoring Lt. Sulu's amputated legs, many of the crew begin to believe that this being may indeed be a deity. In actuality, it is a powerful machine with confused programming (a favorite plot device Gene would use many times), arriving at Earth thinking it is a messiah. Only Kirk remains steadfast in his disbelief.

The script contained elements which would eventually be incorporated years later into the story for *Star Trek: The Motion Picture* — things like Spock spending time as a novitiate with the Vulcan Masters; a transporter accident in which people beam up with scrambled body parts; a disgruntled McCoy beaming aboard after finding happiness in a back-to-nature existence, and a visit to Starfleet Headquarters in San Francisco. In the end, Kirk inevitably goes one-on-one with the Entity, whose Christlike image dissolves into patterns resembling "The Great Deceiver," as Gene put it.

Following the studio's rejection of this script, Gene began writing it as a novel, calling it *The God Thing*. It was set aside when other projects demanded his attention, and the book was incomplete at the time of his death.

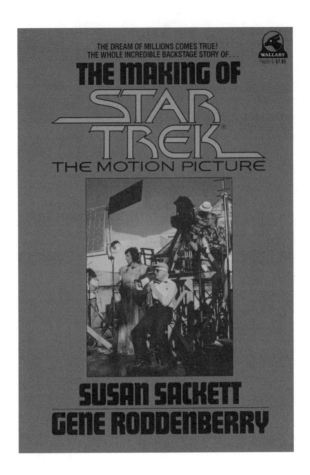

THE MAKING OF

STAR TREK

THE MOTION PICTURE

SUSAN SACKETT

GENE RODDENBERRY

LOG ENTRY 19 : The movie was proceeding on track, but not without its headaches. The studio decided to go with a story that had been proposed for the aborted new TV series, *In Thy Image*, by science fiction writer Alan Dean Foster. Initially, Gene had given Alan a copy of a story he had written years before, called *Robot's Return*. This became the basis for *In Thy Image*. Gene then rewrote Alan's story, but when the studio decided to do a film rather than a TV show, Gene and another writer, Harold Livingston, worked on the screenplay.

Gene's perfectionism caused considerable friction in the office. Nothing was ever simple about this picture. Gene rewrote Harold's rewrites; Harold rewrote Gene's rewrites of his rewrites. This continued ad infinitum, right up until the actual moment of shooting. The actors weren't able to study their scripts and memorize their lines, since dialogue changes were being rushed to the set on an hourly basis. In Gene's words, it was a "writer's nightmare."

When the movie was completed and it came time to award final writing credit, Gene felt he had contributed immensely to the script and should receive major credit; Livingston

Cover of my book, written with Gene Roddenberry: The Making of Star Trek: The Motion Picture

felt otherwise. At one point there was discussion about a possible credit arbitration with the Writers Guild; if Gene wanted screenplay credit, he would have to fight for it. But after nearly four years, the fight was pretty much gone out of him. Gene conceded the point and didn't seek the credit in question.

Working on this first *Star Trek* movie was one of the happiest times in my life. Pocket Books, the licensed publisher, had tapped me to write the behind-the-scenes book, *The Making of Star Trek: The Motion Picture*. I shared the book's writing credit with Gene (although he got the lion's share of the royalties — and rightly so, since it was his baby). The book was due to be released to coincide with the film's premiere. This meant that I had to be on the set nearly every day, asking questions, taking notes, interviewing every-one connected with the film.

It was terrific fun! At various times, I sat down to lunch with George Takei, Walter Koenig, Jimmy Doohan, Nichelle Nichols, the late Persis Khambatta, and Stephen Collins. I brought my tape recorder to the sound stage daily and caught up with Bill Shatner and Leonard Nimoy between takes.

Leonard Nimoy and Bill Shatner both had "favored nations" clauses in their contracts. This meant that they were co-leads, each receiving equal treatment, equal dressing rooms, and equal salaries. However, in my opinion, each seemed to think they alone were the star. I had tremendous difficulty getting information from them for the book.

Interviewing Bill Shatner proved to be the most daunting task. While the other actors were always gracious, Bill was evasive. Once when I approached him on the set with my tape recorder, he said "Get away from me with that thing." I thought perhaps he was jok-ing, as he was known for his ironic sense of humor. Then I realized he was serious. I

George Takei and I were presenters at a Trek convention in Los Angeles. We remain good friends to this day.

explained to him that the book I was writing was fully authorized by Paramount Pictures and that I needed to interview him. He was not very cooperative. He seemed to have changed a lot since my first encounter with him at the recording studio. I never did get a good interview with Bill and had to use his studio bio to piece together the information about his personal life.

Bill hardly ever turned out for dailies (footage shot the previous day); the only time I remember seeing him there was once as he watched, stone-faced, the scene from *Star Trek III* when he delivers the line, "You Klingon bastard, you killed my son!" On the other hand, Leonard Nimoy never missed the chance to watch himself in the dailies. He was a very serious man, although not as stone-faced as his alter ego.

DeForest Kelley (my favorite — how I miss him) was ever gracious and granted me a lengthy interview. I became good friends with him and his wife, Carolyn. I never heard anyone say an unkind word about De. He was a Southern gentleman to the core, much like his character, Dr. McCoy. A few years before the film, I had gotten to know De better when he, Carolyn and I were in Phoenix for a fan convention. We were all at the swimming pool; it was a hot day and I continually dipped in the water to stay reasonably cool. De joked that I looked good in the swimsuit. "Why don't you wear one more often?" Sure, I replied, this would be perfect for the office!

De was always cordial to me. During filming De and I posed for one of my favorite pictures, which I have proudly displayed on my home office wall.

All the actors had one thing in common: when the first draft of the movie script was distributed, they carefully counted their lines. Neither Bill nor Leonard was happy if the other had more dialogue. It was the same with the other regulars — each had to have a scene that featured them, or there would be protests. I remember Gene working hard for several days adding a special scene for Majel in which she shows Ilia (Persis Khambatta) a head ribbon. The scene did nothing for the film, other than giving Majel a special bit.

While working on the book, I talked to everyone involved with the movie. My interview with Robert Wise in his office was a highlight. Winner of several Academy Awards®, Bob was one of the most refreshing Hollywood people I ever met. The best word to describe him is "gentleman." I never heard him utter a harsh word; his presence definitely gave the film an air of dignity whenever he was present

On set, I interviewed editors, grips, gaffers, painters, set decorators, production designers, costumers, special effects people — you name it — if they were on that stage, they couldn't escape me and my ubiquitous tape recorder!

The excitement of doing this book continued when Paramount Pictures and Pocket Books sent me to corporate headquarters in New York to select the photos from their archived slides. They flew me first class, put me up at a fancy Central Park hotel, The Essex House, and picked up the tab for a two-day stay while I spent numerous hours pouring over thousands of slides and stills.

The book was released in two versions — a limited hardcover edition, and a trade-size paperback version, both with beautiful bright red covers. I was thrilled with the way it turned out, and to this day I think it is some of my best work. Of course, much of this was due to Gene's input. Because his name was also on the cover, he took great care to go over everything carefully, making suggestions for changes, deletions, corrections and additions. He also helped me choose from the photos I had selected in New York. And, of

course, it was a rare opportunity to work with him on an equal level.

My other great experience connected with *Star Trek: The Motion Picture* was being an extra for a day. We needed about a hundred extras for the Rec Deck scene, in which all of the crew of the *Enterprise* is supposed to assemble and be briefed by Captain Kirk. Gene wanted to find a way to thank the fans for their support over the years, so after the requisite number of union extras were hired, he asked Richard Arnold, Bjo Trimble and me to round up all the hard-working fans and invite them to appear in the scene. We also included people like David Gerrold (writer of "The Trouble With Tribbles"), Grace Lee Whitney's sons, Robert Wise's wife Millie, a few office personnel, and me!

I got to appear on the balcony overlooking the entire group. If you have a tape and want to find me, I am the third white jumpsuit from the left with the tired, sad-looking face. After standing around for ten hours, it was hard to look perky. Yet Bob Wise spent hours guiding us through our scene with unwavering enthusiasm. "You see it. It's attacking the space station! All your friends are dead! Turn to your neighbor and *react!*" director Wise implored, as we newly-initiated actors looked at a blank screen and imagined all the possible horrors that were happening.

During the making of *ST:TMP*, I was able to get to know all of the original cast members. Most of them were very friendly towards me, and they seemed to care about each

My treasured autographed picture of the late DeForest Kelley. "Just us, Susan," he wrote. What a dear man he was!

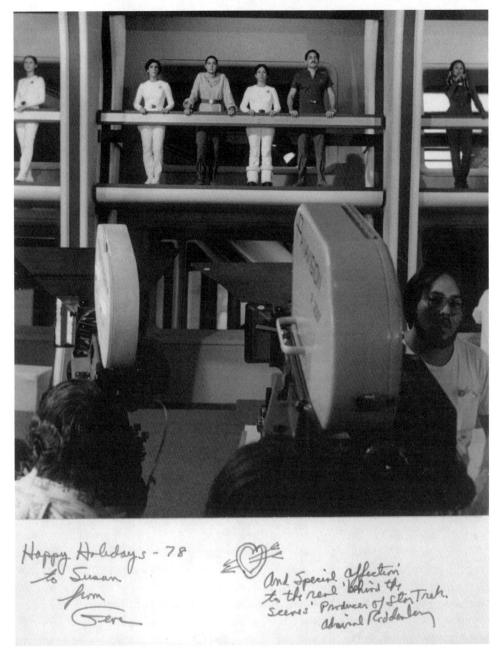

Happy Holidays – 78
to Susan
from
Gene

And Special Affection
to the real 'behind the
scenes' Producer of Star Trek.
Admiral Roddenberry

other as well, as if they were family members. While it's a general misconception that actors in any given show hang out with each other during their down time, our *Star Trek* cast, with the exception perhaps of Bill and Leonard (although this wasn't always true), seemed to have a strong bond with each other. And Gene was very fond of them as well, especially the older cast members like Jimmy Doohan and De, with whom he would often lunch simply because they were friends.

My "balcony scene" from **Star Trek: The Motion Picture**. Gene signed this at Christmastime. It reads: "Happy Holidays '78 to Susan from Gene — And special affection to the real 'behind the scenes' producer of Star Trek – Admiral Roddenberry." Note the two intertwined hearts Gene drew!

LOG ENTRY 20 :

Production wrapped in January, and Gene was completely burned out. His health was beginning to show the signs of this stress. He was in terrible physical shape, and was drinking more than ever. I was concerned for his health; Gene had had a glass of something in his hand virtually all the time I'd known him, and it made me very uneasy.

Early in 1979, he quit smoking cold turkey and began to jog. He seemed very serious about this. I was pleasantly surprised when by March of 1979, he was running up to five miles in the morning before breakfast. I visited him in La Costa, where he proved this to me. While I lazed around in bed one morning, he put on his jogging outfit and apologized for leaving me. "Will you hold and cuddle me when I return, even if I'm all sweaty?" he asked sheepishly. "Of course," I mumbled drowsily as he set out for his morning run along the golf course. It was about six a.m., so I rolled over and went back to sleep (I don't do early mornings well). The next thing I knew, a flushed, damp man was curling up next to me. "That was great!" he gasped, rivulets of water pooling on the sheets. Whatever Gene did, he did it with an intensity and drive that was his unmistakable trademark. He was fifty-eight, and I worried about his heart, but since I myself could barely run half a mile, I was extremely proud of this man, twenty-two years my senior.

There were countless problems with which to contend during post production of the movie. The first organization hired by Paramount to do special effects had failed to produce anything substantial after nearly a year and approximately five million dollars down the tubes. So Doug Trumbull and his team were brought to the rescue, as budget kept doubling.[7] The frantic rush to complete the film by the deadline Paramount had set brought Gene, along with almost everyone else, close to the point of physical collapse.

We would arrive early in the morning to find our offices a makeshift campground, as dozing editors rose wearily to their feet, rolled up their sleeping bags and headed back to their Moviolas. This went on week after week, month after month.

Gene was always an eleventh-hour writer. If there was a deadline in eight weeks, he'd save the big push for week seven, day six. The novelization of the movie was a typical project. I worked right alongside him, editing and polishing, checking for grammar, sentence structure and redundancies (he tended to use the word "now" about six times per paragraph). We didn't have computers in those days. I would type his latest draft, then Gene would pencil in his numerous undecipherable-to-the-uninitiated changes, and I'd do infinite retypes from scratch. Whenever possible, I'd resort to the old cut-and-paste method (using the heavy-duty Xerox) to save wear and tear on my nubs of fingers.

Gene would often forget to eat, downing cup after cup of strong, black coffee. Eventually I'd go out for sandwiches or pizza to fortify us both, or he would have skipped food altogether when he was in this sort of writing mode. We worked this way right up until

---

[7] By the time the film was completed, the final price tag was in the neighborhood of $44 million, the most expensive film made to that date.

three a.m. the morning before the book's actual due date. There were no fax machines either, so we had to send it to New York by overnight delivery. Typesetters were put on overtime, and the book was printed and shipped on time. When the novel hit the bookstalls, it was a huge success, with over a million copies in print.

Star Trek: The Motion Picture was set to have its world premiere in Washington, D.C., on December 6, 1979. I was invited to attend, with the studio picking up the first class tab all the way. It was my first movie premiere, and I could hardly focus on anything else for weeks! I bought a new gown, new shoes, the works. A friend of mine, who was an expert when it came to sewing, offered to make a special evening wrap for me. Gene once told me his favorite color was green and that he thought I looked especially fetching in it, so from that time on I wore green almost exclusively when I was around him. My friend sewed me a gorgeous green velvet hooded cape with white satin lining, an exquisite piece of work. I felt like a cross between Scarlett O'Hara and Count Dracula, but I had to admit it was stunning. When I went to the fabric store to purchase this outrageously expensive material, the sales clerk remarked, "I hope you're not just going to have dinner in the Valley." I assured her I was not.

The Paramount entourage stayed at the elegant Four Seasons Hotel in Georgetown. The premiere itself was preceded by a cocktail party. Robert Wise was so nervous he was scarfing down hors d'oeuvres as if he had never seen food before. I asked him if he was very hungry and he replied, "I always eat like this when I'm nervous." I, on the other hand, who have never had trouble finding an appetite at the slightest excuse, could not swallow a bite, and watching poor Bob Wise gorge himself as if about to become a sacrificial animal made my stomach do a one-eighty deep in my abdomen.

Trek fan and friend Richard Arnold was my escort to the Washington premeire of **Star Trek: The Motion Picture**.

Following the cocktail reception, we boarded limousines for the MacArthur Theatre. I arrived on the arm of my escort, Richard Arnold. Richard was an old friend, and a *Trek* fan friend I had known since the early '70s. He had been helping out in our offices for many years, working on his own time and without accepting any salary (eventually he would be given a full-time paying job as Paramount's resident *Star Trek* archivist). When told I was allowed to invite someone as my guest, I didn't hesitate to ask Richard.

When we arrived at the premiere, it was all I could do to stifle a case of the giggles, as we emerged from the limo to popping flashbulbs and oohs and aahs. I knew people had no idea who we were, but figured we had to be *Important People*, since we were in limos, as were all the stars. So I played the part, smiling and waving to the crowd. Why spoil their fun?

The screening was heavily attended by the press, who were being given their first glimpse of Gene's magnum opus. This made it difficult for me to enjoy the picture as I tried to anticipate how they would react to this or that scene. Following the premiere, we limoed to the National Air and Space Museum at the Smithsonian Institution, where an elaborate party was held in the shadow of Lindbergh's "Spirit of St. Louis." It was indeed exciting, but the highlight for me was the little display case near the entrance. Inside was an actual rock from the actual moon, brought back by actual astronauts! It was almost as fantastic as the film we had just seen — imagine, pieces of the moon, only inches from my face!

I was gaping at this bit of nickel and silicon or whatever when I heard a familiar voice behind me. "I love your outfit. You look fantastic!" It was Gene, who had noticed me in my jolly green cape and white low-cut gown. In his moment of glory, surrounded by

At the premiere, Gene found a moment during the celebration party at the Smithsonian Institution to spend a few moments with me.

press, studio executives, his family (including his mother, who had flown in for the occasion) and an entire entourage of well-wishers and back-slappers, he had slipped from his limelight to spend a few moments with me, not an easy task.

The movie had its nationwide premiere on December 7, 1979, and although some jokingly referred to it as the biggest bomb on that date since Pearl Harbor, it was anything but that. If some of the critics were unkind, the fans couldn't have cared less. It did remarkably well at the box office — in today's dollars it would have to be considered the most successful in domestic rentals of any of the *Star Trek* movies. It was only later that the fans began to dis' the film

The film's main problems stemmed from the fact that it was way over budget. Forty-four million dollars in 1979 bought a *lot* of special effects, and Paramount was determined to use every possible inch of that footage. Subsequently, there were long, lingering, loving looks at starship *Enterprise*; thousands and thousands of kilometers of traveling inside V'Ger's cloud, and many other FX that bored the heck out of all but the most ardent Trekker.

Another problem dealt with the way the movie was produced and overseen by the studio, a film by committee, as Gene saw it. It seemed everyone had a hand in it, from studio executives on down, so that the production eventually became a taffy-pull. Gene's vision was subjected to constant scrutiny and changes at the whim of nearly everyone involved at the executive level, and the cohesiveness suffered.

Despite all this, the film brought out record crowds of fans, hungry for their first look at their heroes since 1969, when the last original episode of the classic TV series had aired.

The decade of the '70s was ending even as *ST:TMP* was making waves at the box office. And riding on the crest of that wave was the man whose name was symbiotically intertwined with the film and all things *Trek*.

Unfortunately, Gene Roddenberry's wave would soon break upon an unknown shore as the new decade would present the biggest challenges he would ever face in his life.

LOG ENTRY 21 :

The new decade dawned even as chapters in our lives were both closing and opening. With the new *Star Trek* movie's release, Paramount took a "wait and see" attitude. If the film proved successful, there would be a series of *Trek* movies. If not . . .

Despite its obscene costs, *Star Trek: The Motion Picture* was indeed a success. A sequel was immediately ordered, and Gene began to work with an intensity that belied his usual eleventh-hour ritual. By the end of May, he turned in a sixty-page outline for a script he called *Star Trek III*.[8]

Some fans familiar with its premise refer to it as the "Captain Kirk meets Kennedy" script. Gene's story concerned the crew of the *Enterprise* traveling through time to 1963 Earth where Klingons, having discovered the "time portal" (from the original TV series episode "The City on the Edge of Forever"), have changed Earth history by preventing the assassination of President Kennedy. Kirk meets with Kennedy, whom he dislikes at first. Eventually, the two develop a mutual trust, with Kennedy even being given a tour of the *Enterprise*. Kennedy refuses to accept his destiny — that he must die according to history's proper timeline — and Kirk allows that there may be alternate universes in which Kennedy does indeed survive. But not in the one we inhabit. In the end, history as we know it proceeds normally, and Kirk has once again saved the universe. This wasn't as hokey as it may sound. There were sensitive moments, even tender scenes with well-developed characters and well thought out science-fiction concepts. Having given the story his all, Gene optimistically awaited a "go" from Paramount to begin writing the screenplay.

Meanwhile, he busied himself with a revived lecture career. His fee had increased substantially, and he now earned at least five thousand dollars per appearance. He was beginning to branch out as a public speaker. No longer expounding upon past experiences as a failed producer of a minor television series or of unsold TV pilots, he reinvented himself as Gene Roddenberry, Twentieth Century Philosopher. People thronged to hear him speak on a concept he had dubbed the "socio-organism." Gene envisioned this as our next evolutionary stage as human beings — humans and their corporations like General Motors, and organizations like the PTA — living, multi-celled organisms, one and the same, their lives intertwined for the higher good of all. It was a profound, controversial and frightening concept, one in which he strongly believed. It provided fodder for his speeches, but did not generate much enthusiasm with his audiences, most of whom (including suposedly intelligent students at such universities as USC and UCLA) were bewildered. Soon he began to downplay his new pet concept and started speaking instead to his concerns for the human species, which he felt was now in its adolescence. We are just emerging from our cradles, barely potty-trained, he told his young audiences, but we're reaching our adolescence. Still, until we learn to put aside our fears of one another, our "petty nationalism," as he called it, the human race cannot reach adulthood.

[8] This number was selected as the third incarnation of *Star Trek*; the original series was, in Gene's mind anyway, *Star Trek I*, and the first movie was *Star Trek II*. However, historically, we now refer to the first movie as *ST I*, the second film as *II*, and so on.

He never doubted that we would achieve this goal; in that aspect, he was an unyielding optimist, a position he continued to espouse throughout his life and his involvement in all things *Star Trek*.

Gene segued from touting the "socio-org" as the next form of life on this planet, to embracing something he now found a more likely candidate — the computer. No longer gigantic room-sized machines requiring an MIT degree to comprehend, computers were just beginning to emerge as a practical tool for far-thinking individuals. As early as 1977, Gene saw the possibility of computers one day being considered a full-fledged life form. Soon he began articulating this on a regular basis in his speeches. And he put his money where his mouth was by purchasing one of the first word processing personal computers on the Paramount lot.

Early in 1980, Gene plunked down six thousand dollars for a semi-dedicated word processor called a Lexorwriter. This state-of-the-art writing computer became an epiphany for Gene. He boasted to all within earshot of its powerful *64k* of memory, the ease with which he could now write his stories, the joys of seeing his typing appear on a screen and just as quickly being deleted, inserted, or cut and pasted elsewhere. Soon he owned a second Lexorwriter, a twin to the first, so that I too could join him in the happy world of computing. Eventually, we both got the hang of these proto-PCs. Gene continually updated his equipment as the years went by and computers became more sophisticated, but he never quite got used to the newer versions, preferring to do his serious writing on the old 64k. I survived the computer revolution with fewer battle scars, and today I can't imagine writing without my modern, high-speed PC.

Learning to use our brand-new Lexorwriter word processor, circa 1980.

One of Gene's speaking engagements that spring took place in the San Gabriel Valley, not far from Los Angeles, and I agreed to drive him out to the small school there. It would give me an opportunity to be with him as well as to hear him deliver the new speech he had been working on. Also, he wasn't feeling too well that day, and he was reluctant to drive himself. About halfway through the speech, he began sweating profusely and appeared to be shaky. I hoped it was a case of nerves, but his pale appearance told me otherwise. He cut short the Q&A period, made minimal small talk with the students following the speech, and practically staggered out to the car.

Something was dreadfully wrong.

On the drive home, his teeth wouldn't stop chattering and he insisted that we put the heat on, although the temperature outside was a balmy eighty degrees. I drove as fast as I safely could, arriving at his house in considerably less time than the usual forty-five minute drive. He claimed he was all right — just a touch of flu — and toddled off to bed. Majel was out, so I asked his household staff to keep an eye on him as I headed home, since working was out of the question.

My phone rang just before 6:00 p.m. "I'm much better now," he said weakly. "I've gotten my temperature down to 104."

"What! What was it before you got it down?"

"Somewhere around 106. I took a cool shower and some aspirin. I'm in bed now, and I'll just rest. I'll be fine."

"You ought to call the doctor." I knew I couldn't force him to do anything, although it sounded as if he needed serious medical attention. He realized this, but wanted to spare

Gene at his home office desk with his latest computer, circa 1988.

me any needless worry, insisting he was going to be fine.

The next morning in the office I received another call. "I don't want you to hear this from anyone else. As soon as Majel came home last night, I asked her to take me to the hospital. I'm at Cedars; don't worry, I'm doing fine."

Don't worry. I hate when people say that! It always means just the opposite. Of course I was worried; what was wrong? What did the doctor think he had? How serious was it? When could I come up there? He told me to give him a day to become stabilized. That night I couldn't stand it any more. I phoned Cedars-Sinai Hospital, expecting to hear the worst. When the nurse answered and said he was fine, I assumed she was covering up. I didn't believe her and pumped her for more information. "You can come up tomorrow and see for yourself," she said. I assured her I would.

I steeled myself, and the next morning I arrived to find Gene in a large private suite, walking about, connected to an IV bottle on wheels. He seemed surprisingly well. Those remarkable recuperative powers again, I supposed.

"The nurse was really taken with your concern when you called last night," he said. "'Your assistant really cares a great deal about you!' she told me." He winked at me. "I just told her, 'I have a very devoted staff.'"

I guess the anxiety in my voice had betrayed me, and the nurse suspected I was more than "devoted staff." I didn't care — I had been frantic to know Gene's condition. Since he seemed so much better, I asked if there was anything he needed. Yes, a candy bar would be nice. So I traipsed across miles of hospital corridor to get him a Hershey bar, not knowing whether or not it was allowed. He assured me it was and explained what the doctor thought he had. At first, Gene said, the doctor's diagnosis had been phlebitis, a blood clot in his leg. But then he began to suspect that Gene had been bitten by a brown recluse spider, a mysterious poisonous critter that inhabits equally mysterious dark and dank places. It seemed so far-fetched, but it made for wonderful storytelling, and Gene began to get more and more into this theory, convincing himself and everyone else that the fateful moment must have occurred when he was working with the swimming pool controls along the hillside the day he became ill.

Who knows? He responded to the treatment of antibiotics and whatever else was in the doctor's IV cocktail and went home in a couple of days. But before I left that afternoon, Gene pulled another one of his "It makes me feel good to be fooled with when I'm sick" numbers. As soon as the nurse left the room, he made sure that what little of his anatomy the hospital gown left to the imagination was no longer imaginary. I was only too happy to oblige since he had seemingly just been pulled back from the brink of death. Hershey bar or me, whatever he wanted was fine now that he was getting well.

Gene recovered completely and began another round of out-of-town speeches. I met him on one — at my alma mater, the University of Florida in Gainesville. I hadn't been back since completing my Master's degree in 1965, so I looked forward to seeing what changes had taken place on the campus of this beautiful, Spanish moss-covered old Southern school. We stayed in a hotel room that overlooked the Suwannee River, made famous in the Stephen Foster song. All weekend Gene and I walked around humming the familiar tune and sharing a secret smile. When he gave his speech in the Florida Gymnasium, an enormous indoor facility that seated twenty thousand, he introduced me from the podium. I rose unsteadily to my feet and ventured a meek wave to the crowd, who filled every one of those seats. I hadn't made any particular impact on UF when I'd attended there; I'd taken all my courses, made a few friends, gotten two degrees, all rather quietly. Now I was a returning heroine, one of their own, being introduced to a group of my fellow Gators, all applauding madly. I sat down and blushed three shades of red while secretly relishing every moment! Another of those moments life, and Gene, handed to me that could never be expected.

Following our Gainesville adventure, Gene and I flew on to visit my parents in Palm Beach. He planned to return to the West Coast that evening. My parents had no idea of my involvement with Gene. They just saw him as the kindly man who was my boss and friend. Friendship they could understand. They were friends with him, too. Gene made a big fuss over my parents whenever they visited me in California. Consequently, they'd been begging him to visit Palm Beach for years. This time he took them up on the offer. My mother fixed a special lunch for him — her famous tomato aspic, chopped liver, and special salads. Cold dishes were in order due to the Florida climate; in Gene's honor, she also served wine with lunch.

Gene hadn't brought a swimsuit with him in his luggage, so we went to one of the local shops where he purchased the first suit he tried on. Then we returned to my parents' modest house a block from the beach. Knowing how much Gene enjoyed the water, I was eager to show off my hometown. The air was warm, but there was a cool tropical breeze by the shore. There are seldom others on this stretch of beach, so we spread out our blanket on the hot sand and listened to the waves crashing a few feet away. We necked for a while (I kept one eye open and trained on the access path in case of intruders), then strolled along the edge of the water. Suddenly a dark shape broke the surface of the waves and I let out a little yelp. It was something I'd never seen from our beach before — a shark! It was less than ten feet from the water's edge, and as I cried out, I instinctively grabbed Gene's hand and pulled him farther up the beach onto the sand.

"What's the matter?" he teased. "Afraid the shark's going to leave the water and make a charge for us?"

I felt pretty stupid. Now he had something else to tease me about — the Palm Beach sharks, the ones that leap up onto the beach to attack people.

We were still laughing when we returned to the house later that afternoon. I drove him to the airport and said a wistful good-bye. How could a day have gone by so quickly? I would be staying on for another week, and I knew I would miss him terribly. I didn't cry until I was in the car and certain he couldn't see my tears as he flew overhead.

LOG ENTRY 22 : Being on the Paramount lot brought us into contact with many of Gene's peers, among them the famous producer-director George Pal. He was in an office across from ours, developing projects for Paramount, when he and Gene discovered each other's presence. They naturally had much in common; Pal was responsible for many of the big screen's science fiction classics, such as *Destination Moon* and *When Worlds Collide*. Soon Gene and George were discussing possible collaborations while Gene continued to await word on Paramount's reaction to his *Star Trek* sequel.

One of their projects was something George had longed to do for many years: a film of the Philip Wylie book *The Disappearance*. The story concerned the world from two perspectives — male and female. From the men's point of view, all the women on Earth have suddenly disappeared. And exactly the opposite has occurred from the women's perspective — there are no more men in the world. Written in the 1950s, it was true to the sociological climate of its time. Women were helpless without men, although they were able to resolve all preexisting military conflicts in a non-violent way. The men were lonely without women but managed to get their sexual fixes — an important necessity for the males — with artificial female companions. The story was badly in need of updating, and Gene began working with George on this. He had a lot of fun delving into the contemporary concepts of male and female roles in that first year of the '80s. Gene was given to a good deal of sexism. Throughout his lifetime, he was never quite able to see women in a completely objective manner, and he brought a lot of excess baggage and hang-ups from his generation. Often, he'd turn to me for input on the female perspective. If he didn't, and I thought him wrong, I had by now become assertive enough to point things out to him. It was great fun working on this project.

Sadly, it came to an abrupt end when George Pal died in May 1980. Gene had met with him over lunch only a few weeks before, so it was a terrible shock when we learned he had passed away. It seemed fitting that I attend the funeral with Gene, as we had both known George well. It was more than a loss of a colleague. George had been a friend. I always enjoyed chatting with him. He spoke gently and softly, in a voice not unlike Gene's, with a charming Eastern European accent. He was always cheerful and quick with a smile; the lot would not seem the same without him.

Eventually Gene acquired the rights to *The Disappearance* and even pitched his script to CBS in October 1981. But like so many of his scripts, this one went nowhere. Eventually, it was moved from our active files to Paramount's storage, to gather dust along with numerous other "failed" Roddenberry scripts.

Gene proved his humanness that summer in a way that did not please me. During the first two weeks in July, I went to Australia, where I was a guest at several conventions. When I returned, Gene seemed particularly eager to see me, and when we got together the day after my return, he was very sexually aroused, more than he'd been in over a year. Although he suffered from impotence almost all the time, there were rare occasions when we actually "did it." This was one such occasion. I was thrilled that he was so pleased to see me.

But I learned within a few days why his libido had suddenly sprung to life. While I was in Australia, he had had a visitor from Hawaii, an aspiring writer who was a friend of his pal, Pat Brown, the ex-governor of California and Rod's godfather. This lady and Gene struck up a friendship, and he found himself excited at the prospect of someone "new," as men often do. He sheepishly confessed to his rendezvous with her. Of course, he would never have told me this if I hadn't noticed the tiny red bites that covered his lower abdomen. Then he acted like a little boy caught with his pants down. I took comfort in the fact that she lived three thousand miles away in Hawaii. And she had made him feel sexy again. It was a one-time thing. He couldn't even remember her last name.

I made an immediate appointment for him to see his old studio doctor in Burbank, who diagnosed crab lice. The doctor gave him some medicine that did the trick. (Fortunately, I managed to escape this scourge.)

I decided not to dwell on this. I had always known Gene wasn't the monogamous sort. He had told me that he'd had occasional temptations early in his marriage — once while visiting a college campus in Alabama with a comely young coed, and on another occasion with a young woman in La Costa. He had no intentions of forming any sort of lasting liaisons during these brief encounters, but, he admitted, there were times when he simply couldn't deny his nature. He had been up front with me from the start, and because of my love for him, I had long ago made up my mind to accept him the way he was — crabs and all.

One beautiful Sunday afternoon, Gene dropped by and took me to the movies. I snapped this photo of him in the dappled sunlight on the front porch of my house in Studio City, California.

Well, almost all. One thing that was painfully distressing to me was his drug use, of which I was becoming aware at this time. Following his constant rejections by the studio, Gene began to suffer great depression. Hoping to distance himself from the humiliation and the pain, he turned to alcohol for comfort, as he had in the past. But its effects only served to make him more depressed. Then one day he told me he had tried cocaine. I wasn't shocked; it was well known that many people in the entertainment industry used drugs, and that cocaine was easily obtainable. And after all, he told me he had only tried it; he didn't plan to use it again. "It made me feel like I could right the world," he said. "I knew this was a false feeling and that this drug could be dangerous." But, as I later learned, Gene had an addictive personality, although he was in constant denial about this.

He used cocaine on and off for the rest of his life. Sometimes he seemed to have a steady supply of it, using it in the office or at our apartment. And once, at his insistence, I agreed to try it. Although I did experience the profound euphoria for which this drug is famed, and it shocked me with how extraordinarily it enhanced feelings of love, I also felt extremely depressed a short time later. I had no desire to continue using this and never touched it again after the first time. Gene, however, carried it around with him in little vials or tiny plastic bags in his shirt pocket. I feared he would get caught someday. Once his daughter remarked about the white powder on his jacket and Gene said something about after-shave talcum.

He insisted on using coke before sex, and it contributed to an even greater impotence, to the point where I finally complained. I never chastised him or made mention of his dysfunction. I realize a man's ego is a fragile thing, and I wanted him to know that I loved him no matter what. But I finally put my foot down when it came to coke. It ruined things. It made having sex with him a chore. Emotionally he'd become excited; physically, nothing happened, though he'd urge me to keep trying to arouse him. I ordered him never to bring it into my house. He agreed, but still would sneak it at his desk. I could always tell when he had been using. A woman knows these things about the man with whom she's been intimate for so many years.

Gene's use of drugs became an unguent to ameliorate rejection. Earlier that year, he had given his all to the Kennedy script and steadfastly believed Paramount would give it a thumbs up. This time he would produce a *Star Trek* movie his way, not like the last one, a film written by a committee and out of control. He would do it on time and on budget. His hopes were high.

His hopes were dashed that summer. After a careful review, the studio decided to pass. There would be no sequel. The studio executives gave Gene and his script a dishonorable discharge. What bothered Gene the most was that they didn't give any tangible reasons for the rejection. "I think they didn't like time travel," said Gene, "which is odd, considering that years later their most successful movie was a time travel story (*Star Trek IV*)."

We were to pack up and leave the lot. Paramount had been our home since 1975; now, five years later, we were shown the gate.

LOG ENTRY 23 : For the first time since I'd met Gene, we were like two

people without a country. It was clear we needed a real office. Never again could we work out of Gene's home — not since our relationship had blossomed. I was quite aware that Majel knew all about his involvement with me. She treated me coolly, and I can't say that I blamed her. I knew Gene was suffering at home; he told me they fought all the time now. But a divorce for Gene was out of the question. He had told me about his divorce from his first wife, Eileen, to whom he had been married nearly twenty-seven years. Gene had begun his affair with Majel while still married to Eileen (which Eileen later confirmed to me), and eventually he left her to marry Majel. Gene also told me the stress of that first divorce had wiped him out — emotionally. It was too painful to even think about. He vowed to die rather than subject himself to an experience like that again. Although he tried to shield me from the pain he was suffering, he broke down a number of times when describing how unhappy he was. At one point, I suggested ending our relationship, rather than see him continue to undergo such stress; in tears, he pleaded with me not to abandon him.

We began our search for a new office. I checked out several suites available for rental, but nothing seemed appropriate. Finally, he received an invitation to share space with a wealthy golfing friend, Mark Tanz, who had decided to become a film producer. Mark had purchased a couple of houses on Fairfax Avenue and reconfigured them as offices. Dining rooms and living rooms had become executive and secretarial suites. One larger area had been converted into a projection room. There were winding brick-lined patios and lots of tropical plants outside our windows. Director Richard Donner was headquartered in one of the houses.

We moved in all our things, including Gene's precious Lexorwriter. Gene was assigned a large room with a comfortable desk. The decor, however, left something to be desired. The centerpiece was a dark green velvet couch and matching chair. Instead of legs, they rested upon rows of steer horns. I was beginning to lean toward vegetarianism at the time, and it bothered me terribly to see the fate of these hapless bovines.

I grew to despise the place. There was nothing physically wrong with it. Mark was charming, the setting was inviting, and we had the run of the kitchen at lunchtime, as well as access to a whole new area of town for dining away from the office. But I missed the studio atmosphere — the high activity level, the hustle-bustle, the crackling creative energy that flowed like electricity through invisible wires.

Gene sensed this, too. He seemed uncertain what to do next. Until now, his attorney and friend, Leonard Maizlish, had acted in the capacity of an agent, arranging his *Star Trek* and other production deals. Now, Gene felt he needed more. He signed on with Rowland Perkins of Creative Artists Agency (CAA), a heavy-hitting talent agency with a top-notch clientele. Perkins introduced Gene to several powerful network executives, hoping something would spark. In an attempt to "package" Gene, he was paired with other fine writers, such as Tom Scortia, who had written numerous science fiction books and several screenplays. The agency had optioned Charles Panati's non-fiction book, *Breakthroughs*, and Gene and Tom began developing a treatment together. Written in 1980, *Breakthroughs* was a thought-provoking work, right up Gene's alley. Predictions included gene therapy for diseases like muscular dystrophy and cystic fibrosis — now becoming a reality, and interactive home computers for use in shopping, booking flights and ordering up the news — another commonplace reality today. Panati also predicted today's modern fax machines, which he called "teleprinters." He missed on a few things — fusion power by 1989; taming hurricanes by 1994, and my personal favorite, a diet aid called *perfluorooctyl bromide*, a compound designed to coat the gastrointestinal tract, temporarily blocking the absorption of food, including chocolates, pastries and the like. I am still waiting for this one, which he predicted would arrive in 1982.

Gene worked up a treatment, but found writing with a partner difficult. He was a man of firm convictions who generally preferred working solo, unless a collaborator agreed with his point of view. Scortia did not, and their pairing ended in a Writers Guild arbitration. Each claimed the work that had been produced was his own. The project was a bust.

He was paired with another CAA client, Robert Joseph, author of the acclaimed book, *Breaking Cover*. Again, nothing panned out. Gene was just not the type of writer who worked well with a partner. A man of conviction, he could be headstrong and unyielding, not ingredients that work well in a partnership.

Other couplings proved equally futile, and Gene again turned to the lecture circuit for income. In August, his lecture agent booked him into the Oregon State Fair in Salem, and Gene invited me along. The speech was planned for the evening, so during the afternoon we checked out a couple of rides at the fair, mindful of Gene's limit, which I recalled from the Disneyland experience years before. One ride spun us up in the air, round and round — and within no time at all, I was queasy and miserable. Gene had great difficulty commiserating with me. He had never suffered from motion sickness in his life, and while we spun upside-down and I turned puke-green, he obliviously regaled me with stories of how he and Jimmy Doohan had spent happy moments being tempest-tossed in Gene's sailboat, the *Star Trek II*. The rougher it got, he said, the more he and Jimmy loved it. His descriptions of the heaving ocean waves did nothing for the upheaval threatening my innards. The Whip, or whatever it was, seemed to go on for hours, and I thought about leaping the hundred feet or so to welcome death below. After what seemed like centuries, we were at last safely down on the ground, and we returned to the hotel.

The next day, Gene made up for this misadventure by taking me on a picnic and drive through the countryside. The Oregon scenery was beautiful on this warm summer afternoon as we drove along, seemingly just an ordinary couple out celebrating the glorious trees and sky.

Early in 1981, Paramount had a change of heart after reconsidering the box office potential of another *Star Trek* film and invited us back onto the lot. There would be a *Star Trek II* movie after all, with producer Harve Bennett in charge. He had a reputation for bringing in his projects — miniseries like *Rich Man, Poor Man* and the TV show *The Six Million Dollar Man* — on time *and* on budget, a high priority for the studio. Gene was not asked to produce; the studio had lost confidence in him because of the enormous budget and lack of critical acclaim of the first *Star Trek* movie. But Gene's contract had a provision that he had to be involved in any production of *Star Trek*. He accepted a position as executive consultant, although it was clear that the production's success would rest squarely on Bennett's shoulders.

Our old offices in Building E had been subdivided into various casting offices (ironically, years later they would be assigned to Whoopi Goldberg during her role as "Guinan" on *Star Trek: The Next Generation*). We were offered three rooms atop Building G. They were much smaller than the ones in E, which I took to be a sign of Gene's diminished status with the studio. But Gene liked the executive office, which had a nice bathroom and good vibes — it had recently been home to actor Chevy Chase. He eagerly accepted.

The suite was on the fourth floor of G, and although I frequently braved the many flights of stairs with weight loss intentions, Gene always preferred to ride the antique elevator. It gave me the willies; its creaking graffiti-riddled door and noisy motor attested to decades of neglect. As often as not, the elevator would lurch to an unexpected stop and its automatic door slide to one side, revealing a floor at eye-level, somewhere between floors!

I'll never forget the first time this happened. As I stepped into this medieval torture chamber, I was joined by a paunchy, jolly-looking middle-aged gentleman with an English accent, who asked me to "Hold the lift, please!" We both pushed the number four, and rode upward in the customary elevator code of silence. The contraption halted somewhere around floor three. The doors parted, and sure enough, there was the third floor, about chest high. I started to panic and said something to my fellow elevator prisoner. He handled it with all the aplomb one would expect from the British. Calm prevailing, he merely pressed "four" again, the doors closed, and up we went. When we arrived safely, he thanked me for my company and headed into the office next to ours. His doorway had been decorated with elegant, Japanese-lettered red and black framework. I knew that Paramount had recently aired the television ratings sensation, *Shogun*. Then I realized who my calm, collected English lift companion had been: James Clavell, the author and writer of the *Shogun* teleplay. I felt a sudden wave of embarrassment and hoped I hadn't been too cowardly. If he noticed anything, he never let on and always smiled whenever we ran into each other.

LOG ENTRY 24 :

It was great to be back on the lot, even if we were somewhat isolated in the corner suite of a rickety old building. I loved Paramount. The Commissary was right next door, and it was great fun meeting friends there or being taken to lunch by Gene a couple of times a week. The Company Store was also handy to our location, and I never tired of browsing for souvenirs with Paramount film and TV series logos. The guards, the workers on bicycles, people passing on their way to and from the sound stages — everyone stopped to smile and say hello. It was a microcosm where we all seemed to share the special secret of belonging.

While Harve worked on his *Star Trek II* script, Gene worked on refining his speech for the ongoing lectures. One afternoon, we were having one of our usual chats about books, literature, films and TV. I told him I had recently watched what I considered the tear-jerkingest movie of all time, *Lassie Come Home*. The mere mention of the title is enough to send me rushing for the nearest box of Kleenex.

"That's by Eric Knight, isn't it?" Gene asked. "You know, he wrote another classic that's never been filmed. It's called *The Flying Yorkshireman*. See if you can find us a copy."

I phoned numerous bookstores, but the book had been out of print for years. Finally, Kellam De Forest Research (a company contracted with Paramount) located a copy for us.

Gene reread the book with a passion. He proffered it to me, and I too shared his enthusiasm. This, he decided, would be his next project. *The Flying Yorkshireman* had been written decades ago, so it took some doing for me to track down the agency representing Knight's elderly widow, who was then living on a farm in Pennsylvania. Gene secured the rights and immediately threw his energy into writing a script.

The story, a delightful fantasy, concerns an English family on vacation in Santa Monica, California. Sam, the Yorkshireman of the title, reluctantly joins his family on a Sunday to visit the temple where an evangelist (modeled after Aimee Semple McPherson) preaches that all things are possible with faith. Sam takes this message to heart, and soon his newfound faith provides him with the ability to fly, to the amazement of his family and some sharp-eyed business promoters. In researching possible locations, Gene and I took a cross-town field trip to Angelus Temple on Glendale Avenue, where the controversial Ms. McPherson had once preached to packed crowds. We were astonished to learn that the enormous auditorium was still being used by contemporary clergy, playing to equally large throngs. We also did some location scouting in Santa Monica, along the Palisades where Gene had written a scene with pterodactyl-like hang gliders whose graceful turns in the updrafts inspire the Yorkshireman to assert his new-found faith and take flight.

Again, Gene gave this script his all. But although there was some interest around town (never at Paramount; a prophet is without honor in his own studio), the project never got off the ground. This was a major disappointment to Gene, since he was hoping to go down in history for something other than *Star Trek*, which had always been something of an albatross for him. He had frequently proclaimed, "I don't want *Star Trek* on my tombstone," and with each new film or TV pilot he produced, he hoped that Hollywood would hand him a blank ticket back from the stars. It was a more unrealistic fantasy than any of his science fiction plots; try as he might, he just couldn't break out of the *Trek* mold.

< < <   > > >

In August 1981, Gene turned sixty, and I planned a special romantic day for him. We always celebrated his birthday a day early since he had to remain close to home and whatever plans Majel might have on his actual birthday. So on August 18, I picked him up in front of Beverly Hills Hotel, but I didn't say where we were going. I headed for the Marina, where I had rented a forty-foot motorized sailboat. There would be no crew, just the two of us sailing around the waters of Los Angeles. I also had packed a picnic basket full of what I considered "romantic" foods — caviar (the only kind I could afford: cheap), canned oysters, fine cheeses and crackers, some vintage wine and other gourmet foodstuffs.

I almost didn't get to share any of it. While Gene sailed like the expert he was, I went down to the galley. Without warning, I got seasick (why didn't anyone tell me about Dramamine?). Back on deck, my stomach settled down enough to enjoy a bit of my carefully planned lunch with Gene. We continued sailing around off the coast, and after lunch Gene decided he wanted a nap. Would I take the helm? So while Gene dozed, I steered the boat, which was a pretty good trick because I had never done this before. His instructions to me, just before nodding off, were to aim towards Palos Verdes (a peninsula on the Southern California coast). He had more faith in me than I did, as he slept on deck like a baby, while I did my damnedest not to run aground. He hadn't mentioned what I was supposed to do when we actually got to Palos Verdes, which twenty minutes later was looming very close.

"Gene! Wake up, for heaven's sake!" I cried, as we seemed in imminent danger of striking the rocks ahead. "We're here!" I had visions of whatever fragments that remained of the boat being charged to my credit card, so I'd spend the rest of my life working off the debt, swabbing decks for the old salts at the boat operating company till my fingers shriveled up . . .

I think he enjoyed tempting fate. He grabbed the helm and steered us out of harm's way without batting an eye. That evening, when we got back on land, I felt like I was still sailing. Trying to get my land legs, I swayed back and forth at our table during dinner at Josephine's, a West L.A. eatery, recovering only sufficiently to drop him back at the Beverly Hills Hotel.

< < <   > > >

Toward the end of the year, Harve Bennett had finally nailed down the script for *Star Trek II*. It would bring back the character of Khan Noonian Singh, from the original series. Gene told me the story of how that character came to be named. Noonian Wang was a Chinese friend who flew with Gene on Pan Am. While Gene was attending classes at Columbia University, he began working with Noonian (whose name meant "the crane" in Chinese) translating Chinese poetry into English. Gene would then take the literal translation and attempt to create elegant poetry while retaining the original meaning. The last time Gene saw his friend was in 1948. Noonian returned to Shanghai just before the Communist Revolution in 1949, and Gene never heard from him again. So he added the name "Noonian" to the Khan character as a signal to his friend, hopeful that one day he

would see *Star Trek* and get in touch with Gene. It was a touching story, but Gene never heard from Noonian again.

When Gene returned two decades later and created *Star Trek: The Next Generation*, he made another attempt to signal Noonian Wang by naming Data's creator "Noonian Soong." Even with open relations with China, there was no reply from Gene's old friend.

The main disappointment for Gene in *Star Trek II: The Wrath of Khan* was the death scene for Mr. Spock. Leonard Nimoy didn't want to be in the film, but Harve Bennett persuaded him to sign by offering him a dramatic death scene. This would do two things: Leonard would have a wonderful acting opportunity, and he'd never be burdened with the character again. It was an offer he couldn't refuse. But to Gene, Spock's death was gratuitous. He felt it was an unnecessary ending not just to a character, but to a child of his. He had been the one who had birthed all the original *Star Trek* characters, and he hated the thought of losing any of them. But Nimoy and Bennett prevailed; the death sequence stayed.

Despite this, Gene thought the film was progressing well and he seemed pleased with Nicholas Meyer's direction as we began to see dailies in November. Gene also enjoyed his visits to the sets. He had a particular fondness for Ricardo Montalban, who had worked for him during his early days as a producer. Being reunited with his old friend seemed to take some of the edge off his disappointment over Spock's death.

I snapped this casual photo of Gene relaxing one afternoon on one of our jaunts away from the studio.

In March, Gene and I planned a trip to New York City. I flew in the evening of the thirteenth, following his speech at SUNY in Stony Brook, NY. It was a dreary, rainy night, and I nervously drove the rental car along the dark, unfamiliar highway to his hotel at the eastern end of Long Island. When I arrived, he had flowers waiting for me, along with the key to a bungalow-like room, complete with fireplace. This was going to be a romantic weekend! He returned immediately after his speech to our room. I was impressed. He really was a true romantic. We had been together now for six years, and he still knew how to act like a schoolboy on a first date. All his "equipment" worked that night, too, which made it very special.

The next day I drove us into the City, actually driving on the streets of New York for the first time in my life. I managed to get the hang of it, even making a U-turn in front of our hotel on Central Park South, where we had an uncomfortably cramped room at the St. Moritz Hotel.

The "Kiss Me I'm Irish" button Gene bought for me at the New York St. Patrick's Day parade.

Gene was such a romantic all weekend. We took a horse carriage ride around Central Park the first evening, embracing and caressing the whole time. The ride was such fun, in fact, that Gene paid the driver to go around again. On March 17, we went to the St. Patrick's Day parade on Fifth Avenue. It was a rainy day, but no one seemed to mind, and we dashed along the parade route to get a better look, away from the midtown crowds. Gene's preoccupation with drinking was in evidence that day. He began hitting the bars early. Most of them were serving concoctions tinted shamrock green, and he tossed down his first such blend right after breakfast. By the time the parade passed by, sure'n he was a loyal son of Erin, too. I joined in the fun by buying a button that read, "Kiss Me, I'm Irish" and used it often that week. When I returned to L.A., I put it on my bulletin board, where it remained for the rest of my Paramount career and brought a number of puzzled inquiries over the years. We bar-hopped along the Manhattan parade route, and eventually detoured a few blocks over to Park Avenue, arriving at the Waldorf-Astoria, where we could warm up and watch the parade better on the hotel bar's overhead TV.

A strange thing happened to me the last evening of our stay in New York. We had smoked a joint before going to dinner, and during the meal at a fine Chinese restaurant, I suddenly felt like the walls were closing in on me. I wanted to rush out into the street for some fresh air and began to panic. He told me to sip a glass of water slowly, which seemed to calm me. I was all right until we returned to our tiny hotel room. I was sitting on the bed when the same thing happened again. This time the anxiety attack would not abate, and I was frantic to get outdoors into the night air. He indulged me; we grabbed our coats and headed for a walk around the block. When we passed the Plaza, Gene insisted we stop off at the bar for a nightcap. I was okay for a while, but then the panicky feelings began returning. My heart was racing, and I gulped water as if it had some magical powers. He finished his drink, and by now he was becoming impatient with me. We returned to the hotel, where I continued to fight these strange feelings. I had no idea what had precipitated this, but it was the last joint I ever smoked.

< < < > > >

The next day, Gene was due to give a speech at the University of New Haven in Connecticut, my childhood home state, and I drove him there. We stopped off in Westport at the Clam Box, a favorite restaurant from my youth, and we also made a detour to Bridgeport, site of my earliest and fondest childhood memories. We drove to my old house, a gray two-story clapboard duplex on West Taft Avenue. It had gotten much smaller over the years, and the sidewalk seemed to have been moved closer to the front door. I knew I was remembering it from a child's perspective, but Gene didn't laugh. He was very respectful of my feelings for this place that was so sacred to me.

Next we drove to Seaside Park, where P.T. Barnum had set up his first circus tent. I had often played there as a child, sitting on the antique cannons that were aimed at Long Island. In my mind, I could still taste the strawberry ice cream cones of my childhood, still see the happy Sunday people walking dogs on leashes or eating picnic lunches. So I was shocked and saddened when we learned that the park was closed to the public due to gangs, drugs and the high crime rate.

I dropped Gene off in New Haven that day, having learned that if you can't go home again, it helps to have your best friend along to ease the disappointment.

LOG ENTRY 25 :

On June 4, 1982, *Star Trek II: The Wrath of Khan* opened nationwide and was a huge success. Gene, along with everyone involved, extolled its virtues, but secretly he was unhappy with the film. He felt as if a death in the family had occurred with the demise of Spock; he hated the *Chocolate Soldier*-like costumes and the quasi-military attitude that permeated the dialogue. And he was outraged over the movie's violence. *Star Trek* had never used blood and gore to the degree portrayed in this film. He especially despised the scene where the alien creature was removed from Chekov's ear and immediately vaporized. "I have always stressed respect for alien life, not 'shoot the ugly alien,'" he told me. He felt they should have studied, not blasted it.

The public didn't seem to notice. *ST II* became a crossover film, reaching a broader audience than ever before — an instant hit. Another sequel in the series seemed inevitable. While this was good news to the fans, it signaled the end of control from Gene's perspective. *Star Trek* had proven successful without Gene Roddenberry at the helm. Gene was devastated.

He immediately threw his energy into a project of his own. For some time, he had been toying with a new character, one he hoped would be everything Spock had been, and more. The creature was a benevolent alien sent to our planet to observe these strange beings called "humans." This detached chronicler was really an alter ego for Gene. Even his name — Gaan — was Freudianly similar. Gene had always said he felt like an alien, who, set down among humans, must try to blend in and go along with their customs. Who among us hasn't felt that way at one time or another? One of Gene's gifts was his appreciation of his audience and their feelings. As he began breathing life into his new alien, he divulged some of what he had written to his lecture audiences. Gaan was shocked, he said, by the savage nature of humans, but he was also amazed when a hundred or more of them could come together in an orchestra and produce exquisite musical symphonies.

Perhaps he was subliminally inspired by the movie *E.T.: The Extraterrestrial*, which opened that summer. He had already seen it once when he insisted that everyone in the office take the afternoon off, so he could treat us to this Steven Spielberg film at the Cinerama Dome in Hollywood. All of us were moved by the little creature from space, and it is likely that "E.T. phone home" planted a seed in his fertile imagination. As the ideas about Gaan began to coalesce in Gene's mind, he decided the best format for his new alien would not be a movie, but a novel he would write.

Over the next several years, Gene worked not *on* the book, which would be titled *Report from Earth* (a concept not unlike "phoning home"), but *at* it. He even gave up golf, ostensibly to work on the novel. He talked about it to everyone within earshot. He told fans it would be done in a year, although there was no publishing deal. The reality was that he only completed seventy pages. Without a deal or the pressures of a deadline, Gene was not self-motivated enough to finish the project.

< < <　> > >

In mid-October, Gene and I went once more to Florida. He had a speech to give in Boca Raton, at Florida Atlantic University. My mother was able to get him a reservation at the Breakers, the finest hotel in town, and I joined Gene for an elegant dinner there. It was perhaps the most beautiful restaurant I had seen since our evening at the Four Seasons in New York, but my heart was not in it. My father was ill, suffering from colon cancer, and I had trouble focusing on anything else. Even making love in Gene's hotel room didn't cheer me. He continued to Miami while I spent a few days more in Palm Beach with my family. Although it went unspoken, we both knew it would be his last visit with my dad.

A few days later, I went on a planned vacation, a four-day Windjammer cruise in the British Virgin Islands. When I returned my father had taken a turn for the worse, and over the next few weeks, we kept a bedside vigil. Gene, meanwhile, was in Hawaii for the Thanksgiving holiday, when on November 25 — Thanksgiving Day — my father passed away. The next day Gene called and for the first time he seemed totally speechless, chiding me for not calling him. "You said you would phone if anything happened," he said, not knowing what else to say.

I couldn't. I was busy. I had to handle all the arrangements, be the strong one in the family. I took care of everything but myself. I was so busy, I forgot to grieve, I forgot to feel — or I didn't want to. Then one afternoon, when my mother was going through some of my father's papers, she started ripping up something in a great panic. I asked what it was, and she became angry and defensive. Determined to see what she wanted to hide from me, I grabbed the papers out of her hands amidst great pleadings and wailings. The papers contained everyone's worst nightmare. There it was, in ancient shreds of black and white. My adoption papers, circa 1944. My father was not my biological father. My father's first wife was not my biological mother[9].

The world was pulled out from under me.

I'd lost my father. I'd lost myself. I became ill. At first I thought it was a bad case of the flu, then I decided I had acquired some rare tropical disease. I felt like hell; I couldn't stop shaking; my teeth chattered constantly; loud noises made me tremble and jump. I hyperventilated on the way to the doctor's office and fainted walking in the door. I was a basket case.

I wanted desperately to get away from Florida, to return to California and my home. Somehow I managed to convince my mother that I was all right and flew back to Los Angeles. There I was met by Richard Arnold, who had been house-sitting for me.

Richard had begun coming into the office on a regular basis, helping with visitors, entertaining fans for Gene, using his vast knowledge of *Star Trek* to assist wherever need-

---

[9] My father's first wife, Bertha, had died when I was four; he remarried her sister (his sister-in-law) Gertrude four years later, when I was eight. To me she was simply my mother — I didn't remember the woman I'd called mother for my first four years. And although I knew Gertrude had formally adopted me, I had always thought I was blood-related; time slipped away, and it became more and more difficult for my adoptive parents to broach the subject. Finally, they decided it was too late, so they never said anything.

ed, all without pay in those days. He'd become a good friend, so I usually asked him to baby-sit my dogs when I was out of town. This time Richard didn't know what he was in for.

I begged him to stay — I was sure I would be well in a few days. But when I got home, things weren't any better. In fact, they got worse. I wasn't able to eat or sleep. My doctor said it was nerves and prescribed a mild tranquilizer. I hated the thought of taking drugs, especially since day by day I began to get worse. I was as taut as a piano wire — touch me and I would surely resonate with pain. I asked Gene for more time off, and, attempting to spare him any concern, told him I was simply suffering from an excess of stress. The office was quiet, so Gene had gone down to La Costa for the month, where he was eventually joined by Rod and Majel. I saw more doctors, then in desperation, I asked Gene the name of the psychiatrist he had seen a few years back. I made one visit to him, received yet another tranquilizer prescription and a referral to a colleague.

I saw the recommended shrink for two weeks and over a thousand dollars' worth of visits that dear Richard drove me to daily. More pills, more sleepless nights. I knew there was something wrong, but what? I sought out a hypnotist for relaxation techniques, and it worked — for about an hour. John and Bjo Trimble came over with a birthday cake on December 18, and I couldn't eat a bite. I was rapidly losing weight — normally a blessing, but now a symptom. I was terrified to be alone for even a minute. Richard had to be away for one night and Bjo took over, sleeping on my sofa so someone would be in the house with me. In my misery, I confided in her, omitting nothing, including my love for Gene. Other than Richard, who was around us constantly and had been taken into Gene's confidence, I had never told a soul.

It was Bjo who eventually set me on the path to the help I needed. She invited me to her house for Christmas dinner, and although I wasn't up to it, I agreed to go. I cried the whole time. Finally, she remembered a writer friend of hers who had been through a similar situation. Her world had collapsed when her husband left her, and she had tried to commit suicide. She'd received treatment from a psychologist working in conjunction with a psychiatrist, and was now like a new person, happy and productive. I practically tore the phone out of the wall calling this writer for the names of her saviors.

It worked. The doctors diagnosed anxiety/depression syndrome — a reactive depression — due to the double shocks of my father's death and adoption discovery. The rationalist in me wanted this illness to be over as soon as possible; I insisted on hospitalization in order to get around-the-clock treatment and attention.

I checked into Glendale Adventist Medical Center, which was more like ten days at a resort than being in a hospital. Patients wore street clothes. We had group sessions and private therapy with our doctors. We worked on crafts, activities designed to get our hands busy and our minds off our troubles. We could read on the beautiful shaded patio. There were organized hikes along wooded trails. At night we could soothe our tired bodies (and mine was sore from head to toe due to tension) in the center's spa pool. To the casual observer, unaware of our inner hells, it looked like a private club. My friends were envious.

It took a few days for the anti-depressant medication to kick in, but at last I began to feel some relief. Apparently this had been coming on for some time. The New York claustrophobia incident with Gene had been the beginning. My father had been ill for two years; I knew the inevitable outcome, and my internalized stress had begun manifesting itself months earlier. As soon as Gene could get away from his family without creating a big flap (which he always avoided at all costs), he came to see me. He brought flowers and a badly needed kiss. He put his arms around me and held me for a long time, and I cried softly against his chest. He seemed on the verge of tears, too. "I'm sorry, so sorry," he soothed. "Some of this has to be my fault. You know, not being there for you . . . not . . ." As was frequently true, I knew what he was trying to say. He was blaming himself for our relationship, for being unable to cast aside his life and start over with me. I assured him I understood, that I didn't mind.

I told him the story of my adoption, and he said it certainly didn't matter to him. Nor should it to me. I was loved and that's what counted. For some reason, this made him recall a strange moment in his past. One time when he was a boy, he was entering the living room in his house when he saw his mother engrossed in a conversation with his aunt. Just as Gene arrived, his mother leaned over and whispered, "Don't tell Gene." He never learned what they didn't want him to know. I know it wasn't anything to do with adoption, but kids always seem to fear this, and perhaps that's what young Gene thought. Anyway, my experience triggered his old memory. After that, I began to kid Gene that the secret was that he was Jewish, since his mother's maiden name had been "Golemon." I joked that I was sure it had been changed from Goldman — who ever heard of Golemon? (No doubt, it's a very common Scottish or Irish name; it was just my way of teasing him.) After he told me the story about the whispered conversation, I had new ammunition for teasing. I had always playfully called him "Roddenberg," as strangers often did by mistake; now I continued to joke about his mother's "Jewishness," giving us something else in common — we both had Jewish mothers!

Gene was totally loving and understanding about the nearly eight weeks I had missed at work. It was a slow time, as December and the holiday season always are, and he was able to get the small amount of mail handled by my friend Cheryl and by Richard. On January 11, I was back at my desk, feeling like a brand new person. And in many ways I was. My psychologist taught me to look at life differently — to explore my own new worlds (yes, he was a *Star Trek* fan). So I began a program of self-fulfillment. I had always wanted to learn tap dancing, and I began adult classes in tap, jazz and ballet. Gene joked to everyone that I was studying tap and urged to me perform "On the Good Ship Lollipop" for visitors. For a while I ventured into transcendental meditation, something Gene said he had tried in the '60s. I attended movies every Sunday, with friends or alone, as I rediscovered my great love of the cinema. I joined Jane Fonda's Workout and began getting into shape physically.

Free of the anxiety and crying jags, I truly felt as if I had been reborn.

LOG ENTRY 26 : In May, Gene was invited to address the C. G. Jung Institute Symposium in San Francisco. He flew up the day before the event to settle into his hotel. That evening I got a frantic call. He had forgotten the Bloopers. Would I get them from the housekeeper, who would be waiting for me at the door, and have them air expressed to him immediately? Before I could answer, he surprised me by saying, "How would you like to bring them in person?" Silly question. I arranged for a dogsitter and caught the first plane out. I later wondered if he had really forgotten them; in any case, it was a happy accident.

I taxied in from the airport and met Gene in the lobby of the sumptuous Hyatt Regency, with its indoor glass elevator that offered an E-ticket ride soaring through an atrium cascading with balcony-draped greenery. He seemed relieved that I had the Bloopers; I think in the excitement of my last-minute trip he was afraid I might forget them.

I was nearly as excited to meet one of the other guests as I was to be there with Gene. It was the first and only time I'd ever crossed paths with George Lucas, creator of *Star Wars*, and it was also the first face-to-face meeting of Gene and George. George was attending as a spectator, not a speaker, since his hero, the late Joseph Campbell, was one of the guest speakers. Lucas was a disciple of Campbell, whose Jungian interpretations of folklore, dreams and the role of myth in the human imagination are said to have had a great influence in the creation of the *Star Wars* saga. I wiped the silly grin off my face as Gene introduced me to George at the catered lunch. I was amazed at how boyish he appeared at age 40. He was slight in build, not at all an imposing man like Gene. I expected legendary giants to be, well, giants. I don't know whether or not Gene noticed that my attention was off him for a change, but for the next hour I was speechless and ate hardly anything, preferring instead to discretely watch George Lucas chomping on a turkey sandwich less than three feet away from me.

After Gene's talk, he mingled with the audience. He stopped when he came to a young man in a wheelchair who seemed to be speaking with a strange voice. The man explained that his voice was synthesized for him, hence the electronic sound. We never learned the reason for his disability. His condition was so severe that he was unable to speak, but he could painstakingly hack out his messages via a computer keyboard, which translated his typing into spoken words. Gene was greatly impressed with this man's courage, and enthralled with the technology. Long afterwards, Gene continued to marvel at the electronics that had made this unfortunate individual's life so much more tolerable. He vowed someday to find a way to work something like this into a story.

Many years later, another man, similarly afflicted, became world famous for his revolutionary scientific ideas. Stephen Hawking, perhaps the greatest mind since Einstein, wrote a book in 1987 called *A Brief History of Time*. Gene and I had become familiar with Hawking's work from his appearance in the 1985 PBS series, *The Creation of the Universe*. A sufferer of Lou Gehrig's disease, more properly called amyotrophic lateral sclerosis, or ALS, the series showed him teaching mathematics in his own voice with the aid of an interpreter. But by the time Hawking's book was released in 1987, he had lost his vocal apparatus to surgery. In his book he referred to his use of a speech synthesizer, donated by Speech Plus of Sunnyvale, California, an area not far from San Francisco. No doubt this is the same source of the device that so delighted Gene back in 1983.

Although Gene Roddenberry and Stephen Hawking never actually met, I'm sure Gene would have been thrilled had he lived to see the day Professor Hawking beamed aboard the *Enterprise*. In 1993, while on a visit to Paramount Studios to promote the video release of the documentary film, *A Brief History of Time*, based on his book, Stephen Hawking expressed an interest in visiting the sets of *Star Trek: The Next Generation*. His greatest joy that day was to be lifted from his own chair and placed in the Captain's seat. But Hawking wasn't satisfied to just sit there. This vital man asked if there was a way he could be in an episode! A holodeck scene was quickly written for him, in which he appeared as an historical figure, and along with Newton, Einstein, and *Star Trek*'s own Data, indulging in a spot of poker. It had to have been one of the high points of the entire seven-year run of *Star Trek: The Next Generation*. Too bad it happened after Gene had died. It's the kind of moment I know would have moved him greatly.

Back in L.A., Gene turned his attention to the next movie. When Spock died at the end of *Star Trek II*, it seemed a given that the character would be resurrected in the next film. Even Leonard Nimoy, who had been signed to direct the third film, was ready to make a comeback. But how? One quiet afternoon I was shooting the breeze with Gene when the solution became obvious to me. Use the Genesis planet, the *Genesis effect*, established at the end of *Star Trek II*. Spock would be regenerated from the effect, rising like a phoenix from his coffin, a clone of himself. His aging, linked to the growth of the planet, would be accelerated. It was a germ of an idea, but Gene liked it enough to take it to Harve Bennett, who was writing the script for *ST III*. My idea about bringing back Spock became part of the third film. And although I was not given any writing credit, both Gene and Harve publicly acknowledged my input, which pleased me greatly.

Filming of *Star Trek III* wrapped in October. Gene and I attended dailies, and although he agreed that Leonard Nimoy was doing a good job of directing, Gene was once again heartbroken about the script. This time yet another main character was killed off. Not a human one, but in Gene's opinion, the character at the heart of everything. The starship *Enterprise*.

He fought tooth and nail to get Harve to change his mind about the ship's destruction. "The *Enterprise* is the home that *Star Trek* lives in," Gene pleaded (a phrase actually conceived by his attorney, Leonard Maizlish). "Trust me," was all Harve would say. "This will work." Whether it did or not, one thing was now apparent to Gene: he had lost control of *Star Trek*. No one listened to his pleadings; if Harve wanted the ship blown up, then that's the way it would happen. Gene could send all the memos, do all the posturings, make all the threats to withdraw his name that he wanted. The *Enterprise*'s stardates were numbered. In the end, Gene yielded, but he ignored the "transwarp" concept the movie tried to introduce into *Star Trek* lore. Warp speed was fast enough, he said, and he never allowed these things to be used later in *Star Trek: The Next Generation* during his lifetime, despite the confusion it caused among the fans.

After the movie's release, Gene even sang its praises. Why cut his own throat? He knew the films were a potential source of income for him. *Star Trek III: The Search for*

Spock was a moneymaker for Paramount, although not as much as *ST II* had been.

Another *Star Trek* movie had been launched, and once again, it was time to play the waiting game. Would there be others? Who would die next? It was while pondering this question that I urged Gene to take a good hard look at his own health. He was badly overweight due to excesses of food and drink, and his blood pressure was dangerously high. If he were to be around for any possible *Star Trek IV*, I knew something would have to be done fast.

At my desk, opening fan mail. We had only been on the lot a short time when this was taken, but already we were getting enough mail that I needed to hire an assistant not long afterward!

LOG ENTRY 27 : "The brochures are here!" I announced excitedly, hoping some of my enthusiasm would ignite the same reaction in Gene.

With Gene's blessing, I had contacted the Pritikin Longevity Center in Santa Monica. I had read great things about the miracles they had accomplished in the field of health. The founder, Nathan Pritikin, was astounding the medical world with his techniques, and I knew their thirty-day residential program of diet and exercise could help get him back on track. At the program's heart was a diet long on complex carbohydrates and low on fat, sugar and sodium — just what the doctor ordered. In fact, many of the patients — residents or guests, as they were called — were sent there on the advice of their doctors. Pritikin had documented success in reversing adult-onset diabetes (which had not yet been diagnosed in Gene — that would come a few years later), as well as heading off surgery in many heart patients who were candidates for arterial bypasses. The Pritikin program reduced serum cholesterol and triglycerides and helped lower blood pressure so that many of the graduates no longer needed their medication.

I wasn't alone in my concern over Gene's deteriorating health and weight gain. The man who once returned to my side glistening with a healthy sweat from a five-mile run now could barely walk across the room without breaking out in beads of perspiration. His backsliding was causing him concern about his lack of energy, and especially his "gut," as he called his oversized belly. So, with the approval of his regular physician, Gene took the plunge and checked into Pritikin on December 18, the week before Christmas (and coincidentally, my fortieth birthday) in order to avoid the holiday season overindulgences. Two days later, I joined him by signing up for their non-resident program called "PM" three nights a week. This was actually the birthday gift I requested from Gene that year. As I turned forty, I realized that I, too, needed to get into shape, and the thought of our going through the program together seemed mutually reassuring. Three evenings a week after work for six weeks (two weeks more than Gene actually resided there), I drove the Santa Monica Freeway from the office in Hollywood to the Pritikin facility, a former beach club on the ocean that had been renovated into a health complex consisting of hotel, dining room, workout rooms and medical facility.

Within a few weeks, the pounds were melting off both of us. Dinner was included with my workout and classes, so three evenings a week, Gene either joined my group or I joined him with his fellow residents for dinner in the dining room. The food bordered on the unpalatable and took some getting used to, although I observed most of the near-starvation level residents salivating over their repasts of broccoli, spinach and string bean casseroles. Gene and I barely noticed what was served. We hurried politely through dinner so we could beat a hasty retreat to his room. The place may have seemed like boot camp, but there were no bed checks. We spent many happy hours enjoying the beach, the TV room, the game room — or the games in Gene's room — with happy abandon.

We played hooky from Pritikin one Thursday afternoon to go to a movie in nearby Westwood Village. The film was *Yentl*, starring and directed by Barbra Streisand. When she sang "Papa, Can You Hear Me?" Gene saw me softly crying and leaned over and whispered in my ear, "Let me be your Papa." "I thought you were Nichelle Nichols's 'Papa'," I replied, referring to her nickname for him — Papa Gene. I also was aware that he had slept with her when she had played Uhura during the filming of the original *Trek* TV series, long before I had met him, so I wasn't pleased with the hand-me-down sentiment. On the other hand, it was comforting that he wanted to be lover and father-figure to me — I had never considered him a father figure, despite the difference in our ages. So I smiled up at him and leaned closer and let him hold me a little tighter. But I never really thought of him as Papa, nor did I ever address him that way.

‹ ‹ ‹   › › ›

Early that year, my 1978 Buick began giving me expensive problems, and I realized I needed a new car. I was still seeing my psychologist once or twice a month, and when I mentioned the car to him, he asked casually, "Well, I wonder if you're going to get some sort of 'daring' car that will show what type of person you are?" I was puzzled. In my years of car-owning I had had my mother's '56 Mercury, a '65 Rambler Classic, a '74 Plymouth Duster and the '78 Buick Regal. If I had to classify my personality type according to the kinds of cars I drove, I'd say I was dull bordering on brain dead. "I just got a new car myself," my shrink continued. I glanced out the window into the parking lot. "Let me guess — the Honda Civic?" "Wrong," he chuckled, then indicated a shiny new red dual-exhaust Porche 944. I was glad to see my payments for his services were going to such good use.

Two weeks later, having sold all my stock certificates and taken out a massive loan from the credit union, I drove up to the Paramount gate in my shiny new red 1984 Nissan 300 ZX, a T-topped, turbo-charged sports car that announced to the world that, yes indeed, I was a fun-loving person (also penniless). Gene offered his congratulations and even told my mother, who by now was convinced I was a complete spendthrift, that I was entitled to have some fun in life. She agreed with this and added, "I guess so, since she doesn't have a boyfriend." I still hadn't told her of Gene's and my relationship.

My California vanity license plate, WRP DRV — Warp Drive.

Gene seemed to enjoy riding in my Z, especially after Rod, now ten years old, told him how cool he thought this sports car was. The TV series *Knight Rider* was airing at the time, and K.I.T.T., the talking car, was a favorite of the younger set. It had influenced Gene's selection of a Rod-pleasing car the previous year. Gene seemed to be willing to do almost anything to win Rod's affection. He leased a white four-speed Pontiac Trans Am with burgundy bucket seats and about a zillion horses whinnying under the hood. Prior to this, he had had Cadillacs and a Mercedes, and I really think he enjoyed the novelty of this toy as much as Rod did. Then one day the horses said "Nay," so off to the repair shop went the Trans Am. Gene caught a ride into the office, then realized he was carless when it came time to go to an off-the-lot meeting. Could he borrow mine? His driving wasn't exactly exemplary, but he hadn't had any serious mishaps, so I took a chance and offered up my new WRP DRV (my personalized vanity plate, short for "Warp Drive"). About two hours later he came back looking shaken. I swallowed and expected to hear about my late, great Z.

"Why didn't you tell me?" he asked. "I was so embarrassed." I hadn't the slightest idea what he was talking about. "That bumper sticker — I got so many stares. People pointed." Expletives followed. Suddenly I remembered — I had recently acquired one of those "I 'heart' such-and-such" bumper stickers which were so popular in the '80s. Except mine expressed my undying love for my favorite TV star at the time — the very hunky Tom Selleck. I burst into unappreciated laughter. I could just picture it — tall, handsome, virile Gene Roddenberry tooling around town proudly in my crimson and black sports car proclaiming to all the world that he loved Tom Selleck. Fortunately, my interest in Tom/*Magnum P.I.* was fleeting, so that by the time Gene needed to borrow WRP DRV again, I was professing my love for dolphins, from his viewpoint a much more acceptable cause.

It seemed to me that Gene's devotion to his young son was the glue that held his marriage together. He'd tell me of the problems he was having at home. But I continued my policy of never encouraging him to think about leaving his wife. It was always difficult for me to remain quiet when I could see the terrible stress he was under.

Rod was his light and his strength. Both parents spoiled their son with excessive gifts and indulgences. What Rod wanted, Rod got. At three, he had his own motorcycle, a miniature version of the one Gene kept at La Costa, and the two would tear around the hills of northern San Diego County. It was a miracle they never got hurt. When Rod turned sixteen, he got the year-old Jeep Grand Cherokee which the Roddenberrys had purchased for the household help to run errands. He customized this twenty-six-thousand-dollar car by painting it with bizarre, teenager-friendly designs. Rod was basically a good kid, and this healthy outlet for the normal frustrations teens go through was fine, with one drawback — it attracted the constant attention of the Highway Patrol, who issued frequent tickets to Gene's young namesake. Other than that, Rod managed to stay out of the kinds of mischief teenagers from celebrity homes so often seem to find themselves in.

Gene enjoyed his son the way all men enjoy having sons, only more so, since this was his "bonus baby." He'd often tell me how he enjoyed observing the developmental differences in boys versus girls. "Girls shriek when they play," he insisted. "Just listen to girls playing and you'll notice this." I did, and they did. But I told him I also thought that a lot of it was cultural — children will do what we expect of them. We may give them slight signals as to proper boy or girl behavior, perhaps without our even being aware.

From the time Rod was very young, he had had a theatrical agent and had been doing print ads and commercials, not unusual for children whose parents are in show business. Often Majel or the housekeeper would take him to his auditions, but one afternoon when no one else was available, Gene asked me if I'd mind taking his seven-year-old son to a commercial try-out. Delighted at a chance to take a break from the studio that afternoon, I picked up Rod at the house. Just as he got into the car, he realized he'd forgotten something.

"I'll be right back. I forgot my teeth," he said.

I was still puzzling over this when Rod returned, smiled a toothless grin at me and inserted his prosthetic front teeth. Apparently, some food companies feel that showing a child with missing teeth might signal to consumers that the youngster broke his teeth biting on their product!

For Rod's twelfth birthday, Gene took his son and six of his young friends to La Costa on the train. I remember how excited Gene was in planning this adventure. I didn't envy him with seven lively twelve-year-olds for the weekend, but I had to hand it to him. He pulled it off quite successfully.

Not so successful was the time that he tried to be a hero to Rod with William Shatner. I remember when he was only three years old, Rod would ask if he could watch "my *Star Trek*." He actually called it that — his *Star Trek*. Gene seemed baffled about where Rod had picked this up. I asked Gene about this and he shrugged, swearing he never mentioned the series at home. *Star Trek* was actually taboo around their house in those days. The whole cancellation experience had left a bitter taste in Gene's mouth. Nevertheless, Rod adored the show from the time he was old enough to reach the knobs on the TV. So when Gene learned that Bill Shatner was down at La Costa one weekend when he'd brought Rod along (who was then about eight or nine), Gene thought he'd play the hero by introducing his son to "Captain Kirk."

Rod was naturally excited at the prospect of meeting his idol, whom he had never met before. Gene phoned up the desk at the La Costa Country Club and was put in touch with Bill. Gene asked Bill if he would mind stopping by to say hello to his son, who was dying to meet him. Or if that wasn't convenient, they'd stop by the Club. According to Gene, Shatner told him, regretfully, he was too busy, his time was limited, and it was absolutely impossible. Faced with the task of disappointing the person he most wanted to impress in this world — his son who saw Dad as a hero who could do anything — Gene was quite hurt by this refusal. He told me that he never felt the same again about Bill Shatner after that, speaking to him only when necessary as required by their business together.

Rod managed to survive, and if his childhood was pampered, he seemed to be quite resilient. He managed to emerge from his rocky teen years unscathed, and during the mid-nineties, he attended college in Massachusetts. He later moved to Toronto and worked with the production company filming the syndicated TV series, *Gene Roddenberry's Earth: Final Conflict* and *Gene Roddenberry's Andromeda.*"

LOG ENTRY 28 :

The summer of 1984 marked the tenth anniversary of my working with Gene, and to celebrate the occasion, along with Gene's sixty-third birthday, we took a day trip to Lake Arrowhead, about an hour-and-a-half drive from Los Angeles. The valley floor was baking under the relentless August sun, but it was refreshingly cool at the 5,100 foot altitude. We even had an afternoon thundershower, a rarity for southern California but not for the mountains. We ate a light lunch at a cafe overlooking the lake. After browsing in a few of the boutiques — Gene was never much of a shopper — we rented a little boat to putt-putt on the lake, viewing the stately multi-million-dollar homes nestled along the water's edge. We topped off our afternoon's adventure with ice cream cones, and I drove the two hours back to the flatlands of L.A. It was a simple celebration of two people who were by now very comfortable with each other. No pretenses were ever necessary — we could totally be ourselves. Gene always enjoyed these birthday playdays so much more than the lavish country club bashes that were thrown for him.

< < <   > > >

Following the Lake Arrowhead sojourn, we had our first experience going aloft in a glider, thanks to the kindness of a fan. *Star Trek* fans who sent us interesting correspondence would easily become friends. One such letter-writer, Doug Perrenod, was a flight instructor who, in return for a chance to visit the standing sets from the movies, offered us the opportunity to go soaring. One October afternoon, we decided to take Doug up on his proposal. We drove in my car, meeting Doug up in Pearblossom, in the high desert where the air currents and thermals are ideal for this sport. Gene took readily to soaring (aficionados prefer the term to gliding) like an eagle takes to the air. He returned to Earth with one of the biggest smiles I've ever seen on his face. Not to be outdone, I became Doug's next passenger, and as the tow plane hauled our glider into the air, I too cracked a smile as I bravely waved good-bye. Once aloft, however, I realized how truly petrified I was. I thought: The tow plane has released us, we have no engine, nothing's holding us up, ergo, we're going to die! It's as simple as that. Gravity always gets you in the end.

Fortunately, nothing of the sort happened; Doug brought us safely back to the ground in a beautiful landing. Again I waved bravely at Gene while he madly snapped pictures. Gradually, I regained enough feeling in my legs to stand and step out of the death trap.

"That was great! Gee, thanks Doug," I blurted out. This will really impress Gene, I thought. No way would I admit in front of him that I was scared when he was having such a good time. Doug, also falling for my faux enthusiasm, immediately asked, "So, are you ready to go up again?" They say there's an evil half lurking within everyone; mine tormented me at the moment by piping up, "Oh, yes!" The next thing I knew, we were up in the sky again — but this time, I managed to steel myself. More than that, I soon found I was enjoying the ride, the view, and the freedom of true flight we were experiencing. Doug set us down like a crate of precious eggs. This time my enthusiasm was genuine (although I graciously allowed Gene and Doug take the remaining rides of that day).

Our next shared adventure took us to Hawaii at the end of October, where Gene was a guest speaker on the Big Island. I met him in Kailua-Kona after he'd finished his speaking obligations, and we spent that evening having dinner at a sidewalk cafe, where we laughed over the feral mongooses that kept poking their heads out of the bushes to beg for food. After admiring the sunset, we walked around a section of town that had some little shops and did some window shopping, then returned to the condo his hosts had provided.

Gene's sponsors had also provided him with a car, so the next day we drove to some nearby sights. We visited a macadamia nut farm, where we ate ourselves silly; walked along beaches of pulverized lava (which gives them the appearance of black sand), and stopped at the spot where Captain Cook was taken prisoner. It was strange, but every time one of us said the name, "Captain Cook," I had a feeling of déjà vu. Why did that name give me those feelings? I wondered. Then it hit me. Captain James Cook. Captain James Kirk. Gene insisted the selection of this name hadn't been deliberate; in fact, he'd gone through hundreds of names for the starship captain before settling on Kirk. But no wonder it seemed right!

The Hawaii trip was our best trip ever. I was pleased because Gene was able to relax, and the change of scenery did us both good. Hawaii always brought back pleasant memories for Gene. "Did I ever tell you that my brother and I played steel guitars when we were children?" he asked me quite suddenly one afternoon when we overheard the strains of this ubiquitous Island instrument. I knew that Gene was very musical, since we

Gene, Doug Perrenod and myself after my successful flight in the "Grob" glider.

used to spend hours singing the old standards and harmonizing on long car rides togeth-er. But until now, he had never mentioned that he played a musical instrument. "When Bob and I were about ten or eleven, our parents would set up appearances for us, and we'd travel all over town putting on performances." I pictured a young, handsome, pre-pubescent Gene Roddenberry, blond hair neatly slicked back by his mom, standing seri-ously over an upright steel guitar, strumming out Hawaiian tunes along with his younger, lookalike brother. They must have made a striking pair.

Our Hawaiian getaway ended with a stay at the Hyatt Regency Waikiki in Honolulu. Gene had been to Hawaii many times in the past with his first wife, Eileen, when their daughters Darleen and Dawn were little, and he wanted to visit his old haunts. One evening we stopped by a hotel called Halekulani ("House Befitting Heaven"). I remarked that perhaps it had been heavenly years before, but the place was all but deserted now and had long since seen its glory days as a trendy resort. A few people were sitting pool-side, finishing up a late supper at the hotel's "House Without a Key" restaurant. We sat down and ordered drinks and listened to the sound of the sea lapping Waikiki beach a few yards from our outdoor table. Soon we were lulled into a state of blissful contented-ness. I realized I was wrong. In keeping with its Hawaiian name, it was truly heavenly.

Shortly after our Hawaiian tryst, Gene told me he had decided to separate from Majel. He drove to La Costa that weekend. I joined him a few days later and spent the night. He seemed relaxed for a change, and I hoped that he would find some peace while spending some time alone, clearing his mind and resting. But the separation didn't last long. By the next week, Majel was down at La Costa. End of separation.

I took this snapshot of Gene during our walk on the beach at Waikiki, Hawaii.

He began turning to drugs again. He had slipped back into his drinking within a few weeks of completion of the Pritikin program. Now he began using cocaine, although I still got angry whenever I caught him doing this at the office. He seemed to be drinking more, too. His weight was up, and he was becoming ungainly. One day he phoned the office to say he was at his doctor's office in Century City, where the housekeeper had dropped him off for some x-rays. He asked me to meet him. I drove as fast as I safely could while trying to remain calm. He said he had been drinking and using coke the night before and had gone downstairs for something. It was dark, but in his hazy state he was sure he knew the way around his own house. He didn't. He tripped over a hassock in the living room and was now suffering pain in his ribcage. Fortunately, the x-rays were negative — just some badly bruised ribs. The doctor ordered a brace for him, which seemed to make it hurt worse.

The incident was enough to scare Gene into resolving never to use cocaine again. He meant it, too. He always did. He didn't realize that he had become dependent on it. I took him at his word, so pleased that he was going to give up drugs and alcohol. Again.

He was in serious trouble, and neither of us realized it.

LOG ENTRY 29 :

With the successful release of *Star Trek II*, Paramount saw the financial wisdom in releasing *Trek* films with clockwork regularity. The labor pains for the next *Star Trek* movie would begin simultaneously with each new picture's release; the contractions were now coming approximately two years apart. No sooner had *Star Trek III: The Search for Spock* been released then plans began unfolding for a *Star Trek IV*. Once again, Leonard Nimoy would be in the director's chair, and Gene was beginning to view the films with greater confidence.

While we waited for the new script, Gene noodled with his novel, *Report from Earth*, and undertook more speaking engagements. These were becoming corporate-oriented rather than college appearances. He was by now commanding a hefty fee, between seven and ten thousand dollars per talk, addressing groups of space age and computer technicians, scientists and business executives.

Meanwhile, things were slow at the office, and I was grateful when Richard Arnold referred me to the licensing division of Paramount after they asked him if he knew of someone who could write the box copy for the soon-to-be-released video cassettes of the original *Star Trek* TV series. I auditioned by submitting a rewrite of their poorly done synopsis of "The Conscience of the King." Hollace Brown, the studio executive in charge of this project, was delighted with my sample, and I was assigned the summaries and teasers for the remaining sixty-nine episodes (ten had already been written, and it was too late to do anything about them). Over the course of the next year, I did my first writing work for Paramount, earning fifty dollars per synopsis. I was thrilled with this assignment, and Gene was very pleased and supportive as usual.

Gene never begrudged me time for my own projects, but since I was paid quite well in my work for him, I always felt my first obligation was to earn my salary by focusing my complete attention on him and the job I was being paid to do. Several visitors to our office during my various vacations had repeatedly told me how Gene went to pieces without me, telling his guests, "I can't wait until Susan returns. She'll know how to handle this." Nevertheless, anytime I asked for a day or two to complete a book by deadline, Gene readily yielded.

My mother came for her annual visit from Florida in early July. I think she looked forward to seeing Gene as much as being with me. By now I had found a way to tell her about our relationship, and although she would have naturally preferred a different situation for her only daughter, she took comfort in knowing that Gene was a decent human being who had always looked out for my welfare and happiness. She never could understand why he was so attentive to her also. "I really like your mother," Gene told me. "I'm not just being nice to her because she's your mom. She's witty and I enjoy entertaining her," he insisted.

Gene always made it a point to take Mom and me to an elegant lunch or dinner whenever she came to town. That summer, he treated us to a lavish lunch at Le St. Germain, then one of the best eateries in the Hollywood area, frequented by top executives from Paramount and other studios. Over the years, Gene entertained us at Chasen's (where he won my mother's heart by having a rose delivered to her at our table), St. James's Club in West Hollywood, La Serre in the Valley, and his favorite in later years, Le

Chardonnay. I think he particularly liked this place because it was named after his favorite wine!

Many of the restaurants Gene frequented might have caused the average person to apply for a second mortgage, but Gene was generous to a fault when it came to picking up the tab. If he was in the party, no one else was allowed to pay. I can only remember one time when he let me treat him to dinner on his birthday, and only because it wasn't very expensive.

Gene loved home cooking, but he was also a dining connoisseur. He appreciated fine French and Continental cuisine that appealed to both the eye and palette. He adored rich foods like pâté de foie gras, French breads loaded with butter, and crème brûlée for dessert. His favorite choice for an entrée was often fish, especially Lake Superior whitefish or sand dabs.

It was these excesses (along with his renewed enthusiasm for the grape) that had been driving Gene's weight steadily upward, and on July 14, he checked into Pritikin again for another month-long stay.

This time, he was much more relaxed about being a Pritikin inmate. Occasionally, he would slip out and meet me for dinner. One evening, he joined Richard Arnold, Richard's mother Denny and myself for a picnic and concert under the stars at the Hollywood Bowl. Denny even went to the trouble of preparing Pritikin-approved foods for Gene while we enjoyed the music from our box seats.

On another occasion, Gene ditched Pritikin to take me to an Explorers Club dinner to meet a very special guest speaker. Ever since I'd known him, Gene had been a member of

Me, with my friend, Star Trek expert Richard Arnold. We are wearing our official **Star Trek: The Motion Picture** t-shirts.

the Explorers Club, an elite group of gentlemen who had done phenomenal things in their lives. The Explorers Club was world-famous for its annual meetings in New York, at which members dined on weird things like yak's tonsils, Bigfoot's toenails and cockroaches rolled in coconut sauce. As repulsive as this sounds, when Gene described it, it had an exotic ring, and I thought it might be fun to become a member. "Sorry," he told me, not really apologetically, "they don't allow women." Later, that rule was struck down, and they did begin admitting women into their sacred ranks, but by then I didn't really care if I joined. Besides, you had to have done some act of derring-do, like hang-gliding off the top of Macchu Picchu, or snorkeling with penguins in their natural habitat — Antarctica, not SeaWorld.

Or scaling Mount Everest. The day Gene checked into Pritikin, his friend George Pappas, whom Gene had sponsored for Explorers Club membership, called to invite him to a special dinner. The guest would be none other than Sir Edmund Hillary, the first white man to scale Everest (in 1953). Would Gene be going? You bet, I replied, *and he's bringing a guest!* Then I informed Gene that I'd made a reservation for him and his guest at the restaurant hosting the event. I hinted that said honored guest be none other than myself. He agreed, but didn't know whether he'd have to refuse me at the last minute in case Majel suddenly wanted to come along. Fortunately, she passed, and I got to attend the dinner, a disappointingly pedestrian chicken. After dinner, Sir Edmund gave a slide talk, followed by a reception. I was speechless, totally in awe as I shook hands with the man who had touched the top of the world.

LOG ENTRY 30 : Late in 1983, I had begun to lobby for Gene to receive a
star on the "Hollywood Walk of Fame." Many people from the entertainment industry
are represented there, and I thought it would be a fitting tribute to someone who had
made an enormous contribution to our twentieth century body of literature via the medi-
um of television and film. Gene was typically modest about this but agreed to attend if
the event should happen.

First I inquired about the cost of a star. Back then, the Hollywood Chamber of Commerce charged three thousand dollars (by 2001 the price had reached ten thousand dollars and was still climbing), and as the sponsor, I was expected to foot the bill. Since I did-
n't have that kind of liquid cash (and I wasn't about to ask Gene to pay for his own
award), I decided the best way to raise the necessary funds would be to invite the fans to
contribute donations. I set up a special savings account and sent out a letter to all fans
and fan organizations, outlining the project and requesting that each fan send only one
dollar. Surprisingly, many fans sent several dollars, along with British pounds, Australian
dollars, Japanese yen, Deutchmarks and Canadian dollars. Even though we lost money in
every conversion, we soon had enough for the star, and then some.

Gene receives his Hollywood Walk of Fame star.

As Gene's sponsor, I was required to submit a massive package of materials, every-thing from a current biography, which I wrote and rewrote with Gene's input, to a com-plete list of all his civic activities. The star selection committee put great emphasis on memberships and charitable activities, and we submitted a long list that included his par-ticipation in things like the Los Angeles Police Band Associates, the L-5 Society, the Plane-tary Society, the Los Angeles Library Association, plus numerous honorary degrees and memberships. Along with this, I compiled an enormous stack of his press clippings, plus a list of his public events such as speeches and prestigious guest appearances. When com-pleted, I had a huge and impressive pile of stuff that we hoped would convince the selec-tion committee that they were out of their collective minds if they didn't award this man a star, pronto.

I was wrong. The first year after I had submitted all this, they sent me a polite letter turning Gene down. They explained that they only awarded so many stars a year, spread out over several different categories — film, TV, music, radio, stage. Sorry, but the TV cat-egory was already assigned for the year. I was welcome to nominate Gene again the fol-lowing year. (Ironically, Leonard Nimoy received his star in January of 1985, but in the motion picture category.) So I went through the motions again. This time it worked, but not because the committee was suddenly enthusiastic about a person at whom they had turned up their noses the previous year. This time, there was something just short of divine intervention — the Writers Guild of America.

The WGA began putting pressure on the Hollywood Chamber of Commerce Walk of Fame committee by insisting there were no writers honored on the Walk of Fame. When the Guild heard that Gene had been nominated, they began lobbying for him to receive the first star honoring a writer. Eventually, there were some front-page articles written about this in *Daily Variety*, with the Writers Guild applauding the committee's actions in accepting Gene as their first honoree.

At last the Chamber of Commerce relented and a day was chosen: September 4, 1985. All summer long I prepared for the big event. I met with the caterers from the Los Angeles Hyatt Regency hotel, Paramount studio administrators regarding security and sound stage facilities for the party, and the wardrobe department so that we could outfit the servers in *Star Trek* costumes. With painters from the Paramount sign shop, I helped prepare a special surprise — a huge banner that read "GENE, YOU BOLDLY WENT WHERE NO MAN HAD GONE BEFORE." We used this as a backdrop for the party that was to be held on the studio sound stage, and later we hung this from the fourth floor of our office building for all the world (well, at least Paramount) to see.

September 4 dawned warm and clear, but that didn't do anything to calm my nerves. The ceremony was to begin at exactly 12:30 p.m. A VIP area had been roped off, and I arrived on the Boulevard about an hour early to shepherd the family and friends into this special section. A huge bank of photographers and people from the media were already jockeying for space when I arrived, clipboard in hand. Soon the crowds began arriving, to the accompaniment of the Los Angeles Police Pipe Band bagpipe music. Then, at precise-ly 12:30, as he had done countless times before, Johnny Grant, the "Honorary Mayor of Hollywood," took to the podium as tinny strains of "Hooray for Hollywood" played over the loudspeaker. Johnny welcomed "Trekkies from all over the world — Japan, Switzer-land . . ." Indeed, fans had come from everywhere. The only one missing from the original

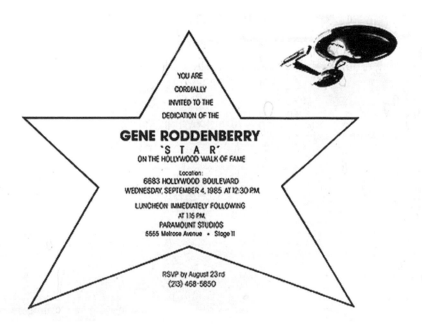

YOU ARE
CORDIALLY
INVITED TO THE
DEDICATION OF THE

GENE RODDENBERRY
`S T A R`
ON THE HOLLYWOOD WALK OF FAME

Location:
6683 HOLLYWOOD BOULEVARD
WEDNESDAY, SEPTEMBER 4, 1985 AT 12:30 P.M.

LUNCHEON IMMEDIATELY FOLLOWING
AT 1:15 P.M.
PARAMOUNT STUDIOS
5555 Melrose Avenue • Stage 11

RSVP by August 23rd
(213) 468-5850

cast was William Shatner, who sent a congratulatory telegram.

Gene's old friend and colleague Ray Bradbury sent a telegram which Johnny read to the throng. In it, Ray played up a decades-old running joke between Gene and him, evoking the public's confusion between these two science fiction writers: "Dear Gene, Everywhere I go I hear your name on the lips of people saying how incredible is the talent of Roddenberry for having written *The Martian Chronicles*. At the same time, everywhere you go, do you not hear the magic name Ray Bradbury, who created *Star Trek*? No matter how you play it, isn't it wonderful? Love to you on this special fine day — Ray Bradbury."

Next someone from Los Angeles Mayor Bradley's office read a proclamation pronouncing it "Gene Roddenberry Day." (Wouldn't it be great, I thought, if someday it did become an official holiday? "No school today, mom. It's Gene Roddenberry Day!")

But it was the commentary by Walter "Mr. Chekov" Koenig that created the greatest stir that day. Called to the podium, he beamed that Gene "is the very first writer to be so honored on the Hollywood Walk of Fame." As soon as he stepped down, Johnny Grant rushed to the microphone, refusing to admit this fact despite the WGA's self-congratulations. "Just to keep the record straight," said the insistent Grant, "he has several colleagues who are already here. There had been such a controversy over this, and he is being honored today for everything he did in television." Off to the side of the podium, Gene immediately picked up this thread by jesting in a barely audible voice (and counting on his fingers in mock enumeration of his "colleagues"): "Oh yeah, Sholem Aleichem . . . " Gene was in jolly humor that day.

Nichelle "Uhura" Nichols' double entendre wasn't lost on the crowd when she stepped to the mike and announced, "My hailing frequencies are always open for you," then planted a big kiss on Gene's lips.

Gene radiated his usual charisma as he thanked everybody and recalled his roots. "I

The invitation to the party celebrating Gene's star on the Walk of Fame .

walked this boulevard on foot patrol, and to have a star here is a double pleasure," he noted.

Following Gene's words to the crowd, his star at 6683 Hollywood Boulevard, the 1,809th star to be awarded, was uncovered. Photo ops followed, with family and cast members.

While this was going on, I rushed back to the studio, where Stage 11 was set up for the lavish invitation-only lunch, which began at precisely 1:15 p.m. I was fortunate in having the assistance of our good friend and *Trek* expert, Richard Arnold, and I was relieved when everything went off without a hitch, since this was the first studio party I had ever planned. Helpful fans, a few of my friends and even my cousins from Seattle pitched in. Lara and Joe Pizzorno came down for the occasion and helped out by checking off guests' names at the door. My friend Cheryl Blythe provided me with the name of a reasonably priced jazz band, "Street Legal," and I hired them to play. The Hyatt Regency from downtown L.A. had catered with the same food stations Richard and I had enjoyed so often at their Sunday brunches (especially the "build-your-own-sundae" buffet), adding *Star Trek* themes to each station.

During the party, I presented Gene with a scroll prepared by Sue Keenan, president of DeForest Kelley's fan club and an excellent calligrapher. Beneath a message that read, "To Gene Roddenberry, You gave us the stars — it's time we give you one. Congratulations!", she had hand-lettered hundreds of names of all the fans who had contributed their dollars and pounds and marks and yen. Unrolled, the scroll stretched halfway across the stage. Gene was visibly moved by this. He became even more emotional when I presented him with a check for the Make-A-Wish Foundation, the charity Gene himself had selected to

Gene's family and friends at the Hollywood Walk of Fame star ceremony.

receive the excess of funds collected. I, too, choked as I made the presentation for this organization which helps sick and dying children realize their fondest wishes.

It had been a perfect day, and I was walking on air. And there was more that evening. Majel invited a busload of her country club pals from La Costa, plus the ones from Bel-Air to assemble for a big evening party at the Bel-Air Country Club. The amazing thing was that somehow Gene convinced her that I had to be on the list — after all, if I hadn't worked for two long years to get his star, there wouldn't have been a celebration. So I was invited to the Bel-Air party, and I invited my cousin Carl Kugel, a TV director and former executive at Fox, to be my escort. Carl and I stayed an appropriate hour or so until a testimonial roast by Gene's friends, planned by Majel and emceed by a Korean comic named Johnny Yune, really did me in. Maybe it was because I was exhausted from the day's marathon of events; maybe it was Yune's exotic accent, which I didn't have the patience to understand. When I started nodding off, I finally decided to call it a day, excusing myself and cousin Carl, and headed wearily home.

We had lots of time together now with no deadlines and no immediate project on tap. Gene was spending time in La Costa, and my visits there were frequent, ostensibly to have him sign the weekly checks for his bills and to deliver his mail. Even if he wasn't able to maintain La Costa as the bachelor pad he longed for, he did enjoy getting away there as much as possible.

Whenever he was in town, he took things easy, too. We enjoyed long lunches and planned special adventures. For instance, on November 6, at the ungodly hour of 6:30 a.m., Doug Perrenod, Richard, Gene and I drove to Edwards Air Force Base, where Doug had arranged for us to view the landing of a space shuttle. Ever since the rollout of the *Enterprise* back in 1976, Gene had wanted to watch either a launch or a landing. Once, we'd missed a launch in Florida by only hours. So we were excited about seeing this landing in the high desert.

We viewed the event from an outdoor grandstand. Loud sonic booms heralded the big spaceship's approach. Everyone searched the skies trying to be the first to get a glimpse. And then, suddenly, there she was, dropping from above and gleaming white in the sunlight. The ship touched down perfectly and taxied to a stop off in the distance. It would be a while until the astronauts left the craft and were debriefed, so we decided it was time to return to town. Before going, I took one last look at this wondrous object that had been in space only moments before, now presenting itself for inspection on the runway. Alone, silent, waiting — the shuttle seemed out of place here. It belonged in space, not earthbound on a desert runway. As we headed toward the parking lot, my thoughts were of the happy day when she would "slip the surly bonds of Earth" and once again be spaceborne.

LOG ENTRY 31 :

January 28, 1986. I always have the TV on in the morning when I'm getting dressed. Usually I pay very little attention to it, but for some reason that day it caught my eye. It was around 7:00 a.m., and a newscaster was saying something about the weather in Florida and "icing up." I turned toward the television and saw the familiar image of a space shuttle, poised on the launching platform, its nose aimed skyward.

I felt a sudden dread, but I dismissed it. I'm sure they'll do the right thing, I thought, and continued drying my hair and applying my eyeliner. The TV droned on, but I ignored it. I finally turned it off, leaving the bedroom for the kitchen and my cup of Earl Grey.

A little after 8:00, I switched on the TV in the living room and sat sipping my tea. There it was again. In the background, I could hear the countdown. Nine . . . eight . . . seven . . . The pang I had dismissed earlier returned with a vengeance. I can't watch this, I thought. Something's dreadfully wrong. No, I mustn't think that. Everything's fine, I reassured myself; yet I knew it wasn't.

. . . Six . . . five . . . four . . . My hand was sweating so much I couldn't hold the cup. Are they really going to launch? Maybe they'll stop.

. . . Three . . . two . . . one. There! It's going! It's okay! Then, why was I still shaking inside? Why this irrational sense that something was not right? Moments later, I knew. Instead of flying as a unit, one of the rockets suddenly flared, the boosters veered off in two directions trailing brilliant yellow fire and white curlicues of smoke, and seven astronauts bound for the heavens fell instead to their watery graves in the impersonal sea below.

I kept screaming, at the same time reaching for the telephone and dialing Gene's home number, unsure whether he or Majel would answer.

"Hello . . . ?" his sleepy voice said.

"Gene, quick, turn on the TV. The shuttle just blew up!" I was yelling into the receiver. He hadn't been watching; he'd gone back to sleep after his customary morning read of the paper. I could hear his set as it came to life. Miles apart yet together, phones pressed to our ears, we watched in silence. What could we say? Our minds were as one during those long moments.

At last Gene broke the stillness. "Take the day off if you want," he said softly. He could hear me crying.

"No, I want to be around people. I want to see you, if you feel up to it."

"Of course," he agreed, and later we met at the office, where we sat glued to the TV, consoling each other and the staff for most of the day. "This is an unbelievable tragedy," Gene said, shaking his head in disbelief.

The demise of the space shuttle profoundly affected the entire nation; indeed, the whole world mourned the tragic loss of life. But for Gene and me, the loss went even deeper.

The space shuttle was the one whose landing we had so recently cheered in the desert: *Challenger*.

< < <   > > >

A few weeks later I visited Gene in La Costa, where he was supposed to be working on his book, *Report from Earth*, but was really loafing. On this occasion, we decided to make a run for the border, i.e., the Mexican town of Tijuana. We parked on the American side and walked over the bridge where we caught a taxi into town.

T.J. is not exactly the most attractive of cities, but our taxi driver did his best to show us the sights. We were surprised to learn that there is a community of upscale homes, which our driver pointed out with great pride, where the well-to-do reside. We were actually even more surprised to learn that there *were* well-to-do residents in this border town, which has a reputation for being on the seedy side. At Gene's request, the driver took us back toward town to visit the bars. Thus fortified, Gene thought it would be fun to have our pictures taken with one of those poor burros painted to look like zebras. (What ever possessed the first person who did this?) The burro owner/photographer crowned us with straw hats. Mine said "Linda Tijuana" — beautiful Tijuana — while Gene's hat bore the caption "Drunk Again." We spent the rest of the afternoon shopping for souvenirs. I spotted a warm cotton knit hooded pullover that Gene insisted on buying for me, and just before reaching the U.S. border, we had our taxi driver stop at a pottery stand, where I bought a Pinocchio piggybank and a seated ceramic frog that held a tiny potted houseplant. When we re-entered the U.S., I kidded Gene that we should say, "All we bought is a little pot!" He told me if I said that, he'd make sure they sent me back to "my people" in Mexico.

On another trip to La Costa later that winter, Gene greeted me at the door with a terribly worried look on his face. He told me that he had had some rectal bleeding and had spots in his shorts. He seemed truly frightened. I insisted he see a doctor right away. We

Atop painted burros in Tijuana, Mexico, 1986.

returned to Los Angeles the next day, where he saw his regular physician, who sent him to a specialist. The specialist checked him over and decided Gene needed surgery. It was a simple procedure at Cedars-Sinai, done on an outpatient basis. Early one morning in February, I went with Gene to the hospital. They sedated him, and the doctor removed what turned out to be a cancerous polyp from his colon. The procedure was similar to one then-President Reagan had undergone at about that time, only not quite as complex. I sat with Gene in the recovery room for an hour or so while the anesthesia wore off. Then I drove him home where he slept the rest of the day.

I spent a lot of time worrying about Gene and his various ailments — perhaps too much, but I think he enjoyed my Jewish mothering. I would bandage his cuts, give him Alka-Seltzer or Pepto for his stomach aches and aspirin for occasional headaches. At his insistence, we had a complete over-the-counter pharmacy in his office's private bathroom: Stomach and cold remedies, sprays, salves, hydrogen peroxide and Band-Aids, contact lens solutions for those eye emergencies (we both wore lenses that were constantly slipping), shaving cream, razors and razor blades for Gene. There were several electric razors at any given time — Gene had a passion for these gadgets. Every time we went to an appliance store, he would add another to his collection. He always seemed to be in search of the perfect electric shaver and, in addition to the ones at the office, he kept a couple at my house.

Gene had a fascination with all sorts of gadgetry. When I first knew him, he was particularly interested in unusual clocks and timepieces. He had one of the earliest digital quartz watches on the market, an original Pulsar. (One of my first assignments when I went to work for him was to take it down to Bullock's and have it repaired. Gene's high-tech toys seemed to have a high rate of entropy.) In his house, he had a clock that turned different colors as the minutes progressed. Another one had an array of lighted dots that required expertise to decipher. Still another, a silver mushroom-shaped piece about five inches high, chimed the hour and minutes when you grasped the cap. Since he enjoyed clocks and watches so much, it made shopping easy when it came time to give him a birthday or Christmas gift. One year I presented him with a talking watch. At the mere press of a button, the watch brightly announced the time to anyone within earshot. This was fine if he was alone, but didn't go over too well with people in movie theaters or at concerts. Like most gifts I gave him, he used it with great gusto at first, but soon moved on to other passions. When I asked what had happened to this watch, he confessed that Rod had shown an interest in it, so he gave it to him. Another watch I gave him had a complete calculator and rolodex in the wristband. I think it met with a similar fate.

For seventeen years, I strove to find unusual gifts for this man who, after all, could purchase anything he ever wanted. Once while on a visit to New York City, I spotted a lamp on the desk of *Starlog* magazine editor Kerry O'Quinn. "Where did you get that?" I excitedly demanded of my bewildered editor. I explained that this lamp with its swirling, sparking bits of mylar that reflected the colored light shining from below would make the ideal gift for Gene. Kerry sent me scurrying over to a store called Brazil Comtempo, on Madison Avenue, and I returned with what turned out to be one of Gene's very favorite gifts. Back in those days of working on the first *Star Trek* film, we would toke up at the end of the day, then sit in a darkened room and stare at the incredibly hypnotic kinetic lights and colors and be dazzled for long, relaxing moments. Many years later when the lamp finally burned out, I scoured the streets of L.A. for a replacement and finally landed a close cousin, a Gemlite manufactured by the folks who produced the popular '60's lava lamps. Gene enjoyed my Gemlite in his office until his final year, when I took it home after he became ill and was no longer able to come to the office. For months after he died, whenever I would begin to feel lonely, I would remember the warmth we felt those nights at the office so long ago, and I'd turn out my living room lights and turn on the sparkle lamp. It was such a comforting feeling, as if he were nearby basking in the colorful glow.

LOG ENTRY 32 :

One Christmas I actually gave Gene the stars. Well, one star, really, named after him. I heard about a company called International Star Registry that lets you name a star for someone. (And, as far as I know, no one from the any of the stars has contacted Earth to object.) They register it, record it in their archives, and send you a parchment certificate along with star-locating charts. Somewhere out there in a distant quadrant of the galaxy is star "Gene Roddenberry." Ironically, that same year, my friend Cheryl gave me a star, too (named "Susan Sackett," of course) — which wasn't anywhere near Gene's. Had I known I was going to receive one as well, I would have requested adjoining stars! I had Gene's official document framed for the office, and since we had run out of wall space, we agreed the logical place for it was on his bathroom wall, where he could admire it several times each day.

His most treasured gifts were the numerous books I gave him over the years. He was a reading shark, sinking his teeth deep into the pages of anything in print, chomping through it with a bloodlust, gorging himself until sated, usually in one long sitting. In this manner, he tore through several books a week. His appetite ran from history to sociology, from best-selling novels to literary classics. Nothing was safe. If he especially enjoyed something, he would reread it numerous times. One of his favorites was *The Rise and Fall of the Third Reich* by the late William L. Shirer. Gene was fascinated by World War II and anything that had to do with Hitler. He spent much of his spare time trying to understand this most powerful and dangerous man of the twentieth century. We spent long hours discussing his fascination with Hitler. Whenever I would mention how evil I thought Hitler was, Gene would disagree.

"Evil doesn't exist," he would argue. "There really isn't such a thing as evil."

I knew Shakespeare had said the same thing when he wrote in Act II of *Hamlet*, "There is nothing either good or bad, but thinking makes it so," but my common sense and indignation over Hitler's treatment of the Jews and other minorities made me cry out.

"How can you say that about a horrible man who murdered millions?" I'd protest.

Gene's reply: "But it is our interpretation of these actions that labels them evil. Certainly Hitler didn't think he was doing evil. He thought what he did was for the *good* of his country." And so it would go. It wasn't that he liked old Adolph or was a neo-Nazi or anything — he detested the things Hitler had done — but he was captivated by this major historical figure. He had a Spock-like curiosity about what made this madman tick.

Gene's quirky point of view often puzzled me. He would talk about the Russian system, extolling the worthy goals of communism — no hunger, no unemployment, everyone medically cared for and housed, and freedom *from* religion, an important concept for Gene — yet when I would ask if he was a communist, he would always reply with a resounding "No, but I admire the concept." Of course he wasn't a communist — he was a flourishing capitalist in the truest sense, enjoying a Beverly Hills lifestyle that included the finest of houses, cars and other rewards of our American work ethic. But he was always tolerant and pleased with the finer points of communist ideals at a time when the president of the United States was railing against the "evil empire." It was a great gift Gene had, to be able to look at things from the other side, to challenge the accepted viewpoint and prevail in his logic. He wasn't just playing devil's advocate; he truly was

able to see beyond the propaganda and make decisions for himself.

His eccentricity seemed genuine. He thought drugs, for example, should be legalized. He despised the Pledge of Allegiance. "How can you pledge to a piece of cloth?" he'd ask. And he came down especially hard on organized religion.

Until the time he was nine or ten, Gene had been given a Protestant religious upbringing by his church-going mother. He told me that all ended one day when he was about to take communion and thought, "I've been put here among cannibals! They want me to eat a body and drink blood!" After that, he refused to go to church and maintained that attitude throughout his adult life. He saw religion as beliefs based in superstition, although he did have respect for some ceremonies. The first year I knew him, he had been invited to a Jewish Passover dinner by his next door neighbor, and as a joke, I taught him the "Four Questions" — in Hebrew. Under my tutelage, he memorized them by rote and made a huge impression on the assembled guests. Oddly, when I first met him, he told me that he respected all religions, and at his infant son Rod's "Welcome to the World" ceremony (definitely *not* a christening, he insisted), he had invited a priest, a rabbi and a minister to preside.

This is a picture I took of Gene in our offices at Paramount in the mid-'70s, shortly after we arrived on the lot. You can see some of the supplies in the background, including our stationery we used at the time, with the original Enterprise in pale blue on white envelopes. I really like Gene's smile here; we were just about to embark on the great adventure of reviving Star Trek and you can see from his expression how happy this made him feel!

At that time, he said he leaned toward Eastern philosophies of religion and believed in the "All." I asked him what he thought "God" was and he said simply, "Thought." But his beliefs progressed towards agnosticism over the years, and although publicly he sometimes professed and cheered atheism for its iconoclasm, many of our conversations concerning his ideas of life and death found him maintaining a concept of our being part of a greater whole, a drop of water merging into a larger pond. You could take out a drop of water (the individual), but once the drop merges back into the pond (death), you might be able to remove another drop, but it would not necessarily be the same (reincarnation).

Once, following a particularly enjoyable afternoon of lovemaking, I asked him if he really did believe in reincarnation. The answer was much less profound than his "drop in the pond" philosophy. He said simply, "I don't know. But if I do come back, I'll spend the first fifty years looking for you!" We both laughed over this, although I felt that deep down he was quite serious.

Gene always took life, and life after life, quite seriously. His agnosticism found him constantly questioning the existence of a supernatural being, but to him this in no way conflicted with the possibility of the continuity of consciousness, a subject about which he frequently wrote as well as read.

His reading material wasn't always this philosophical, however. When he wasn't devouring heavy metaphysical treatises or tomes about Nazis or communists, his favorite light reading was anything in the Horatio Hornblower series, and he mentioned frequently that Capt. Kirk was based on Hornblower. He especially enjoyed *Beat to Quarters*, which he once eagerly offered to me. I tried desperately to read it but couldn't get past the first few chapters. Frequently, however, we would exchange our favorite books with each other. We were both fans of Richard Bach (whom Gene knew well and I had had the pleasure of meeting a couple of times), and we were taken with his 1984 romantic autobiography, *The Bridge Across Forever*. We also shared all the current best-selling novels, as well as books relating to scientific endeavors, like Charles Panati's *Breakthroughs* and Lyall Watson's *Supernature*. And since there never could be enough hours to read everything in the world, which seemed to be Gene's goal, he began ordering from Books on Tape, a company that shipped audio cassettes of recited books that could then be played on one's car tape system. I remember spending long hours driving to and from work listening to tapes Gene had completed — things like *Peter the Great* and *Moby Dick*, which I might never have bothered with otherwise.

One important book Gene shared with me early in my writing career was *The Art of Dramatic Writing*, by Lajos Egri. Originally published in 1946, this book has become a classic for anyone interested in becoming a good writer. I was surprised to hear that Gene had actually studied writing. I had always assumed it came naturally to him. But he swore by Egri, whose basic premise was simply that *all good drama must have a premise*, as well as *good characters* and *conflict*. His own copy of this book was so thumb-worn, I immediately purchased one of my own, which I still treasure.

LOG ENTRY 33 :

Star Trek IV: The Voyage Home was in full swing, and for once even Gene seemed to be getting behind this film. Although the premise was a bit far fetched (whales have communicated with extraterrestrials in the past; now the cetaceans have all died out, and the aliens trash Earth searching the oceans for them), I enjoyed the Save the Whales theme and was pleased when Leonard Nimoy asked for my input. I supplied him with several hours of videotapes that I had collected over the years as part of my longtime interest in the subject. Gene and I attended the dailies, and when he was out of town giving talks to universities, I very often saw the footage alone and reported to him on it. I could tell from the start that this movie was going to be a hit.

Of all the *Trek* films, the cast and crew seemed to have the most fun making this one. Even Leonard Nimoy seemed to be more relaxed, and could often be seen joking and smiling with his fellow cast members. He was more confident in his second directorial venture, doing considerably more acting in *Star Trek IV* than his brief appearance in *ST III*. But, Leonard told me, "It would be much easier if I were only doing one job or the other. It was tough. I wouldn't recommend it."

The secondary actors were all much happier with their roles in this movie. Walter had been very dissatisfied with his minor part in *Star Trek III*, but reveled in his expanded role in *IV*. "Chekov was a delight for me," he told me.

George Takei was thrilled to be given a chance to ad lib; the scene in the Huey helicopter, in which he accidentally activates the windshield wiper, was improvised with Nimoy's blessing. George was disappointed, however, when another sequence that he especially liked was cut. Harve Bennett had written a scene in which Sulu meets his great, great, great, great grandfather, who is seven years old. But the scene was never filmed in order to maintain the shooting schedule.

The film differed in tone from the other films, with the action taking place not in outer space, but in present-day San Francisco. And it boasted a sense of humor that was absent in the previous adventures, giving it added audience appeal. In one scene, Nimoy directed his own associate producer, Kirk Thatcher. Kirk appears as the annoying boom-box punk on a San Francisco bus, whom Spock dispatches with a Vulcan neck pinch, a gesture wildly applauded by his fellow passengers. Kirk, a part-time musician, wrote and performed the song, *I Hate You*. It is one of the comedy highlights of the movie.

Much of *Star Trek IV* was filmed on location, and one afternoon I drove out to Will Rogers Park in Pacific Palisades. A mock-up of the ramp to the Klingon ship had been built, and they were shooting several scenes with Kirk, Spock, Dr. Gillian Taylor (Catherine Hicks) and other *Enterprise* crew members. Although there had been some scenes shot on location in San Francisco, this local park was doubling as Golden Gate Park. The cast did several takes going up and down the ramp, and Catherine did the scene where Gillian drives her truck while talking to Kirk. But the most interesting scene was when Gillian is supposed to be touching the cloaked spaceship. It looked like a Marcel Marceau number as Catherine placed her hands up against the air, pretending to feel the invisible ship. In science fiction, much of acting consists of reacting to what you *can't* see; the *Star Trek* cast could write the book on it.

Back at Paramount, it was time to film in the B-tank. This large area usually served as

a spare parking lot, but for this occasion, the cars were removed, and the whole area of several acres was flooded. A portion of the crashed renegade ship *Bounty* was built to protrude from the tank and set into the water. Industrial Light and Magic (ILM) had built magnificent radio-controlled humpback whales, which could move through the water and give the appearance of monstrous size. With wind and wave machines churning, our cast was placed into the water to splash about and laugh for joy at the sight of the whales swimming. They did this for hours, no one complaining. Then, shivering, they completed the scene and wrapped in their warm terry robes. It was a memorable afternoon, even though many of us spectators got a bit damp from the spray.

In October 1985, I had tried out for the TV game show, *Jeopardy!* The producers congratulated me and told me I would definitely be on the show, and the following August, I got a call. On August 5, I told Gene I wouldn't be able to work that day as I was going on *Jeopardy!* to win enough money to pay all my outstanding bills. His eyes squinted with a combination of amusement and disdain as he bellowed with laughter. "Susan," he said, wagging a finger at me, "you've got to be kidding. That's the dumbest thing I've ever heard you say." Two days later, I made him eat those words. I'd won sixty-four hundred dollars, plenty to cover my debts, and as the returning champion on the next show, I'd added an all-expenses-paid trip for two to Hawaii to my haul of prizes. Gene was contrite,

Gene and I share a moment at the 20th anniversary party for Star Trek, held at Paramount Studios.

happily adding this bit of lore to his repertoire of tales about me, in which he delighted.

My first *Jeopardy!* appearance aired on Monday, September 8, 1986, a fortuitous day indeed. It was the twentieth anniversary of the television debut *of Star Trek*, and immediately following the broadcast of my episode, Dawn Roddenberry and her husband Richard Compton picked me up in a limousine for a spectacular *Star Trek* anniversary party on the Paramount lot.

The whole original cast was there, with their spouses and loved ones; there were food stations named after the characters, and lots of self-congratulatory fun from crew and staff, as everyone mingled as equals — grips and with actors, lighting technicians with producers. The transporter set was lit, and guests were invited to pose for souvenir pictures on the transporter pads.

These parties were always a success and this was no exception. Between the party and my *Jeopardy* airing, this was the culmination of one of the most memorable days in my life.

And yet, two weeks later, something even more memorable happened. After all the years of urging Gene to get treatment for his drug and alcohol problems, he had finally agreed to take what amounted to a gargantuan step, and just in time for the next turning point in his life.

LOG ENTRY 34 : I was convinced Gene's drinking had become excessive.

He had wine with lunch; drinks in the afternoon at his desk; cocktails before and during dinner, and occasionally would even toss down liquid Nyquil (twenty-five percent alcohol in those days) at bedtime.

Gently, as always, I told him I thought he needed help. I was elated when he agreed, and at my suggestion, he allowed me to send for information from the Schick-Shadel Hospital for alcohol and drug abuse. The material arrived in a plain brown wrapper. It described the facility, located in Santa Barbara, about a two-hour drive up the coast from Beverly Hills. Gene consulted with his internist, who agreed that it was important for him to get treatment. On Sept. 21, 1986, Gene left for Schick-Shadel in Santa Barbara for a fourteen-day stay.

Over the next two weeks, I drove up the coast to check on Gene's progress. The hospital was more like an unglamorous one-story motel with rooms circling a central courtyard. I had been given clearance to phone and visit along with only two other people — Majel, and Leonard Maizlish.

The first time I arrived, Gene gave me a quick tour. One of the treatment rooms he showed me was half-jokingly called "Duffy's Tavern," after the popular radio show of the '40s. It looked for all the world like a neighborhood corner bar — bottles, coasters, swizzle sticks, posters, neon — the works. But to the residents at Schick, this room was more akin to Hell. The treatments, Gene told me, consisted of aversion therapy. In order to deter the urge to drink, patients were given medication that caused vomiting whenever alcohol was consumed. They were brought to Duffy's and told to order their favorite libations. Drinks were downed. Drinks came back up. Soon, drinking became associated with vomiting. And very soon, patients no longer wanted to drink. They were forced to repeat the experience *ad nauseum*, to reinforce the pattern.

This was no twelve-step program. No one was told they were powerless, or had to depend on group support or some outside "higher power." This meshed perfectly with Gene's agnosticism, which is one of the reasons he agreed to participate in the program.

After a few "Duffs," as the treatments were known, Gene told me he never planned to take a drink again as long as he lived. He also swore off cocaine forever, having seen the horrors of patients receiving treatment for that addiction. It seemed an epiphany.

During his stay at Schick, Gene also received counseling. He talked with his therapists about his need for support once he got back home. The counselors urged him to continue to get help, and that most importantly, he needed to continue with the follow-up treatment the facility provided.

Gene emerged happy and confident, clean and sober. A month later, he was supposed to return for a weekend of reinforcement therapy. He was still off the booze, but he was about to embark on a speaking tour to a number of important groups around the country. He was unable to attend, but promised to check back with Schick as soon as he returned to town.

The talks included a convention in Wichita, Kansas; the Ruth Eckerd Hall in Clearwater, Florida, and Info Systems of the U.S. Air Force in Washington, D.C. His newly updated speech was entitled "The Shape of Tomorrow," and covered the computer revolution, his latest pet topic.

When he returned to L.A., I again mentioned Schick. The doctors and administrators had been very solicitous, I told him. They had phoned several times, urging me to remind him that his program was not completed, and he needed the follow-up procedures. Gene dodged this very successfully, and there was not much I could do about it. This time, he had a legitimate reason.

The reason was called *Star Trek: The Next Generation*.

Shortly before Gene went into Schick, Paramount Studios presented him with a written treatment for a new television series, *Star Trek: The Next Generation*. The studio executives in charge of this production had hired an outside writer to create this new incarnation of *Star Trek,* and they wanted Gene's opinion. Gene mustered a self-control I didn't know he had as, politely, he told them to which end of space they could go. "When I read what they had written, I almost threw up," Gene told me. If the studio wanted a new *Star Trek,* he was their boy, not some outsider who had populated a new starship with a bunch of "gee whiz" space cadets.

"But Gene, you've always said you'd never do *Star Trek* again," proclaimed the baffled brass.

"True, but if anyone's going to do a new *Star Trek,* it's going to be me. If not, I'll sue." Simple, fighting words.

There were, of course, certain requirements. Gene insisted first and foremost on total creative control. No Jeff Katzenbergs, no Harve Bennetts. He would create and executive produce the new series, which would be sold into syndication (not to a network), giving him freer rein than ever before.

It was with this guarantee in mind that he took the plunge at Schick, knowing full well that before he could breathe new life into the *Trek* concept, he needed to revitalize himself. (Unhappily, he never found the time for the mandatory follow-up treatments, despite numerous calls from the concerned staff.)

With a clear head and renewed enthusiasm, Gene returned from his brief speaking tour with the energy of a power plant. I have never seen him more in control, more empowered.

Paramount held a press conference to announce the development of a new, exciting series that would debut in less than a year's time.

It was time to get to work.

LOG ENTRY 35 :
Gene's first step toward creating *Star Trek: The Next Generation* was to develop a brain trust. In October, Bob Justman and David Gerrold were among the first to come on board. Justman, sixties, salt-and-pepper haired and thickly moustached, had been associate producer and eventually producer on the original *Trek* series, and Gene wanted him on the team from the start. Ditto writer David Gerrold, of "The Trouble with Tribbles" fame, a highly popular episode he'd written when he was in his teens. David was still baby-faced and full of boyish enthusiasm, and his imagination and creativity were much admired by Gene. Others who soon joined the team were former *Star Trek* producer Eddie Milkis, plus a smattering of studio executives and Gene's attorney Leonard Maizlish.[10]

Gene spent mornings working at his desk, hammering out the new series. It would be different, but within the parameters of the old *Star Trek*. The spin-off would, for example, utilize the familiar home of *Star Trek,* a new, greatly updated incarnation of the beloved starship *Enterprise*, NCC 1701-D, eight times the size of the original. There would be a captain, first officer (but not a Vulcan), doctor (this time a woman), plus a crew of Starfleet officers. Familiar terminology would include the ship's quarters such as the bridge and sickbay, and transporter room for "beaming;" weapons and gadgetry would still bear the designations phasers, communicators, tricorders and photon torpedoes; and those bad guys we loved to hate, the Klingons and Romulans, would still be around. With *détente* and *glasnost* fresh in his mind during those years, Gene decided that the Klingons would now be Federation members.

Each day at lunchtime, Gene and the gang, including myself, would meet in Paramount's executive dining room to develop the new characters and the show's "bible."

Captain Jean-Luc Picard[11] was the first character to be created. Gene wanted him to differ from Kirk in a number of ways. He wouldn't rush down to the planet on every mission, thus putting himself at risk. Instead, his First Officer, Commander Riker, would in essence be a co-captain, in charge of Away Teams and planet explorations. I recall Gene telling us, "The Captain's job is to operate the ship, and the First officer's job is to present the Captain with a well-operating ship and a competent crew. Riker feels that it is *his* ship which he has loaned to the Captain." Another departure from the original series was that Picard wouldn't be a superstud like Kirk; consequently there would be a lot less space bimbos. This was a captain with a serious attitude.

Creating the character of Data wasn't as difficult for Gene. He admitted to using Questor, the android from his TV pilot, *The Questor Tapes*, as the blueprint for Data (orig-

---

[10] Gene's omnipresent attorney caused a great deal of consternation to the creative team, yet Gene refused to proceed without Maizlish at his side. He and Maizlish were best friends as well as having a working relationship, and with the treatment Gene had gotten at the hands of the studio in recent years, he felt more secure with his attorney by his side.

[11] Jean-Luc Picard was originally called Julien Picard, but this sounded too much like the watchmaker, Lucien Piccard, so it was change.

inally pronounced with a short "a"). The most difficult part was getting the make-up peo-ple to follow Gene's wishes. In the trials, he'd tell them he wanted Data to look very white, but the makeup people would do it more normal skin toned, more brown. Gene stuck by his guns, telling them each time, "No, I want him whiter." He didn't want to explain every week that this was an android. Eventually Michael Westmore, the show's make-up artist, settled on opalescent gold makeup, which photographed as white. Brent Spiner, who played Data, was also given yellow contact lenses, as Gene wanted his eyes to appear non-human.

The addition of a Ship's Counselor was another departure for Gene. He thought that counselors ought to be part of twentieth century corporation structure and would certain-ly be present on a starship, helping to "lubricate friction between people in the way oil smoothes out friction in an engine," he told me.

Marina Sirtis was startled when she learned she'd won the role of Counselor Troi; she was in the midst of packing for a return to England the afternoon when she got the phone call telling her she'd gotten the part. Marina had been considered for the role of Tasha Yar, the ship's Chief of Security[12], and Denise Crosby, who eventually won that role, had been up for the part of Troi. Gene decided to switch blonde Denise and brunette Marina, totally the opposite of his initial image of the characters, and it worked.

Having a female doctor was a true departure for Gene, but he didn't want to do a retread of Dr. McCoy. And he needed a high-ranking woman on the ship. The doctor fit the bill nicely. Gates McFadden had been working in theatre as an actress and choreogra-pher when she won the part as Dr. Beverly Crusher. When we met her, she had been using the name Cheryl McFadden, and this went out in all the press releases announcing the new cast. A week after the announcement, she decided Cheryl was too pedestrian; from now on, she would be billed not as Cheryl, but Gates, and the press kit had to be rewritten.

Gene wanted Dr. Crusher to have a son, Wesley, but the staff wanted more female roles. "I thought it might be a little bit of a stretch for today's audience to believe that a young female would have passionate feelings about matter and energy, which was part of the characterization," Gene told me. For a time, the character of Leslie Crusher existed in the series description, but stories involving her usually saw the character as weak and helpless, either being attacked or having to defend her virtue each week. They went back and forth over the Wesley/Leslie character, and eventually Gene decided on Wesley after seeing Wil Wheaton in *Stand By Me*. "He had the right look; I could see him someday as a young lieutenant," Gene commented.

Early in these development meetings, the staff decided that a physically handicapped person should be prominently featured in the main cast. To that end, Lt. Geordi LaForge was created. The character was named after a fan of the original series, a young man who had been a regular attendee at conventions and was well known to Gene, David Gerrold and others. The youth's name was George LaForge, and he was wheelchair-bound. Geor-di would represent the disabled and physically challenged population as a blind person, although assisted by a prosthetic device. And as a unique dramatic device, Geordi would

[12] Natasha "Tasha" Yar was originally called "Macha Hernandez," a knock-off of the butch character in the 1986 movie, *Aliens*.

be the *Enterprise*'s navigator – a blind man flying the ship!

I was delighted when Gene encouraged my input at these brainstorming sessions. He cautioned me, however, not to speak out too frequently in the meetings. Gene seemed to suffer a bit of confusion over my status, especially in the eyes of those whose respect he craved. *He* knew I was more than just his executive assistant, but he told me he was concerned that he might appear weak in the eyes of the development committee. I guess he wanted them to view him as more exalted, not receiving advice from a lowly female assistant! So in the beginning I was only present to take notes. Later, as everyone grew more comfortable with my presence (I was the *only* female at these meetings — Dorothy Fontana was employed elsewhere at the time), I began to offer my input. Mostly, though, I took my best shot when Gene and I were working alone in the office.

My contributions weren't large, but I was pleased at being taken seriously. Gene even honored me by making one of the main characters my namesake. *Deanna* Troi bore my middle name, and Gene decided to name *Wesley* Crusher after himself — Eugene Wesley Roddenberry. This entwining of our middle names was our personal secret.

Not every suggestion I made was welcomed with undying enthusiasm. I told him I didn't think the concept of children aboard the ship would work — and many of the fans and critics later agreed with me — but he refused to drop this, comparing the lengthy voyages of the *Enterprise* with pioneers moving their wagons west across the American frontier of the 1880s. I countered with, "Yes, but the *Enterprise* crew aren't space settlers, they're explorers. They'll be going home again." It didn't wash with him, and the concept remained. I also suggested that by now the Federation would have developed the technology for the Romulan cloaking device and could use this freely, but he countered with the fact that this would preclude a lot of drama (and I had to agree with his reasoning). What about a personal cloaking device, something an individual could use? This he nixed too, and rightfully so, or we'd have been doing *The Invisible Man* every week!

One thing for which I did fight very hard was an updated opening narration. Gene was perfectly content to stick with "To boldly go where no *man* has gone before," while I lobbied heavily on behalf of my gender, eventually persuading him to change the prologue to "To boldly go where no *one* has gone before." A subtle difference, but vital, I felt. It wasn't easy to persuade Gene to make this kind of change. For all his liberalism, he seemed to have an underlying mistrust of women. Then too, he came from a time in our century that had treated women as second-class citizens. There was a kind of lag between his idealism and the reality of his actions. If I'd say, "You've got to stop thinking of women as a different species," his rejoinder would be, "I have a great affection for them, but they *are* different." I would constantly catch him saying things like "the woman doctor," or "the lady pilot on my flight to Denver." Gene finally relented on the "where no *one*…" idea when the other members of production team told him how much they liked this newer version, and I breathed a sigh of relief, knowing that this would go over much better with an '80s audience.

LOG ENTRY 36 :

Like Captain Kirk in *Star Trek II* when he was able to take back control of the *Enterprise* after being stuck at a desk job, Gene was happier than I'd ever seen him. It was as if he, too, had been given command again after a long period of being grounded. Here was the Gene Roddenberry in action that I'd heard so much about — gathering the best minds around him, encouraging creativity from his brain trust, rushing to meetings with studio brass, giving interviews to Larry King, *Time* and *Newsweek*.

Sandwiched between his morning and afternoon writing marathons and the lunchtime jam sessions, Gene and the team screened dozens of science fiction films. For me, it was heaven, as we saw virtually every contemporary (and some not-so-recent) SF film — *Aliens, Ice Pirates, Brazil, Enemy Mine, Outland, Blade Runner, Dune, Explorers, Robinson Crusoe on Mars,* plus all three released *Star Trek* films and a rough cut of the upcoming *Star Trek IV*.

Unfortunately, during this frantic time of screening potential producers and writers and assembling a new cast, writing scripts and launching a new series, our time together suffered and our relationship nearly succumbed. It was at once an exciting period in my life and one of the lowest ebbs in our relationship, which suddenly was relegated not just to the back burner, but to some burner on another planet. He had simply found another passion — his first and constant love — creating. How could I argue with that? Of course, he never articulated this, but it was readily apparent that his new mistress was really an old friend, one he had never quite forgotten. His work was his life. How could it be any other way? You can't be the creator of a twentieth century phenomenon and have a casual relationship with your progeny. For me, it was a lonely time, as our moments together became fewer. While I cried many a tear for my late, lamented love life, I wouldn't have traded places with anyone.

Many people wanted to trade places with me. Our office was inundated daily with résumés from showbiz wannabes of every sort — artists, writers, editors, set designers, and many, many secretaries slavering for a chance to work in our office. It was the kind of job to kill for, and I felt fortunate to be in my own shoes. For example, one of the perks I had enjoyed for years was the joy of being on a studio lot. I'd had the opportunity to meet not only the original *Star Trek* cast members, but at various times since our first tenure there, I'd been privileged to have chatted up many celebrities, including Michael J. Fox, Robin Williams, Henry Winkler, Michael Landon, Kirstie Alley and dozens more. I never tired of this aspect of Hollywood glamour.

Now, with the casting for the new *Star Trek* series, I had the opportunity to meet the stars before they became household names. Each was unique, and I have memories of my first encounter with each of them.

Patrick Stewart, for instance, had a warmth and charisma that could not be denied. But, until the first time he walked into the office, I feared for the sanity of Gene and Bob Justman, who were backing him for the role of the Captain. What had possessed them to court a bald, middle-aged Englishman?

When Bob first told Gene about his discovery, Gene wasn't the least bit enthusiastic. Patrick had been appearing as part of a lecture series at UCLA, reading from Oscar Wilde and Noel Coward. Bob and his wife, Jackie, were in the audience, and as Patrick began speaking, Bob turned to her and said, "We've found our captain." When Gene saw Patrick's picture, he was astonished. "I'm not going to have a bald Englishman for my French Captain," he said. But after Patrick read for him and Gene saw his acting ability, he changed his tune. "The more I saw him, the better I liked him."

I had to admit I, too, was wrong. The first time Patrick greeted me as he went past my desk to Gene's inner office, I was instantly converted. Later, as I got to know him better, his usual effect on me was to render me nearly speechless. Anyway, who wanted to talk when you could listen to that magnificent voice or gaze at his superbly unadorned pate?

I remember when Jonathan Frakes was up for the role of Riker, along with one or two others. He sat in my office (which was somewhat of a waiting room for those about to meet with Gene) rubbing his hands together, then pacing the hallway, then returning to his seat and asking me, "What do you think? Do you think I'll get the role?" What could I say? I didn't have a clue as to who would get the role, but he seemed to want it so badly. "Of course you'll get it, you're a shoo in," I confided. "They loved your reading."

LeVar Burton, on the other hand, was at peace with himself and the universe when he came for his callback for Lt. Geordi LaForge. He exuded a mystical calm, most likely because of his New Age interests. He told me he'd recently been to some mountaintop in Sedona for the "Harmonic Convergence," that he'd climbed to the top of a hundred foot pole somewhere for the experience, and that crystals were very important things. It didn't matter that I thought all this a bit on the far side — he believed it, and it worked for him. He got the job.

A year later, when Whoopi Goldberg was added to the cast, I again had trouble finding my tongue. But amazingly, she was the easiest person of all to talk to. I guess I was expecting one of her outrageous stage personae, but this quiet, unassuming lady calmly asked for a drink of water. "Wow! She drinks water, just like the rest of us!" I thought, hoping my awe wasn't too apparent. She quickly became my favorite actor in the cast. Whenever we watched her in dailies, it was time to get ready for a treat. She was a gifted dramatist. From viewing years of dailies, I know that most actors will give the same reading, the same inflections, the same gestures with each take of a scene. Not Whoopi — her readings were always fresh and varied and consistently excellent. She also loved to catch her co-stars and the crew off balance by ad-libbing bawdy jokes and one-liners whenever she flubbed a line. Those of us back in the office watching the daily video footage of her scenes lived for these moments! I never tired of my good fortune at being a part of all this.

Gene, now busier than I'd ever known him, was aware of our dwindling time together, but he did his best to find special moments for us to get away and have lunch at places like Butterfield's, a charming outdoor patio restaurant on the Sunset Strip, and Columbia Bar and Grill, a trendy Hollywood eatery owned by Wayne Rogers (of M*A*S*H fame).

We no longer had our place on Wilcox, but now and then he'd suggest we dash off to a hotel where we could be alone for a couple of hours. Sometimes these were classy places, like the Hilton on Vermont, where we went when my mother was in town and we

couldn't use my house. Sometimes they were whatever was nearby, like the Players Motel on Vine Street, or Arthur's Hideaway in Universal City, a sleazy quickie place that made my skin crawl. Gene had once spotted this motel and admitted he had always wanted to try something with closed-circuit XXX videos. I indulged him, but I found it a loathsome spot, and I think he was too chagrined to admit his mistake. He enjoyed the challenge of making a getaway from these places without being recognized. In some ways, our whole relationship was a challenge to him, a dangerous game that he delighted in constantly winning. It made me nervous and uncomfortable at times, and I think he enjoyed that, too.

Early in the production, it became apparent we would need to move out of our space in Building G to accommodate our ever-increasing staff. We were relocated to Building L, later renamed the Mae West Building. I hated our offices there. I went from having my own room adjoining Gene's spacious one in Building G (later renamed the William S. Hart Building), to a tiny space in an outer office, shared with several other assistants and desks. Eventually, these were separated into cubicles thanks to padded section dividers, but I felt downgraded. It was hectic and noisy to boot. Gene's office was a comedown too,

On the day I was on **ST:TNG** as an extra, Jonathan Frakes ("Riker") and Brent Spiner ("Data") posed for a photo with me. I had no idea they were being so silly until I saw the print and realized they were sticking out their tongues! When I asked them to autograph the picture, Brent wrote, "Susan, You are a woman of infinite taste, Love, Brent" while Jonathan simple scrawled, "Hmmmm."

although I think he was too busy to notice or care. He had one window high up, with which he constantly fiddled, trying to adjust the flow of air. The air conditioning controls for our offices, however, were located on the other side of the wall separating our suite from producers Bob Justman and Eddie Milkis' digs. Somehow, when the brilliant Paramount engineers had wired the rooms, they had cross-connected the thermostat controls, so ours controlled Justman's and Milkis', and their thermostat controlled our rooms. It was either freezing in our offices, or hot as Vulcan.

I was grateful when we left Building L after production began, since this space was no longer adequate. By the spring of 1987, Gene, the writers and I had returned to Building G (renamed the William S. Hart Building), Gene and I now headquartered on the ground floor instead of the fourth. The production team acquired their own space, a group of temporary offices set up in a massive trailer at the opposite end of the lot. The production trailer had no plumbing facilities, and I shuddered every time there was talk of our having to move there. Fortunately, we never did; instead, the production team was eventually moved closer to us, in the Gary Cooper Building across the way.

LOG ENTRY 37 : By Christmas of 1986, preproduction for *Star Trek: The Next Generation* was in full swing. Gene had given the creation of this new show every- thing he had in him, and it was taking a toll. He began drinking again over the holidays, the Schick aversion therapy long forgotten. The only consoling thought was that at least he was sober during the crucial first few months of start up on the new series.

Gene's time was becoming so limited that I had to make appointments to see him dur- ing the day. We actually set meetings on the calendar — lunchtime, late afternoon, and so on. More often than not, these would have to be postponed, as the exigencies of the new show and all its ensuing problems were more demanding than meeting with me, although my ideas were certainly important to him.

At one of our meetings late in 1986, I pitched my first story idea, about a child whose dreams materialized, putting the ship into danger in an unknown part of the universe. He thought it wasn't believable enough. ("How did the child get these powers? Why was she suddenly manifesting them?") So imagine my surprise when, a couple of months later, the show bought an episode that bore remarkable similarities. Its title was "Where No One Has Gone Before." It involved a character called The Traveller whose thoughts were superimposed on the ship and tossed it into *galaxia incognita*, a dreamlike universe.

This was my first experience with Hollywood producers' *modus operandi*. They may not always remember who pitched what, but when something strikes them just the right way, *that* writer makes the sale.

For example, very early in the show's first season, Gene and I had lunch at our favorite Continental restaurant, Le Saint Germain, a refined Melrose Avenue eatery that we both adored and whose loss we mourned when it folded (hardly anyone could afford its pricey menu). Over watercress salad appetizer (mine), pâté (his) and crisp French bread, I told him I wanted to write a story about a group of renegade Klingons who had not seen the wisdom of the new order in which Klingons (long the weekly heavies in *Star Trek* and in the movies) were now loyal adherents of the Federation. In the story I pitched, Worf, the Klingon crewmember of the new *Enterprise*, would be severely tested. Was he Klingon? Did he truly belong with the *Enterprise*? Or did his destiny lie with his ancestors? As I laid out these rough ideas, Gene kept nodding his head. When I finished he said simply, "It won't work. Not on this show. All Klingons are now loyal." End of discussion. Not even Gene could foresee the direction the Klingon story arc would take. Of course, as any fan of the show knows, over the next several years, some of the best stories written for the series revolved around Worf, his family, his moral tug-of-war, the Klingon leaders and the decidedly hesitant Klingon faction which seemed temporarily resigned to Federation membership.

This was just one example of my frustration in offering the show what I thought were good ideas, only to have them shot down and then later emerge in the hands of another writer. Another example: In 1990, Fred Bronson and I pitched a Western, a holodeck- gone-wrong story, and were told that under no circumstances would the show ever con- sider a Western; then in 1992, the episode "A Fist Full of Datas" appeared. In 1991, we pitched nearly ten show ideas. The last one was an idea about a *female* Ferengi, a kind of "Yentl" (as in the Barbra Streisand film), posing as a male in order to utilize her natural intelligence and skills to the fullest, eventually enabling her to rise above her oppression in male-dominated Ferengi society. I jokingly called it "Fentl, the Female Ferengi." The assembled writing staff laughed and laughed as they escorted us out the door. That was the last we heard of our "Fentl" until 1993, when we learned that this concept had been placed on the producers' "cliché board" in their office. According to the October, 1993 issue of *Cinefantastique* magazine, one of the categories on this board was listed as:

FERENTYL — A female Ferengi who is passed off as a male.

The article noted this comment from one of the writers: "A Ferengi *Yentl*, groaned another staffer."

Okay, it was good for a laugh. So again, imagine our surprise when we saw the "Rules of Acquisition" episode of "*Star Trek: Deep Space Nine*'s second season which featured a female Ferengi in the "Yentl" mold.

I never actually believed that such coincidences were out-and-out plagiarism, nor did we request any arbitrations by the Writers Guild. Yet on the few occasions when we did venture to point out the many similarities to our stories, we were told that "Several people had pitched that idea" or "This one was different," or "The writers found a way to make it work." Hollywood! It was frustrating, to say the least.

< < <   > > >

Filming for the first season of *ST:TNG* began on May 29, 1987, a Friday. The first scenes were of Data (Brent Spiner) and Wesley (Wil Wheaton) meeting for the first time in the holodeck. They were shot on location at Griffith Park, and Gene and I drove together to the set. On the way, he confided that he was still stumped for a name for blind navigator Geordi's visual device. Suddenly it just popped into my head. "How about VISOR?" I asked. "Great!" he replied, "but what does it stand for?" I improvised frantically. "Why, Visual Instrument and Sensory Organ Replacement, of course. Or, it could be Visual Instrument and Sight Organ Replacement . . ." I was beginning to realize that a little thinking could be a dangerous thing and decided it was time to quit while I was ahead. He liked the first one, and as soon as we arrived at the glade, he accosted Rick Berman with the acronym for the device (which was actually a modified banana hair clip).

Gene was quick to give credit where credit was due, which pleased me greatly. When I asked for a weekly credit on the show's "crawl," he wholeheartedly agreed and asked me what I thought it should be. I suggested Production Associate, a title I had been eyeing as a possibility since 1976, when we began production of the first *Star Trek* film. I'd seen it on a number of prestigious series, including some of our favorite British PBS shows. Gene thought that was a good choice, and told me to put it in the form of a memo to his attorney, Leonard Maizlish. I was surprised, since I didn't think this was the kind of thing that was memo-worthy, but at that point in the show's formulation, Gene was still terribly insecure and wasn't making any sort of move without first running it by Maizlish.

I had never been particularly fond of Leonard Maizlish. I'd met him when I first began working for Gene and wasn't impressed. He was then in his late '50s, had slicked down, thinning dark hair, dressed in wrinkled shirts that were not always tucked in, and a wore a perpetual look of melancholy. He reminded me of Mr. Magoo, scrunchy-faced and pudgy. He'd known Gene for years and they had become best buddies. Maizlish had handled all of Gene's contracts with Paramount, and as far as I could tell, Gene was his only client. To me, he was a leech; to Gene, a lifeline. He depended on Maizlish to guide him through the mire of Paramount executives who wanted to take advantage of him. Had Gene believed in a personal savior, Leonard Maizlish would have fit the description.

I drafted a memo to Maizlish, telling him where I had heard of the terminology and how innocuous it would be so as not to step on anyone's ego-swollen toes. I got my credit, which remained my title throughout the nearly five seasons I worked on the show.

June 1, the Monday after the glade sequence, was the first day of filming at the studio, on Stage 16, the largest sound stage at Paramount. Fred Bronson, my mother and I were thrilled to accompany Gene as they filmed the first setup, the "Encounter at Farpoint" shopping mall scene with Gates McFadden. Her characterization wasn't quite down yet, and she played Dr. Crusher with an attitude. "I'll take the whole bolt," she announced imperiously to the sales associate. "Send it to Dr. Crusher on board the *Enterprise*," she demanded, sounding like Queen Elizabeth ordering up supplies for Buckingham Palace. She later looped (re-recorded in a studio) her lines, with her characterization greatly softened.

After my mother returned to Florida, construction began on an addition to my house — a new master bathroom. To celebrate the addition's completion the following spring, I had a "bathroom warming" party. It was on a weekend, and Gene managed to slip away from home. In months to come, Gene and I would use the sauna and, occasionally, the oversized whirlpool tub (which took so long to fill, we rarely used it). He really enjoyed the sauna, odd for a man who perspired heavily without additional help. I was concerned about his heavy sweats. His forehead would bead up and feel cold and clammy to the touch, but he ignored this. It was simply a part of him, due, I assumed, to the burden of carrying around his excess poundage. Once when I asked him about his heavy perspiration, he jokingly used the opportunity to quote an old adage his mother taught him when he was a child. "Horses sweat," she told him, "men perspire, and ladies glow." I laughed and told him I was working up a good glow in the sauna.

He was uneasy because my sauna heater did not have a guardrail around it, so he bought me a wooden framework protector. He was also apprehensive about the bathroom floor having two levels. He said that *my mother*, who made an annual trip from Florida to stay with me, would most likely have difficulty navigating since the tiles created the optical illusion that it was all one flowing floor. I think he was reluctant to admit that he was becoming unsteady on his feet. At his insistence, I added decals to mark the four-inch drop at the end of the tile on the higher level.

The new series premiered on Sept. 30, 1987, to good reviews, and Gene seemed to relax a little. We were able to get away at least once a week now. Our dinners out had become more and more special, and I had added an unwanted twenty pounds. On Saturday, October 10, I enrolled at a weight-loss clinic called the Diet Center. Naturally, Gene chose that evening to surprise me by inviting me to dinner at Chasen's, the most elegant restaurant in Beverly Hills. How could I say no? Of all days to begin a diet!

Gene had promised me I could have a walk-on part in the new series if I stuck to my goal, and I stayed with the program so that by the end of the season, I had lost enough weight to turn a few heads. I held him to his promise, as reported in Army Archerd's column in *Daily Variety*, (March 23, 1988):

> Susan Sackett, Gene Roddenberry's exec assistant, dropped 22 pounds on a bet with Gene — her prize — a walk-on in the "Neutral Zone" seg of *Star Trek*.

Although I am generally content to remain behind the scenes, I must admit that going before the camera has its pleasures. Gene saw to it that I received the full glamour treatment: makeup by Michael Westmore (who has since won several Emmys), hair styling by the show's skilled hair dresser, plus complete wardrobe fitting under the guidance of the late Bill Theiss, our very gifted costume designer. Unfortunately, the life of an actress is all hurry-up-and-wait. I arrived for my call at noon, as required. Then I waited. And waited. Finally, at 6:00 p.m., the director announced that they were ready for my scene. And so, under Les Landau's splendid direction, I made my walk-on debut as "Girl in Turbolift Who Exits and Turns Right." Don't look for this in the credits. In fact, don't blink at all for five seconds about three-quarters of the way through the show, or you'll miss me.

And now, Mr. Landau, "I'm ready for my close-up!"

LOG ENTRY 38 : By the time the first season was completed, Gene was a changed man.

It had been a year of supreme accomplishment for him, but not without exacting an enormous toll on his emotional and physical health. With his reputation on the line, he insisted on writing and rewriting the first eleven episodes (although he only took credit for his original ones). His efforts may have helped with the show's continuity, but it cost him most of his staff, who vehemently objected to the constant scrutiny and revisions. The producers and writing staff also had a difficult time dealing with Gene's insistence that his attorney, Leonard Maizlish, participate in every production meeting. They felt even more resentful when it became clear that Maizlish was aiding Gene with a good deal of rewrites. He would sit on the sofa in Gene's office, mark up pages and hand them to Gene, who would then look them over and hand them to me to type up and give to the writers.

Members of the *TNG* writing staff notified the Writers Guild that a non-member was working on scripts, a big no-no. Maizlish was asked to leave the Paramount lot, and for a while he laid low, although by the next season he had eased his way back onto the lot.

Gene refused to cut Maizlish loose. In his determination not to have this new series fail, he relied on whatever advice his old attorney gave him, and confrontations by the writers on staff did no good. Eventually, frustrated writers and producers chose the only course left to them: they walked. By the end of the season, there had been a mass exodus

One of our many memorable evenings "out on the town."

of creative staff. Still others were fired when they failed to measure up to the standards Gene (and Maizlish) had set. By the end of the season, our revolving doors had seen the comings and goings of a large percentage of the WGA membership. The disenfranchised writers included David Gerrold, Dorothy Fontana, Bob Lewin, Johnny Dawkins, Herb Wright, Sandy Fries — a seemingly endless procession of quality talent was chewed up and spit out by the shakedown cruise of *TNG*'s first new season. Saddest of all, perhaps, was the loss not only of the talents of Gerrold and Fontana, but of their friendship with Gene.

It was a rift that would take a long time to heal.

After the departure of Gerrold and Fontana, things never returned to status quo between Gene and them. David even filed grievances with the Writers Guild against Paramount and Gene over a number of claims, including the creation of the show itself. Gene had charged David with the awesome task of finalizing the series' bible, utilizing Gene's notes. To David, this was akin to co-creating the new series itself, and indeed it was a monumental work when completed. To Gene, however, this was nothing short of Lucifer asking God for co-credit in creating the Universe — it just wasn't about to happen, no way. David also had written what he felt was an excellent script, only to have it axed by Gene and the production staff. The studio eventually settled with him, but it would be years before there was renewed civility between the two.

Shortly before Gene's final illness, David sent him a letter asking if they could put their differences behind them. Gene was uncertain of himself by that time and asked me what he should do. I looked at him, seeing his health slipping away and knowing he couldn't go on forever. "It's always better to have a friend than an enemy," I offered. By this time, I was having to draft nearly all his correspondence, and Gene asked me to compose a letter from him to David, agreeing that it was time to make peace. He would not, however, fulfill one of David's requests: to put in a word with Michael Piller (the head writer/producer) about his script. Gene said, "I'll be happy to be your friend, but I've put my trust in Rick Berman and Michael Piller, and I don't tell them how to run the show." David's story was not produced, but at least Gene and he mended their fences. I was delighted by this, as I've always thought David was a terrific guy, full of humor, and a very gifted writer. (And I'm good friends with his sister, Alice, who was my realtor on a couple of homes I bought and sold.)

If the series was difficult from an emotional point of view, financially Gene was able to relax for perhaps the first time in his life. With the advent of the first season of *TNG*, he had purchased a bigger, newer house in La Costa. Only the year before, he had been told by his accountants that he probably ought to sell the $400,000 one he already owned there, as it was economically unwise for him to continue to pay for this without a larger income. But he loved his La Costa hideaway on Almaden Road. Indeed, it was lovely, with a cozy den, bright kitchen that faced out to the pool, and large bedroom with radiant ceiling heat that never really warmed the room. I spent many happy overnights there curled up in his arms as we warmed each other. I much preferred our combined body heat to the kerosene space heater he frequently refueled in the bedroom. It gave me the jitters every time I read about another Californian dying from fire or fumes caused by such devices, but with the radiant ceiling such a dud, there was little choice.

What I enjoyed most in those days was the opportunity for us to be alone together, sharing quiet times around this tranquil pool. I'd sit with a book of philosophy, quoting aloud from time to time while Gene busied himself watering the hanging plants and flowers. Some months later, he installed an automatic irrigation system with little plastic tubes connected to each plant, so they all were watered simultaneously. I missed seeing the domestic, nurturing side of him. I still get a warm feeling when I picture him shirtless, in shorts, dashing from plant to plant, seeing that each had just the right amount of water. These were idyllic times, those long lazy summer afternoons at La Costa.

Most of this abruptly ended with the beginning of the new show. He had only an occasional day or two to dash down to La Costa once the series was in full swing. When he told me he'd bought a new, larger house there and had put the Almaden place on the market, I felt a real twinge of loss.

His new house became a pet project. He hired a decorator from a prestigious firm and began working with her with almost the same fervor he had on the new TV series. Nearly all the planning was done by Gene and the decorator, everything from furniture to floor coverings and wall decorations. Later in the year, Gene finally found time to get away for a few days. He invited me down, and I got my first look at the new La Costa digs. I could never tell him this, but I honestly disliked that house. It was built in the shape of a U, with the entrance at the open space. The house surrounded a Romanesque swimming pool, which could be accessed from any of the rooms. At the back right side of the U was the master bedroom — large, but not overwhelming. The best part was the bath area, which had separate tub, shower, closet, dressing room and toilet. The shower was large enough for several bathers if necessary, although I didn't ask about this. Gene showed me how to work the steam vents, and I especially liked the sitting bench in the shower.

Staying at La Costa always made me nervous, whether it was at the little condo in the early years, or either of the houses. I usually slept fitfully, fearful that Majel might burst in and find us there. I couldn't understand how Gene could be so relaxed. He'd snore away blissfully, while I'd have nightmares that she was standing in the room. It was a perfectly plausible scenario, and I rehearsed many a getaway in my mind over the years. The next day, before departing, Gene would always ask me to be sure I didn't leave anything behind, like bobby pins that might have fallen out in the bed. Bobby pins? I never used them! Had this been a problem in some previous relationship? I didn't want to know.

LOG ENTRY 39 :
August 19 was Gene's sixty-six birthday, and I planned a small party for him on stage, where we were filming the second season of *ST: TNG*. When I ordered the cake, someone reminded me that it was Jonathan Frakes' birthday, too, so we had dual cakes and a surprise party for both. One problem — Gene almost didn't show up. He was dining with then-Paramount Domestic Television President Mel Harris in the commissary, and was having such an enjoyable lunch that the two of them got completely carried away. Mel lost track of the time and forgot that at 1:30, he was supposed to suggest to Gene that they segue to the stage and watch some afternoon filming. As the clock ticked away without Gene's appearance, producer Bob Justman began pacing the stage frantically, staring at his watch and noting that the crew were all being paid to stand around and do nothing. Since production costs were approximately nineteen thousand dollars per hour, this was probably the most expensive birthday party in *Star Trek* history! Eventually Mel steered Gene to the stage, where the relieved cast and crew sang the appropriate tune, Gene and Jonathan sliced their respective cakes, and Bob Justman's nerves returned to normal.

< < < > > >

Early in December, I spent a couple of nights with Gene down in La Costa. When I returned to town, I discovered that despite having two large dogs, plenty of fences, and

Jonathan Frakes takes time out from playing Commander Riker to chat with Gene. Ironically, the two men shared a birthday – August 19th.

locks on my doors, my house had been burglarized. It was clearly an inside job, perhaps a disgruntled gardener I had recently let go, one who knew my dogs would greet him as a friend. I was minus a couple of portable TVs and a stereo, but I was thankful that my dogs were safe. Gene was greatly alarmed at this home invasion. "Get yourself a good security system and I'll pay for it," he insisted. By Christmas, I had new burglar alarms in place plus a private rent-a-cop surveillance company. Ever since I'd known him, Gene had lived in his own fortress, protected by the Bel-Air Patrol, a similar company and system, but I was new to the world of homeowner paranoia. Still, I did feel violated, and I was grateful that he felt this protective toward me.

That year, Gene decided to revive the time-honored Hollywood Christmas tradition of giving gifts to each person in the cast and crew. The show was providing special crew jackets for everyone, and although Gene and I designed these together (and I assumed the horrendous job of trying to coordinate one hundred and seventy-five jackets to fit everyone), he also wanted to give each crew member something he'd personally purchased for them. It became a challenge to think of something memorable and unique each year. The first year, Christmas 1987, the gift was a hastily planned afterthought; Gene had far more pressing problems. But even with only a month's lead time, we came up with popcorn canisters with three flavors and a "Gene Roddenberry" signature and ST:TNG logo on the can. Subsequent years saw these crew gifts becoming more and more elaborate: logo-emblazoned beach towels and tote bags, leather embroidered fanny packs, and leather-like duffel bags, all paid for personally by Gene. Christmas was everyone's favorite time of year, when Gene once again could play Santa. We always looked forward to the gifts from the show, too. Besides the jackets, the production paid for gorgeous deep blue terry bathrobes with a pocket logo (I still use mine every day to towel off after my shower), and a second season edition of jackets. Some years later, as money got tighter, the show gift dwindled to a baseball cap.

We also had elaborate Christmas parties (the first few years, at least), a chance for the cast and crew to kick back and mingle — producers with grips, executives with gaffers, actors with office staff. Egos were checked at the door and disputes over stories and scripts were forgotten. At the first two parties, there was a blooper reel, in the tradition of the original series. Bob Justman prepared the first one, and it was a classic in the making. But somehow, it had gotten outside the audience for which it had been intended. Tapes began appearing in dealers' rooms at conventions, and the actors were dismayed to have their outtakes gawked at by total strangers. The following year there was again a blooper reel, but it was tightly guarded, with only the executive producers allowed anywhere near the existing copies. After that, no one seemed to take the time to produce bloopers, which is a shame because there were so many funny moments in dailies, especially once Whoopi, an outrageously talented cut-up, was aboard.

Brent Spiner was also a clown, often doing Jimmy Stewart and other impressions to amuse the crew. But Brent could be temperamental as well. He especially disliked having unannounced visitors on the set; it broke his concentration to look up while delivering his lines and see a number of strangers gawking at him. He compared it to having office workers surrounded by people staring over their shoulders as they did their desk jobs. This was his job; he was at work, and visitors were not particularly welcome. According to set protocol, all guests had to be cleared and approved in advance by the production office. The guest list was sent to the set each day and the guards only allowed those visitors whose names were on the printed list. If Brent was working, guests were rare. Temperamental actors were nothing new in Hollywood; we were just fortunate that the majority of our cast members didn't have these hang-ups.

LOG ENTRY 40 :

After Christmas, Gene seemed a bit edgy, which I attributed to the stress of having to live like a gypsy in his home. Earlier that winter, Majel began a redecoration project on the Leander house, where I had first worked for him back in 1974. They had lived there since the early '70s, and it was sorely in need of redoing. But there was more to this than met the eye. At first, Gene told me they were looking for a place to rent while the Leander home underwent renovations. By February, there were workmen swarming all over, and Gene was becoming desperate. He did not look forward to going home in the evening to the mess that had once been his home. No matter — soon the plans were changed. They would purchase another house, and the newly redecorated Leander Place home was put on the market.

Gene confided in me that he was perfectly content living on Leander Place in Beverly Hills, but he graciously agreed to move. All their spare moments were spent in checking out the wealthier sections of Los Angeles County — Beverly Hills, Bel-Air, Brentwood, Westwood, Highland Park, and even Encino in the San Fernando Valley. And as they looked, their budget soared like the national debt. They finally settled on an English Tudor home in Bel-Air that had once belonged to Cary Grant. The Roddenberrys bought this property from Marty Pasetta, the producer of several Oscar® award presentation shows. Just a golf club's swing from the Bel-Air Country Club, but unfortunately, Gene no longer had time to play golf.

From the moment they moved in, the renovations began. Gene's attorney, Leonard Maizlish, jokingly referred to this house as "a four-million-dollar fixer-upper." He told me that at least another two million dollars were poured into the renovations — a downstairs master bedroom with separate his-and-hers bathrooms and room-sized walk-in closets (the upstairs master bedroom was turned into a guest room), and a new office for Gene, also downstairs. These two groundfloor additions were a good idea, since Gene admitted he was starting to have difficulty using the stairs. And he needed a real office, rather than the makeshift one he had improvised on the upstairs landing.

Rod's upstairs bedroom was the next thing to be upgraded. But instead of a makeover, it, too, became a guest room while a whole new suite for him was added over the garage. His virtually separate apartment was composed of a bunkroom for eight of his friends, with an adjoining sitting room complete with pool table and fireplace of its own. It was done mostly in black — Rod's color of choice (he was going through a kind of Steven Seagal/Goth phase, with his naturally blond hair dyed black and worn in a ponytail and his wardrobe of all-black clothing).

Even the downstairs guest bathrooms (again his and hers) got a facelift. During one rare trip to the house to interview Gene when we were working on our jointly-written twenty-fifth anniversary book, he told me that the "Hers" guest toilet had cost fifteen thousand dollars, whereupon I got an overwhelming urge to pee. The basement was converted into Majel's office (not Gene's; his was upstairs), with a jungle motif. The walls were covered with paintings of tropical foliage, the furnishings had leopard prints, and I believe there was a black-light effect. I think sound effects could also be summoned at the touch of a button. One of the housekeepers told me they actually called it "The Jungle." In the backyard, there was a spa with a natural rock waterfall; a greenhouse, landscaping

— the renovations were still going on at the time of Gene's final illness.

Gene was beginning to live a lifestyle that was completely alien to me, one which I had always thought would be alien to him, too. He had never cared much for the trappings of a successful Hollywood producer, but now it seemed he was being swept along in some current of lavish living. I told him I thought this wasn't the real Gene Roddenberry. He assured me he hadn't changed at all, that he was still the same old Gene, but I wasn't so sure. About a year before the move, he had purchased a previously owned Rolls Royce for twenty-five thousand dollars. It was a late '70s model, with richly polished wood interior paneling and leather seats that were beginning to show a bit of their age. Gene enjoyed this car immensely, and I was sad to see him sell this Rolls in early 1988, when he traded up to a brand new cream and tan Silver Spur. It was beautiful, of course, but to me no car is worth in excess of a hundred thousand dollars when there are people living on the streets and children starving. On the other hand, he had earned it, and I was pleased that he could relax in such comfort.

And he needed to relax. He seemed to be spreading himself much too thin. He was on the board of a number of organizations, generally in an honorary position, but not always. For instance, he was a member of the board of directors of the Police Band Associates, a group of prominent and socially responsible citizens — a bank president, a college professor, a surgical nurse, a high school principal and others — who planned charitable events featuring the Los Angeles Police Department's different bands. The pipe band had played at Gene's star ceremony in 1985, and the organization also boasted mariachis and a con-

On special evenings when Gene got together for formal dinners with his Police Band buddies, they would dress in full Scottish regalia (in honor of the Police Pipe Band). Gene stopped by my house after one such occasion, dressed to the hilt – in a kilt!

cert band. Each year they held an annual concert, usually at the Police Academy, and not only was Gene expected to purchase a table for ten, but he was invariably called upon to supply the master of ceremonies. One year it was Jimmy Doohan; another it was Charlton Heston. This took up a great deal of his time, but he thoroughly enjoyed the company of these people, some of whom became his close friends.

He was also on the board of governors of the newly formed Sci-Fi Channel on cable TV, which was just beginning to draft plans for its operation. This was an honorary position, with his name adding credence to their letterhead. Gene never actually attended any board meetings, nor was he part of the decision-making.

All this would have given any producer more than enough to fill what spare moments of time he might find on his hands. But there was more. The second season of *Star Trek: The Next Generation* was plagued by a writers' strike, which began in March of 1988. Under the strike regulations set forth by the Writers Guild (to which *Star Trek* and all major television shows were signatory), no members were allowed to write during the strike, and no producers could accept new scripts. It was frustrating for Gene and co-executive producer Maurice Hurley, who were both producers *and* writers. Presumably hyphenates (i.e., talent with hyphens between their job descriptions — writer-producers, producer-directors, writer-directors, etc.) were supposed to picket themselves!

With production at a standstill, I suggested to Gene and Maury that they consider some of the old scripts on file since 1977, back when we were stockpiling for the proposed new *Star Trek II* series. I went to Paramount's basement storage, where the boxes containing several scripts were kept with our other stored things, and dragged these up to the office. I spent several weeks reading and evaluating these old scripts for possible use as episodes. I then sent my recommendations in writing to Maurice Hurley:

> TO: MAURICE HURLEY
>
> FROM: SUSAN SACKETT
>
> DATE: MARCH 16, 1988
>
> SUBJECT: SCRIPTS ON FILE FROM 1977

Here is my report on the scripts which Paramount bought back in 1977 for a then-proposed *Star Trek II* television series. You will note that there are some characters which can easily be adapted to our new crew.

THE DEVIL'S DUE, by William Douglas Lansford. In my opinion, this would make an excellent episode, very visual, good characterizations, not very expensive. It is long (70 pages) but could easily be trimmed and adapted to our Teaser and Five Acts format. It's good science fiction in the tradition of many of the original *Star Trek* episodes.

THE CHILD, by Jaron Summers and Jon Povill. Another excellent story, probably the most easily adapted. Very science-fictiony, good emotional use of characters. Highly recommended.

Unfortunately, I cannot find much to recommend in the remaining four scripts . . .

With their hands tied, the writers could do little but long for an early settlement to the strike. It didn't come until August 7, twenty-two weeks after it had begun, which caused the start of production on the second season to be delayed several weeks and resulted in a twenty-two episode season rather than twenty-six. Hurley (who preferred being called by his surname only) quickly reworked "The Child" as soon as it was legal, and it was rushed into production as the first episode of the second season. "Devil's Due" got its due years later; it wasn't used until sometime in the fourth season, when Michael Piller found a way to rework it with our *TNG* characters. Even so, the cast was puzzled by the timbre of this show, sensing that this was somehow different. Several of them expressed their confusion over the characterizations in the episode. When I ran into some of the cast members on the set and told them its history — that it had been written as a "Captain Kirk saves civilization as we know it by outwitting the godlike alien" story — they understood why it seemed so strange. Kirkian though it may have been, it was one of the highest-rated episodes of the fourth season, perhaps proving there was nothing wrong with an occasional "Picard goes mano-a-mano with the creature of the week and outwits it" premise.

LOG ENTRY 41 :

Gene never let his success go to his head, and he always found numerous ways in which to express his generosity. He often donated to the homeless of Los Angeles during holiday appeals, the ones with ads in the newspapers showing a starving, unkempt person being served a turkey dinner with all the trimmings. This never failed to get to him, and he always pulled out his checkbook and sent them a large donation.

His other pet charity involved the organization called Save the Children. I was the first to succumb to their ads showing sad-faced kids suffering from neglect or starvation, and had requested that my contributions be used to help a needy Native American family. I figured that charity begins at home, and if I could only afford to sponsor one child, it should be from my own country first. I received information about Nellie, the little girl I was to help, along with a picture and note from her mother. I was so excited that I shared this with Gene, who immediately decided he would do the same. He requested a little American Indian boy, also from the Pueblos of New Mexico. I corresponded with Nellie, and Gene did likewise with his boy, Loren. Our friend, writer Sonni Cooper, who had a lifelong interest in the Pueblo Indians, made annual treks to New Mexico and frequently reported firsthand on "our" kids. Gene also sent checks at holiday time, and later, when the boy was old enough, he invited him to L.A. to visit with his family and meet Rod, who was about the same age. Just a few years ago, while visiting Sonni (who, with her husband, Ralph, had retired to New Mexico), I finally met my "child," Nellie, now a grown woman with kids of her own!

That summer, Gene decided that he wanted to hire a driver, as he was beginning to tire of having to drive himself. I suspected that he wasn't feeling quite up to par, and these concessions to his advancing age and declining health scared me. On the other hand, Gene was not as alert behind the wheel as he had once been. His absent-mindedness seemed to be carrying over into his driving. He would do things like pull up to a red light, stop, then begin to proceed, as if it were a stop sign. His wanting a full-time chauffeur made me relax a lot.

By August, he had narrowed his choice of driver down to two people — a Teamster who had chauffeured famous celebrities and was currently working at Universal Studios, and a man recommended by my friend and writing partner, Fred Bronson. Fred's friend, Ernie Over, had been working for the Super Shuttle, an airport taxi service, so he had the driving experience, but not the requisite Teamster affiliation that would have made it easier to get reimbursement from the studio.

Gene asked me which driver I thought would be best for him. Ernie was fortyish, short, with a Pillsbury Doughboy body and a jovial laugh. Like my friends Fred Bronson and Richard Arnold, he was also openly gay. Ernie had once worked as a radio announcer in his native Wyoming, and I thought his pleasant voice would be a plus. I told Gene that Ernie seemed superior in intelligence to the other fellow. "It would be nice to have someone to talk to," Gene commented, and Ernie was hired.

I remember the first time Gene asked Ernie (which Gene always insisted on spelling "Earnie") to drive him home. I walked them out to the car and was surprised when Gene climbed into the back seat! He was determined to get his full chauffeuring benefit. He settled in and took out a script to read and acted as if it was the most natural thing in the world for him to be driven around in his Rolls. But I knew he was secretly smiling inside at the absurdity of it all. Within a week, he was sitting next to Ernie up front, chatting away, discussing world politics, religion, and all the topics Gene enjoyed most.

He kept that car (to which he affixed his GENE R vanity license plates) until his death, and I enjoyed several memorable rides in the Rolls with Gene, Fred, Ernie and others as we went to lunch (or just with Gene when we would go to dinner). To this day, I can't see a Rolls Royce Silver Spur without thinking of how much pleasure Gene got from his.

December was a busy month for parties. There was the *ST:TNG* cast and crew Christmas party, Gene's and my office Christmas party (which I always took delight in planning), and that year there was a wrap party for the latest movie incarnation, *Star Trek V: The Final Frontier*.

Gene hadn't participated much in the making of this film. More than anything, it was the story that distressed him. His own script, "The God Thing," had been turned down by the studio years before, and he was still smarting from that rejection. He felt that *Trek V* did a much poorer job of portraying an encounter with God than his own story, that it was much less imaginative, limited in scope and depth. He had seen a few of the dailies, then threw in the towel and refused to attend anything further until there was a rough cut. He found the raw footage so depressing that he stopped attending the screenings, pleading "too busy with our TV series." I remember one of the sequences that particularly irritated him — several minutes' worth of shadowy, pounding horses' hoofs. I think, after that, he decided it was Harve Bennett's problem.

December also marked my birthday. Since it is a week before Christmas, I'm used to becoming lost in the shuffle. But the assistants and other workers in the office had an unwritten rule that everyone had to have a surprise birthday party. We prided ourselves on inventing creative ways of distracting the birthday boy or girl while the party was set up. While my surprise party was being deployed this particular year, I was summoned to the production trailer to sort through the Christmas beach bag and towel gifts. I tried to solve the problem quickly so I could get back to work — it didn't dawn on me that this was a diversion. As soon as I'd check over the list, someone would point out yet another name that had been omitted or some other minute problem. Eventually, I tired of this cumbersome nonsense and said I was going back to my office. However, they had kept me occupied just long enough — when I returned to the Hart Building and our office in room 101, I was greeted with a chorus of "Surprise!"

I should have guessed. It was a variation on a scheme I had devised myself. Surprise birthday parties for staff were always held in Gene's office. Everyone knew the routine. After lunch, the birthday person was ordered to an important meeting in Gene's office. "Gene wants to see you" generally meant that a birthday party was imminent, as the victim sheepishly entered the inner sanctum to be "surprised." This time, however, I was totally unsuspecting, hoisted by my own petard.

Gene held off on my Christmas gift until after the New Year, as I was in the process of buying a new 1989 Isuzu Trooper. The day after I got the car, he presented me with my belated Christmas gift — a cellular car telephone. I had always sworn that I'd never get one of those "durn infernal contraptions" — probably the same thing people had said a hundred years ago about having phones put in their homes — but it did seem like a good idea in case of emergency. It turned out to be one of the best gifts he ever gave me. I often used it to call him from the road to remind him of appointments as I headed to the office, or to check with Jana Wallace, our secretary, to see what was going on as I battled the traffic on the Hollywood freeway.

By now, Gene was starting to relax more and more, realizing that the show was on track with the writers' strike settled, and he began to think about enjoying life more. One of the first things he knew he wanted to do was to return to the South Pacific, to Guadalcanal, where he could chase down some old World War II ghosts that were still haunting him. Gene wanted closure.

The trip was planned for May, and his friend and attorney Leonard Maizlish would accompany him. It was fortunate that he made the trip that year, for he would never in his life be able to undertake such a journey again.

LOG ENTRY 42 :
The Solomon Islands are composed mainly of the peaks of old volcanoes and coral atolls. They are not routinely visited by tourists. Journeys there are usually arranged only by experienced travel agents, and even then, there are typically delays with flights, poor accommodations and the possibility of tropical diseases in this remote South Pacific nation with only one telephone for every forty-four people.

Gene, however, was determined to return to Guadalcanal. Fortified with anti-everything inoculations, he and Leonard Maizlish set out to revisit the places of Gene's memories from nearly fifty years earlier. After landing in Honiara, the nation's capital on the island of Guadalcanal, the pair spent two and a half weeks visiting old battle sites, memorials and mosquito-infested lagoons. They even had a special visit with a tribe of islanders credited with being the world's original bungee jumpers. This particular group of natives, in order to prove their prowess, tie ropes made of vines to their ankles and plunge hundreds of feet off a rickety tower. Most of the time the ropes hold. What traditionally was a time-honored test of manhood for the locals has recently become a bizarre and dangerous worldwide craze — an appropriate word, to say the least. Gene and Miazlish didn't take the plunge, but their very presence at this event was unusual, as it is not generally open to tourists.

Gene returned from the adventure contented, his heart's uneasiness about the past at last laid to rest. Miazlish, however, was not well during the trip, and after seeing his doctor, announced that he had suffered a stroke.

At about the same time, Gene was beginning to exhibit signs of decreased vigor. He had been diagnosed with diabetes in 1988, and his health had become a constant source of concern to me. There was nothing dramatic, no sudden changes, but there were subtle differences. He was walking more slowly, and his right arm was stiffly bent at an angle by his side, not swinging as it should in a normal stride. In July, my cousin Lara from Seattle visited me with her new baby and her husband, Joe Pizzorno, a naturopathic doctor (ND) and then-president of Seattle's Bastyr University, a highly respected training center for NDs. They had met Gene many times in the past and had even assisted me at the studio party the day Gene got his Walk of Fame star. So when Joe, a medical professional, said to me, "Gene's not walking right and he doesn't look well," alarm bells began going off. At the same time, I vehemently denied anything was wrong. Gene himself seemed eager to concur. When I asked him about the arm stiffness, he said it was merely an old habit, one acquired in his police days when he kept his arm at the ready to draw his gun.

I was only too happy to buy this, but even as he was insisting that all was well, I noticed he was beginning to have difficulty with his handwriting. The first hint of trouble came when he asked me to order Number One pencils, with broader graphite in them, rather than the finer point Number Twos, which were standard issue. It was not apparent to me at the time, but this was his way of dealing with his lessening ability to control his handwritten notes.

< < <   > > >

Star Trek V: The Final Frontier opened in June, 1989, and Gene was not pleased with this film. His foremost objection was to the premise — Captain Kirk faces off with "God," who — surprise! — turns out *not* to be God after all. Since there were so many similarities to Gene's own storyline in "The God Thing," I worried that Gene was perhaps just being curmudgeonly.

He seemed to be exhibiting this behavior more frequently, and I was worried. He was getting on in years, and there had been definite personality changes. He was less patient than when I had first known him. He seemed more forgetful, too. Until now, I hadn't given Gene's age much thought. For a long time, he had not looked his age. Usually, this is genetic, but Gene also dabbed on a bit of Grecian Formula hair color in the late '70s and early '80s, admitting to me that he was concerned with appearing younger for his son Rod's sake. It must have been difficult for him to be fifty-three years older than his son, and I know he at least wanted to keep up a youthful appearance for the youngster. Gene's daughter Dawn once confided in me something her half-brother had said to her at a Christmas celebration. "Rod told me," she said, "'You're lucky — you had Dad when he was young.'" "You have got a point there," I told her, astounded that Rod had had such insight, since he was less than ten at the time.

Gene's sixty-eighth birthday was approaching, and I wanted it to be special. Something told me there wouldn't be many more. Our birthday playdays had become a thing of the past. He had difficulty getting away for a whole day and quite frankly, he couldn't handle the daylong activities we used to undertake. The previous year, my old friend Fred Bronson had taken Gene and me to a special lunch at the Paramount Commissary. As we sat in the corner of the executive patio, Gene grew curiously sentimental and thanked Fred profusely for having brought me into his life. The next year, Fred asked if he could plan a special day in honor of four converging occasions — Gene's birthday, my employment anniversary, and Gene's driver Ernie's birthday and anniversary.

Fred booked us a private room with a fantastic view from the fiftieth floor of the Bank of America Tower in downtown Los Angeles. Appropriately named Floor Fifty, the restaurant, normally patronized by wealthy bankers, business people and their clientele, was decadent in its elegance. Servers hovered over us as if we were gods, and the food echoed this attitude. The menu printed especially for that day included cream of tomato garlic soup, one of Gene's favorites, along with sautéed Maryland crab cakes, steamed mussels in opal basil sauce or New York strip steak. Since Floor Fifty didn't have a liquor license, we first had to stop at a liquor store to purchase wine to go with lunch. After this repast, we tried to avoid the dessert, as we were all so stuffed, but at our server's insistence, most of us opted for fruit and light sweets. Gene, however, insisted on a rich carrot cake, which we tried to talk him out of, since we had a surprise party with carrot cake waiting back at the office! We returned to the office in time for the staff to surround Gene with birthday wishes and a small party, and while it wasn't quite the same as our celebrations had been in the good old days, he seemed contented, so I was gratified.

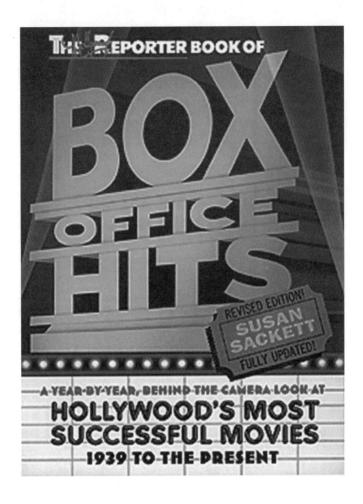

THE REPORTER BOOK OF
BOX
OFFICE
HITS

REVISED EDITION!
SUSAN SACKETT
FULLY UPDATED!

—A·YEAR·BY·YEAR, BEHIND·THE·CAMERA·LOOK·AT—
HOLLYWOOD'S MOST
SUCCESSFUL MOVIES
1939 TO THE PRESENT

LOG ENTRY 43 :

Early in October, I went to France for two weeks with a friend of mine, Marcia Rovins, who had done a smashing job of researching my book, *The Hollywood Reporter Book of Box Office Hits*. Before I left, Gene hadn't been feeling well. Several times when we were at lunch, he had complained that he "had a bubble" in his throat and couldn't swallow properly. He'd excuse himself from the table and head for the men's room. After a while he'd return to the table and say everything was all right, but I was certain something was wrong. While I was in France, I phoned Jana, our secretary, and learned that he had had a doctor's office procedure to open up his esophagus. I was much relieved to learn about this and relaxed a bit, knowing that he did not have some dread disease, like throat cancer.

A few days later, I again phoned from France and was told that over the past weekend, Gene had attended a Roddenberry family reunion in Tallahassee, Florida. Dozens of Roddenberry kinfolk from Cairo, Georgia and the northern Florida area attended a weekend of football games and picnics. Gene's Roddenbery cousins, the one-"r" branch of the family, were well known throughout the South. Their name can still be found on Rodden-

One of my books about show business: **The Hollywood Reporter Book of Box Office Hits.**

bery pickle relish, boiled peanuts and other regionally popular products. The patriarch of the clan had been Julien Roddenbery, who was nearly one hundred when he had died a few years before. Gene himself was a hero to the family and was well acquainted with many of Julien's grandchildren and great-grandchildren, especially Lucretia Roddenbery (what a great name!) and Mardi Roddenbery. These were colorful folk, to say the least, so Gene was very gung-ho about the giant clan gathering in Tallahassee.

When I phoned the office from France this second time, I expected to hear all about the antics of his favorite cousins. Instead, Gene admitted that things had not gone well, and that he had become quite ill during the trip. He couldn't put his finger on it, but he told me he knew something was not right. Gene seldom complained about health, so there I was in France, ready to get on the next plane. He assured me he was fine, but when I returned a week later, I learned that he was in the midst of a series of medical tests, including MRIs. The doctors discovered several areas of Gene's brain that appeared to have been sites of minor strokes. He downplayed this, insisting he was fine. But it was becoming apparent that he was bluffing.

His limping became more pronounced. He was having difficulty with his handwriting. He could no longer sign his name legibly without considerable concentration and strain and asked me to sign his mail. And he began seeing a barrage of doctors in an attempt to find relief.

Although Gene's most obvious trouble started after his October trip, the following year Leonard Maizlish began to speculate that he and Gene had both suffered their strokes at the same time, while they were on the trip to the South Pacific. Leonard seemed almost pleased with this idea, as if this were some sort of male bonding adventure. I tried to tell him of Gene's insistence that his problems had become pronounced during the weekend in Tallahassee, but Maizlish appeared to derive a weird pleasure out of this perceived shared problem and kept insisting they both had had their strokes during their vacation together.

Gene had been using uppers for years, with a prescription when he could get it, without a doctor's prescription when he couldn't obtain what he wanted through proper medical channels. Since the '70s, I had observed him taking various drugs, including Ritalin, Tenuate Dospan, Valium and Dalmane. He told me that many of these were readily available in Mexico without a prescription, and that a friend had been able to procure them for him. He also claimed that he could not write without chemical help, and that this had been the only way he had been able to get through the first *Star Trek* series. Then, late in 1989, after he'd suffered this apparent series of strokes, he began seeing a neurologist/psychiatrist who gave him the prescriptions he wanted, including amphetamines. Gene said the doctor "understood." This physician had told him, Gene claimed, that perhaps he had been born lacking something that other people have naturally in their brain chemistry, and it might be perfectly all right for Gene to need these uppers simply to put him on a par with the average person. I was shocked to learn that this doctor, agreeing with Gene that it might be something he needed, actually prescribed the amphetamine Tenuate. How had Gene managed to convince this member of the medical profession of such a thing? Gene suffered from hypertension — high blood pressure — and from everything I had read (and by this time I had begun to read plenty), Tenuate was certainly counter-indicated. You don't give such a serious amphetamine to a high blood pressure sufferer, especially one with the history of drug abuse that Gene had.

Gene seemed to have become a walking pharmacy, which was bad enough. I feared that all this coupled with his increasing alcohol use had turned him into a human time bomb. Frantically, I tried bringing this to his attention. I left magazine articles on his desk pointing out the dangers of cocaine. I confronted him with the evidence of his usage that he thought he was hiding from me so well. He became annoyed and angrily dismissed me. He was by now having terrible mood swings and uncharacteristic outbursts of violent temper, which baffled me. He had never been verbally abusive to me before. I felt helpless in my efforts to get him to see what he was doing to himself. I didn't realize that I was powerless to help him; in fact, I could have been the poster child for Co-Dependents Anonymous. I realize now that all those years of trying to get him to drink iced tea, to give up drugs, to not use salt (bad for his hypertension; I'd grab the salt shaker out of his hand and scold him like a child), were expressions of my co-dependency, of which I was totally unaware.

Gene appeared to be chemically imbalanced, and was constantly attempting to find solace in pills or booze. It is possible that addictive disease ran in his family. He told me his sister and father had been heavy drinkers. Or maybe it was a classic case of the depressed literary genius. Writers and artists have been suffering for their art for centuries.

The debate still rages in the medical world over whether depression leads to drinking, or drinking causes the depression. Gene knew he suffered from both problems and had sought help from his doctor, who prescribed various drugs, including Prozac. But Gene never truly addressed his alcoholism, which continued to manifest itself with the number one symptom of this disease — the alcoholic's denial of the problem. According to the Feb. 3, 1993 *Journal of American Medical Association*:

> Alcoholism is described as a primary, chronic disease with genetic, psychoso-cial, and environmental factors influencing its development and manifestations. The disease is often progressive and fatal. It is characterized by . . . distortions in thinking, most notably denial . . . the alcoholic's denial is essentially the inability to accept the loss of control over drinking, the psychological dependence on the drug, and the eventual need to abstain.

The article seemed to hit the nail on the head when it went on to quote E. P. Nace, who had authored a book on the subject (*The Treatment of Alcoholism*): "Denial is a process that protects the option to continue to drink, which is for the alcohol-dependent individual, the sustenance of life itself." No wonder strong drink is sometimes called "aqua vitae" — the water of life.

I struggled to understand Gene better, to realize that creative people have flaws just like anyone else. I recalled that Gene had advocated more lenient treatment for drug offenders. He railed against what he called the "throw them in jail and throw away the key" mentality of the government; declaring a "war on drugs" was in his opinion declaring a campaign against people in emotional distress. He argued that there is a reason why people do these things, and you've got to get to the heart of that reason to understand why they find drugs so necessary to overcome the unhappy circumstances of their lives. Sadly, no one realized that he was speaking autobiographically.

LOG ENTRY 44 :

I was elated when one suggestion I gave Gene did spark some interest. I recommended he try Pritikin once again, and he seemed to look forward to returning there. Late in November, 1989, he checked in for a two-week stay. But he was having great difficulty walking, and the treadmill workouts didn't help much, since he had to be careful not to go very fast. He ate the healthful food served there, but his spirit wasn't into it.

His increasingly poor health was taking its toll on our sex life. I knew that his chronic impotence was mainly caused by his alcohol and drug usage, and he admitted as much to me. I mentioned this to my gynecologist when she asked me what I was doing for birth control, a routine question. I told her "abstaining," and explained it was not my choice. She suggested several sex therapists, but when I mentioned this to Gene, he said only that he'd think about it. I never mentioned it again. But I could tell he wasn't happy about his decreased libido. Early in 1989, he had begun receiving weekly injections of testosterone from his regular physician. Gene hoped the shots would improve his libido; he really meant he hoped it would cure his impotence. It didn't, of course; between his diabetes and alcohol and drug use, there was little that could be done. I was disappointed, but after so many years, I had very few expectations. I think I was always pretty good in covering any disappointment, and I tried to let Gene know that it really didn't matter. I honestly enjoyed being with him, cuddling, hugging. We were occasionally having oral sex, but he was no longer responsive in this area that for years had been his only source of true sexual pleasure.

About this time, Gene had started meeting with a computer programmer and writer from Santa Monica who was an extremely intelligent woman, something Gene highly admired in his select circle of friends. Gene found her childlike stature (she was barely five feet tall) coupled with her intelligence very attractive. I assume she was likewise attracted to Gene for all the reasons I was — his intelligence, his warmth and his humor. I'm also sure she was flattered to find this famous man expressing an interest in her. The two had what he thought was a clandestine rendezvous at the Beverly Hills Four Seasons Hotel. Gene loved the hotel, with its gorgeous furnishings and lavish minibars, and one afternoon when we hadn't had much time together lately, he booked us a room. I drove there with him in his Rolls, and the staff acted pleased to see him. I was puzzled when he seemed to know all about the place, the in-room honor bar, the location of the phones in the bathroom and so on. When a bill arrived at the office a few weeks later with *two* dates on it, I knew something was up.

I confronted Gene with this and he admitted his tryst with this other lady. His one or two past indiscretions that I knew of had been fleeting. I reminded him of our long-standing friendship and relationship, that I never expected him to leave his wife for me, but that I did demand loyalty. I had sacrificed much for our relationship, including the possibility of a husband and children, and I felt that we had a commitment to each other. If he felt differently, that was fine. We could end our friendship then and there. It was the only serious fight I'd had with him in all our years together. I was angry and terribly, terribly hurt.

I confided my distress to Leonard Maizlish. He knew my feelings toward Gene, although I'd never expressed them openly to him before. I hoped he would give me some advice, but all he said was that Gene was having a delayed mid-life crisis and one last fling as old age set in, and that if I were tolerant, it would quickly pass. It did indeed pass, although not quite that quickly. They had two more meetings, which Gene tried to cover with a faked get-together with his Police Band buddies. He forgot I was the one who made and confirmed all his appointments.

But I bided my time. I began to feel less threatened. After all, what was I fighting for? I knew in my heart that Gene loved me unflinchingly. I also knew that he was old and impotent. I say this not to be cruel; these were the facts. His latest fling would realize this, too. And since his life had been so unhappy and his health was so precarious, I soon began to feel pleased for him. I knew that I didn't own him. No one can own someone else. I would not fall into the possessiveness trap.

On my birthday that December, we had lunch in Santa Monica. Ernie drove us and ate with us at a small but elaborately decorated Mexican restaurant. The purpose for the drive to Santa Monica was an appointment Gene had with a dermatologist who was treating him for large acne-like pimples and boils on his scalp and the back of his neck. The doctor prescribed something topical and mentioned that it might be an allergy. My own suspicions were that it was a side effect of the Tenuate Dospan he'd been taking. I had seen these symptoms in him before, and the two always coincided. This possibility was confirmed when I checked my copy of the Physician's Desk Reference. I kept my mouth shut, but I was nonetheless uneasy at the prospect of his continued drug usage.

Later in the week, when Gene was able to get away for our annual birthday dinner, we had a true celebration at Camille's on Ventura Blvd., one of our special places. We had been going there for many years and the maître d' always greeted us like long-lost friends. The food was elegant and beautifully prepared; the settings and ambiance were unsurpassed. A guitarist softly strummed the theme from M*A*S*H and other requests while we dined by candlelight in our favorite booth. We went there as often as Gene could get away. Once, we ran into TNG actor Wil Wheaton's parents, an odd chance encounter, since they lived about twenty miles from there. Wil was not with them, and Gene politely introduced me. I wondered what they thought we were doing out having such a fine dinner together in the evening, but if they suspected something clandestine, they never indicated it.

This birthday celebration was to be our last. The next year, in 1990, Gene was just not feeling well enough, and by then I didn't relish the idea of his driving. About a year after Gene died, I was passing by Camille's, dreaming nostalgically about the good times we'd had there, when I noticed that it wasn't there. I stared at the writing on the exterior — "Japanese cuisine" and "Karaoke" were loudly proclaimed by the signs and little musical notes painted on what had once been a classy exterior. It nearly broke my heart. I was glad Gene never saw the sad fate that had befallen our favorite little rendezvous.

LOG ENTRY 45 :

When I worked at NBC, a friend there once told me, "You can have anything you want, once you set your mind to it." I suppose that's true. I had wanted to live in Los Angeles since I was eight years old, and here I was. I wanted to work in television, and I had done that, too. Even more, I had wanted for many years to write for television. And now, after continually pitching ideas to Gene and to the writing staff, with and without Fred Bronson as my writing partner, that goal was finally to be realized.

Early in 1989, Fred and I sold our first story to *Star Trek: The Next Generation*. Gene loved our premise about a female Starfleet historian from far in the future who *returns* to the 24th century in pursuit of a time-traveling renegade. This story of intrigue, romance, mystery and time travel was my first sale, and I was thrilled. Since it was purchased at the end of the second season, Fred and I expected to be given a go-ahead to write the script before the kick-off of season three. But over the summer, Maurice Hurley departed the show and a new head writer/producer, Michael Piller, was brought on board. Michael had his own ideas about what he wanted in the way of stories, and ours was not on his priority list. Even though Gene loved our story, he was cautious about making demands on the new producer. And so I learned that sometimes being on the inside could be a curse instead of a benefit. Later, we attempted to resurrect our tale by offering it to Pocket Books as a potential novel. The editors liked it immensely, but by the time we began talking about deals, several episodes with similar storylines had been produced, and our book never got off the ground.

Undaunted, Fred and I enrolled that fall in Truby's Writing Workshop, a class in basics for screen and television writers and writer-wannabes like us. Actually, Fred was already a credited writer, having written for the animated version of *Star Trek* ("The Counter-Clock Incident," under the pseudonym John Culver) and for some of Dick Clark's television specials. I, of course, had the inside track to Gene Roddenberry and the *Star Trek* staff — a circular track, since it seemed to take me on a journey to nowhere every time I drove on it. But, armed with Truby's tips and with what we thought a natural idea, Fred and I approached Gene one more time.

It was understood that each year there had to be a script starring Gene's wife. That was a given. One evening during our writing class break, Fred turned to me and said simply, *Ransom of Red Chief.* An image formed in my mind, like in a cartoon strip where a light bulb clicks on over a person's head. As Lwaxana Troi existed at that time, she was an over-the-top, caution-to-the-wind loose cannon. Anyone foolish enough to kidnap her would find himself wanting out, as in the O. Henry "Red Chief" story of the little boy whose kidnappers must pay a ransom to get rid of him. The story was perfect for Majel's character. We refined the concept and pitched it to Gene, who liked the idea immediately. He encouraged and guided us along the way as we drafted our story, although he still couldn't guarantee its purchase by Michael Piller, who was certainly under no obligation to buy it. If it were to sell, it would have to do so on its own merits. Fred and I poured ourselves into the story, and by the time we presented it to Michael, it was so tightly written that he actually admitted to liking it.

During the Christmas season, Fred and I put the finishing touches on our story outline,

now titled "Ménage à Troi," and by February, we had completed the first draft of the script. We were delighted to learn that Rick Berman raved about our first draft script; Gene told me Berman called it "one of the cleanest I've seen this year." Still, the writing staff felt the need to polish it until March 19, when our episode finally went before the cameras. For me, it was the culmination of a lifelong dream. Even though I had written several books, I still had the fantasy of seeing my name in the opening credits as a "legit-imate" television writer. The staff writers told me I was insane. They felt that having your name on a book cover was eminently more prestigious, but I held onto my vision. Like the man at NBC said, I usually got what I wanted.

It was ironic to have written a script for Majel. I had always made it a point to be polite and even chipper on the phone or if our paths crossed, but we had spoken only when necessary, such as to relay a message or phone call to Gene. There was no way of avoiding each other on the set, however. In an awkward moment for us all, Majel approached Fred and me to offer her gratitude. "Thank you for writing such a good script for me," she said, her eyes focused on Fred. It was our only conversation during the eight-day shoot.

Fred Bronson, my lifelong friend and writing partner.

That winter, Gene was the recipient of the Jack Benny Memorial Award at the annual fund-raiser dinner given by the March of Dimes on Feb. 24. The event was held in the Grand Ballroom of the Sheraton Grande Hotel (now owned by Marriott) in downtown LA. Ray Bradbury was the Master of Ceremonies, and Jane Wyatt introduced the evening's events, which included appearances by all the *Next Generation* cast, plus originals DeForest Kelley, George Takei and Grace Lee Whitney. Prior to the award, a special film recapped highlights of Gene's life. The film was to end with an animated autograph of Gene Roddenberry as it materialized across the screen.

I knew Gene was beginning to have handwriting difficulties, but I hadn't realized how serious it was until the preparation of this film began a few weeks before the event. When he was asked to autograph a blank sheet of paper for the animators to edit into the film, he turned to me in the presence of the promoters and said, "Susan, you do it. You do my signature so much better than I do." So I smiled as if this were the biggest joke in the world and signed his signature for the film.

By now Gene had cut back on his denial, telling everyone that he had suffered a minor stroke. The truth was that he could barely hold a pen and was having me sign all his correspondence. Each week our secretary, Jana, would bring me a pile of letters for "his" signature. I no longer felt guilty signing, since Gene himself had sanctioned my doing this. Indeed, I signed his name almost perfectly by now — the wide stroke on the G followed by quick, short strokes for the e-n-e. The R in Roddenberry gave me some problems. It never seemed quite right, but perhaps that was because Gene himself had varied this from time to time, sometimes looping it, sometimes almost printing it. The rest was a kind of scrawl, ending with a downstroke for the final letter. I had perfected this so that it

Fred Bronson and I on location during the filming of our Next Generation episode, "Ménage à Troi."

became almost automatic, like my own signature. On more than one occasion, Jana would hand me a letter to sign with my name and by mistake I would do Gene's. She'd just sigh, reprint the letter and quip, "It's not easy being Gene!"

I was surprised the doctors were not giving Gene any physical therapy for his lost dexterity. My feeling was that he denied any problems, to himself as well as his doctors. Most likely he had sweet-talked his way out of therapy, convincing them that he was fine. I could see the need for rehabilitation of this lost motor skill, but I had never met his new doctors. To contact them and offer my medical opinion would have annoyed Gene, and I would have been perceived by his physicians as an office assistant overstepping her bounds. Instead, I drew on my experience as a former teacher of young children, and tried to get Gene to take some steps toward recovering his handwriting skills. I prepared sheets of exercises, repetitive blocks of letters for him to practice. At first, he seemed genuinely pleased because I cared enough to make this effort, but after a while he stopped trying. I think it was because of his frustration at not making any serious progress.

Gene asked me to do virtually all of his correspondence, even his personal letters to friends like Rupert. I had no problem getting into his style after working with him for sixteen years. For instance, he had a streak of modesty when writing about himself and seldom used the personal pronoun. He would write sentences like, "Had a nice visit with you last week," or "Hope you are recovered from the flu." This was not an accident; he once told me he thought it was very egotistical to constantly use the pronoun "I." (*I* find this impossible to overcome!)

LOG ENTRY 46 :

Gene was beginning to have more and more trouble with his gait. He had been dragging his right leg slightly since the previous summer. By the spring of 1990, he was moving only with great difficulty. He began getting routine massages at home every morning and hired a personal trainer to lead him through a series of exercises designed to strengthen his muscles. All the while I kept asking him if he shouldn't be getting physical therapy from a professional, medically trained, licensed therapist, since he said the doctors suspected he had suffered a stroke. But he was unwilling to explore any of those avenues. Despite the workouts, which he kept canceling, he continued to drag his right leg. Once, while visiting him in La Costa, I suggested he try to *think* while walking, like a child who might be learning for the first time. "Instead of leading with your left leg and then dragging your right along, try leading with your right." He did, and suddenly months of leg-dragging melted away. He appeared to be walking normally! However, it took a conscious effort to continue doing this. Who thinks "right foot, left foot" when walking? It's as automatic as "breathe in, breathe out." Soon he would slip back into his right leg-dragging motion. "Lead with your right," I'd encourage whenever I'd see him start to walk. Then he would resume a normal pace. This was exactly the kind of therapy he should have been getting professionally, but I wasn't trained in this, nor was I around him as often as necessary for him to derive the best results. Soon he lapsed into what was comfortable for him without his having to concentrate. He never regained a proper gait.

Gene was the recipient of the Jack Benny Memorial Award at the annual fund-raiser dinner given by the March of Dimes on February 24, 1990. Left to right: Me, Gene, Fred Bronson, Richard Arnold. In the background is a framed portrait of Gene they presented to him as part of his award.

It was breaking my heart to see him declining like this. His deteriorating health also meant less time for us, although we still managed to get together once a week or so for a bit of hugging or petting. I knew how important it was for him to feel that he was still loved, that I still cared. And I did. It may not have been the passionate, hearts-on-fire romance we once knew, but we still needed each other's company. It was a comfortable marriage of minds that we both recognized for the special entity it was.

Ironically, this was the most hectic and exciting time in my writing career. I busied myself with as much writing as I could fit into my schedule, and it helped fill the gap while his health continued to spiral downward. I had recently seen the publication of my sixth book, *The Hollywood Reporter Book of Box Office Hits*, and on April 7, ten days after the filming of our episode wrapped, I held a party for my friends and many of the office staff to celebrate the book's publication. In keeping with the theme of the book, everyone dressed as his or her favorite movie character. Scarlett O'Hara mingled with cowboys and Humphrey Bogart lookalikes, while I elected to be a film director, complete with mega-phone, ascot, riding crop, boots and jodhpurs. I gave out "Oscars" — little statuettes I had found in the Universal Studios gift shop. Awards were for best costume, best make-up, and best actor and actress in a scene my guests had to perform. People I hadn't seen

With Gene on the set of Star Trek: The Next Generation.

in years were invited, as well as associates from the *Star Trek* office. It would mark the last time I would get together socially with some of these people from the show. The only one missing was Gene, who was not well enough to attend.

In April, I had decided to spend part of my vacation time attending the annual conference of the American Humanist Association in Orlando. I had belonged to this organization for a couple of years, and I soundly believe in their principles. The four-day weekend would comprise a series of award banquets and seminars, culminating in the Humanist of the Year Award to entrepreneur Ted Turner. I suggested to Gene that he might enjoy attending the convention, and he readily agreed. I knew Gene would appreciate these events since he was also a member of the AHA. Their tenets meshed perfectly with his beliefs — that we as humans must take responsibility for what happens in our lives rather than attributing consequences to an invisible, supernatural being; that the universe and its events evolve in a natural way, without interference by a rule-breaking "celestial butler." Although much of the membership professes atheism, at that time I tended to take a more open-minded approach, that of an agnostic. (Agnostics believe that perhaps there is a god force behind the universe; perhaps there isn't.) I knew Gene felt this way too. One of his pet peeves involved those who, upon receiving an award or winning a sports event would announce, "First, I would like to thank God." He always felt those people sold themselves short. If a prize fighter won a match, did that mean God wanted him to beat the other fellow to a bloody pulp? Gene used to become terribly upset whenever President Jimmy Carter spoke about his born-again religious beliefs. "I worry about a president who claims he has a personal relationship with God," he said.

During our trip, Gene was walking with pronounced difficulty. He insisted on hiring a wheelchair to take him to the airplane, rather than navigating the L.A. and Orlando airports on foot. On the plane to Orlando, he downed the free-flowing drinks in our Delta first class cabin. Yet despite my suggestion that he keep his drinking to a minimum because cabin pressurization doubles the effects of alcohol, he continued sucking up V.O. Manhattans.

We stayed at the Harley Hotel — "a member of the Helmsley Group," as the logo proudly proclaimed on the matchbooks and amenities, and I conjured up images of notorious "Queen of Mean" Leona, who at that time was on trial for income-tax evasion. Our suite had two adjoining rooms, for decorum's sake, but I appreciated having my own bathroom and extra closet space for my clothing.

The oppressive sub-tropical Florida heat and humidity, already beyond belief in late April, were taking a serious toll on Gene. He perspired profusely, and on the first day after our arrival, he complained that he wasn't feeling well. He spent most of the following morning in bed, but by afternoon he had recovered enough to hire a taxi to be at our disposal for the weekend. Our driver, an ardent Trekker, took us to a shopping mall, where Gene immediately purchased some shorts and cooler shirts. I begged him to lay off the booze for the duration of the trip. He must have been feeling really terrible, because he agreed, and indeed it made him feel better. His doctor back in L.A. later diagnosed his problem as hypoglycemia, an adverse reaction to drinking due to his diabetes. Thankfully

Gene was a type II, non-insulin-dependent, diabetic, or he might not have been so fortunate, since a hypoglycemic reaction can be a prelude to a diabetic coma.

The first night, our taxi driver recommended a restaurant called Church Street Station, in a revitalized area of downtown Orlando. After a lovely dinner, throughout which we held hands and slowly sipped the glass of wine Gene insisted on, we rode around town in a horse-drawn carriage. It wasn't exactly Central Park, but it put us in a romantic mood, and both of us always opted for that.

The next evening's main event was the Awards Banquet. Just before Ted Turner was to receive his award, Gene spotted him seated across the room, along with a lady by his side. He excused himself from our table and went over to introduce himself. He also spoke to Ted's date and told her how glad he was to see her again. She was completely baffled. Gene had thought this lady was Jane Fonda. She was not, although there was a slight resemblance. Ted wasn't married to Jane at the time, which may explain why he was decidedly cool towards Gene. When he returned to our table, Gene told me of this debacle. I felt embarrassment for him, but especially because of Ted's attitude. Who was he to not worship at the feet of this American icon, the creator of *Star Trek*? I could see the hurt in Gene's eyes and was almost sorry we had made the trip. Even Ted's humorous acceptance speech didn't change my feelings.

At one of the awards dinners that weekend, Gene met a man named David Alexander. He had just been appointed editor of *The Humanist* magazine and asked Gene if he could interview him for an article. I thought he came on strong but was most cordial. After that, he insisted we join him and his wife Penny at their table, which was much better positioned than our own. If Ted Turner was aloof, David more than made up for his lack of enthusiasm. By the end of the conference, it became clear that David was fascinated by the Gene Roddenberry mystique. He arranged to meet with Gene back in Los

Gene gets direction before filming his introduction to the Universal Studios tour Star Trek promotion.

Angeles and told Gene that he wanted to propose his name for the next year's Humanist Arts Award. Naturally, Gene was flattered.

Following the convention, our taxi took us to the Orlando airport, where I continued on to Palm Beach for a week while Gene, again in a wheelchair, headed to his gate for the return to Los Angeles. I was terribly concerned about his condition but grateful for the time we had spent together.

It was to be our last trip alone.

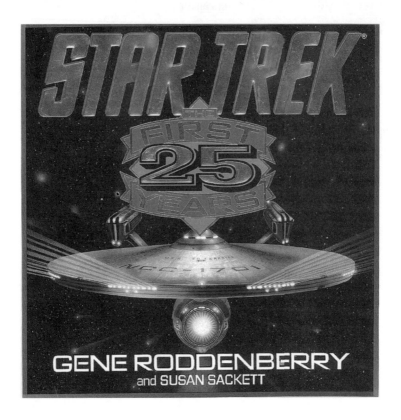

LOG ENTRY 47 :

In 1984, two years prior to *Star Trek*'s twentieth anniversary, I had proposed a commemorative book honoring the upcoming occasion, but for some reason, the licensee, Simon & Schuster/Pocket Books, never reached an agreement with Paramount, Gene and myself. Disappointed but undaunted, I immediately proposed a book for the series' twenty-fifth anniversary in 1991. Towards the end of 1989, my contract for *Star Trek: The First 25 Years* was still being hammered out, but it seemed a certainty, and with Gene's blessing I began to work on what would be my magnum opus to date. In February 1990, I had signed a contract for the book to be delivered at the end of the year. I immediately scheduled interviews with everyone connected with the original series, which would be the main focus of the book. It was ostensibly co-authored by Gene and myself, but it was understood that I was the sole writer. Gene's name, plus first person quotes from my interviews with him would lend credibility as well as sales clout. It would be our second book together (*The Making of Star Trek: The Motion Picture* had been our first), and once again, my name on the cover — although only one half the size of his — would be linked to his by the word "and," rather than the typical ghost-written "with." I was especially pleased with this, as well as gratified by this new opportunity in my writing career.

I began interviews with Gene in May. Over the course of several months, we discussed the history of the series, along with his philosophy and beliefs, but it progressed

The cover of my book, **Star Trek: The First 25 Years.** The book was on the presses, ready to roll, when it encountered legal problems, and was never printed.

much more slowly and painfully than I'd ever imagined. I would set up my tape recorder at Gene's desk or at his La Costa home and ask him questions from a prepared list. Often, his mind would stray, or he would lose his train of thought, or he simply wouldn't recall the episode in question. On more than a few occasions, he asked me to turn off the tape recorder and postponed our session. In his words, he'd be having "a bad day."

He seemed to be having more and more of these. To me and to others, Gene's thought processes were unusually strained. I would remind him of his favorite anecdotes, hoping to elicit these in his own words so I might use them as material for the book, and he'd gaze blankly at me as if I were discussing someone else. It was very disheartening. I hated to see his mind slipping like this.

I mentioned this to David Alexander, who had begun interviewing Gene late in June for an article in *The Humanist*. He sympathized with my struggle, which he also seemed to be enduring, and volunteered to fax me his raw interviews. From these I was able to extract a few sentences, especially about Gene's early life and religious beliefs, but the subject matter was only peripherally suited to my book's needs.

My interviews with Gene were conducted wherever I could catch him. He wasn't coming into the office as frequently as in the past, since he had pulled back from the show, allowing the team of producers and writers to do as they felt best. Several of my meetings with him took place at his home in Bel-Air, where I was given the tour of the newly redecorated rooms. His office was done in a rich dark wood, and everything he needed was within easy reach — his phone, intercom to the kitchen, and, of course, his beloved Lexorwriter (which he kept nearby for a sense of security, since he wasn't doing any writing). I was pleased to see that the portrait of him done for the front cover of the *Philadelphia Inquirer* Sunday Magazine in the early '80s was on the wall opposite him, where he could admire it while seated at his desk. I had bought him this gift with the stipulation that he will it back to me,[13] since I thought it truly captured his essence.

One of the happiest moments that year was when our episode of *Star Trek: The Next Generation* aired on June 3. Fred and I had received an advanced copy of the tape, but there is no way to describe the excitement of seeing your first teleplay actually aired (complete with those nasty commercial interruptions). We were guests of honor at a special screening organized by Ernie and some other pals of Fred. We each invited our friends and guests to the bash held in a projection TV auditorium at the Beverly Garland Hotel in North Hollywood. Afterwards, these kind people gave us a lovely party. It may not have been a searchlight Hollywood premiere, but I couldn't have been more exhilarated from the rush the experience gave me.

The next day I departed for my vacation, this time to England and Wales for a "theme" trip. One of my favorite TV shows has always been *The Prisoner,* which had been rerunning that year on *CBS Late Night*. My friend Darlene Lieblich was equally crazy about this surrealistic program, and together we made a pilgrimage to "The Village" in

---

[13] He kept his promise, and this portrait now hangs in my home's entryway.

Portmerion, near an unpronounceable seaside town in Northern Wales. Standing there, viewing the actual location where this '60s series had been filmed, I was filled with a sense of awe, and I suddenly knew what it must feel like to be a serious *Star Trek* fan. Here we were, two reasonably intelligent professionals in the entertainment industry, jumping up and down and giggling like schoolgirls, all the while chanting, "We're in the Village, we're in the Village!"

During the time I was away in Britain, Majel and Gene went on a week-long trip to Bermuda, a place they had visited in their happier days. I was pleased that Gene was having a chance to get away for a few days and relax. But I was shocked at what I saw when he came home from his trip. He arrived back in town shortly after I returned from Britain, and he was now walking with the full-time use of a cane, which he had bought in Bermuda. I was terribly concerned, and wondered if he was doing everything he could to regain his health, which seemed to be so rapidly slipping away from him. But I also tried to make light of it, and for his birthday in August, I sent away for a special gift, a very elegant hand-carved cane with a hidden sword. He adored this novelty, which made his perceived stigma of using a cane easier to overcome. He used this unique cane every day. A few months later, he told me it had been confiscated as a "concealed weapon" at some event where scanners had detected the sword. I forget exactly what happened, but it was never returned to him in good condition, and he had to rely on the use of other canes, and shortly thereafter, walkers and wheelchairs.

LOG ENTRY 48 :

That fourth season of *TNG*, I tried desperately to get Gene to take a more active role in the show. Scripts were beginning to come in, and I hoped that Gene would start to emerge from his depression if he became involved in the series. He had paid scant attention to the show during the third season, not caring much about the scripts and doing no writing whatsoever.

The new first draft scripts were in serious need of his attention, so I had them delivered to him down at La Costa. When I told him how poor I thought some of them were, he asked for my comments. The studio had supplied him with a fax machine for the La Costa home, and I faxed him lengthy memos on the first drafts of "Devil's Due" (June 12, 1990; full of anachronisms and twentieth century clichés and superstitions); "Clues," (June 22, 1990; I had no comments on this second draft — it was a good one from the start); "The Loss" (June 18, 1990, for which I had a few minor comments), and a confidential memo on the first draft of "Suddenly Human," which I sent on June 28. By that time, a rewrite had been ordered, but I urged Gene to read the script carefully to be sure several problems were addressed:

> TO: GENE RODDENBERRY
> DATE: 6/28/90
> FROM: SUSAN SACKETT
> SUBJECT: " SUDDENLY HUMAN,"
> First Draft Script, 6/1/90

Gene, this needs tremendous work . . . My main problem [with it] is the premise. Picard must find a way to persuade the human young man in the story to rejoin the human race, as if this is so important. It's jingoistic, chauvinistic and a few other -istics. It's also wrong. It's racist. In short, it's not *Star Trek* . . .

Specifics:

Page 6 — The description of Jono letting loose a "high-pitched BEDOUIN-LIKE CRY" (referred to several times throughout the script) puzzled me. What *is* a Bedouin-like cry? If these people appear too Arabic, this show will be taken as a racial slur . . .

Page 9 — Don't understand Picard's angry remark about their "antiseptic excuse for a culture." This is a prejudicial remark and not in character for our captain. Our show is about contacting other life forms and civilizations, not putting them down for not being like us. . . .

Page 11 — Geordi's speech near the bottom. "I say off with his turban! Holo-zap him to a beach party! Show the man he can tan!" HUH??? What in the world is this? . . .

Page 17 — Why does Picard turn his own quarters over to this boy? This is never made clear in the script. He obviously hates this idea. He can feel paternal to him without offering him his own bed (and volunteering to sleep "next door in the ready room" — what ship is this? Not ours!)

Page 18 — Picard's speech about his hair is absolutely out of character and not appropriate to 24th century thinking. "You're fortunate enough to have an abundance of growth up there. God knows I've tried everything." Since when is Picard desperate to grow hair? Why should he be? What an insult to all the bald, beautiful men in the world (like PATRICK STEWART!). If he wanted to grow hair in the 24th century, he most certainly could. Why should he want to? This speech makes me sick. (I know, that's an unprofessional comment. Tell that to my stomach.) . . .

Page 31 — If Troi says a line like, "I am half-Betazoid, half human . . . Yes, and all woman," our audience will be laughing so hard they'll miss the next bit, which is even funnier. Really, having the boy touch her tits and having her explain "They're breasts. Infants nurse on them." Can I have the towel concession to sell to the drooling, slavering men in the audience — after they stop laughing? Come on, Deanna Troi's breasts are already a joke, what with her push-up underwear she describes at every convention. I'm sure this scene will bring the loudest unintentional laugh we've ever had . . .

Page 45 — More unintended comedy. The character of "Diedre" comes off as a spaced-out Valley girl, interested in the newcomer's hair and clothes. "You're kind of cute though . . . just got to do something about your hair." Our teenagers aboard the Enterprise aren't airheads. And her second speech on down the page, "Oh beam me to heaven! What a heartbreak!" is grody to the max! Gag me with a spoon . . . Aside from the above, it's a great script. Just kidding. Wanted to see if you're paying attention.

Unfortunately, Gene wasn't; he was beginning to exhibit signs of mental difficulty. His interest in the scripts was practically non-existent. "I'm sure it will be fixed," was all the enthusiasm he could muster. The scripts did indeed undergo major rewrites that addressed most of the problems. Gene was fortunate in that he had selected top people for the production staff who fixed most of this stuff without our help. Still I continued to try to do the job Gene had asked of me, which was to read and comment to him on scripts. It was painful and frustrating to have to sit on the sidelines while my efforts fell on disinterested ears.

Gene's efforts on behalf of the show had by now dropped off almost completely. His calendar consisted mainly of lunch dates with friends or cast and many trips to La Costa, where I often joined him to try to conduct interviews. Unaware of the seriousness of his illness, I tried desperately to pull him out of his depression and downward spiral, a futile effort that was beginning to pull me down as well. Gene did, however, attend viewings of the rough cuts of episodes. Rick Berman would call when it was time for Gene to head over to the production office, often commenting to me, "I think Gene will really like what we did with this one." I hadn't the heart to tell him that Gene had not even read the script.

When Gene did manage to come into the office to attempt to answer his mail, he would sit at his desk, shuffle a few papers around, then try to buzz me on the intercom. We had had a new telephone system installed and Gene never got the hang of it. After a few frustrating tries, he would completely bypass the new com lines by yelling loudly,

"*Susan!*" He seemed to grow more and more detached from everyday life. He didn't care if his mail piled up. He would take long naps on his couch after lunch, probably due to the wine he would have with it. After this, he'd switch on the TV and watch dailies, if they were in, or just anything if they weren't. Sometimes I'd open the door and see him staring at whatever channel happened to be on the TV: a game show, a talk show, the news, a cartoon, a soap opera — he seemed oblivious to what he was watching. This behavior seemed very odd to me, and very distressing.

Until this time, my life had seemed on a steady course, but now as I peered into my own future, I was beginning to see a cavernous void stretching before me. My friend and writing partner Fred Bronson had for years been recommending a workshop to me in which he acted as a "facilitator" — the '90s term for leader. I had held off on participation in this, since it seemed to be geared mainly towards gay men and women who were having difficulties coping with their relationships or realities of their sexuality. Gene's assistant Ernie had taken the workshop, and Richard Arnold was signed up for the upcoming one. However, Fred assured me that straight participants in "The Experience Weekend," as it was called, generally found it very beneficial, too. I was still reluctant, but I signed up for the same weekend as Richard, August 3-5. My main concern was my bleak future. I was in denial about Gene's health, although a part of me realized that his decline was permanent and that I'd better start thinking of how I would get on with my life once he was gone.

Fred was right. From the moment the weekend began with the playing of John Lennon's "Imagine," I knew I was doing the right thing. As I listened, eyes closed, to the lyrics of that song (which is my all-time favorite), it seemed to me that it was describing Gene Roddenberry. Lennon invoked a world with no countries, no religion, no heaven, no hell — just people living in harmony. When he said, "You may say that I'm a dreamer, but I'm not the only one," I immediately thought of Gene. These were two twentieth century dreamers, cut from the same cloth. Too bad they never met. I began to cry softly. I just couldn't imagine a world with no Gene Roddenberry.

By the time I had completed the weekend, I felt revitalized. "Empowered" was the buzzword of the event, but I truly felt that way by Sunday night's graduation. I was strong, I was invincible, and I would carry on with my life when the time came.

Following the workshop, Fred and I, along with his father and my mother, took a week-long Caribbean cruise aboard the *S.S. Norway*. When I told Gene what ship we were going on, he seemed to get a vicarious pleasure in hearing about my trip. Many years before, the *Norway* had been the *France*, and back in the '60s he had sailed to Europe with his first wife, Eileen, and their two girls. His trip had come at a crossroads in the days of sea travel, when steamships were more elegant — no bikini-clad young ladies or loud-mouthed men in floral shirts laden with camcorders. After my cruise, Gene hung on my every word as I told him that the ship was still as lovely as ever, with its richly paneled library and tastefully decorated cabins, dining rooms and so on, without mentioning the loss of elegance that had overtaken her passengers. I didn't want to spoil his happy memories.

LOG ENTRY 49 :

On August 23, Fred Bronson, Ernie Over and I drove with Gene to his sixty-ninth birthday party, which was held that year at the Ritz Carlton in Laguna Niguel. This enchanting new hotel offered a spectacular view from its main lounge set on a cliff overlooking the Pacific. As we proceeded to our table outside on the patio, we had plenty of time to take in the sight of the waves breaking on the shore below the rocky cliff. Gene's difficulties in walking were even more pronounced, his slow shuffle making it seem like a mile-long hike. He spoke very little during the lunch — small talk, mostly. Our scintillating mealtime conversations now seemed a thing of the past, and there were many awkward silences. Gene also said very little in the car during the hour-and-a-half drive in each direction. To fill the void in the conversation, as well as to compensate for my sadness because of Gene's poor health, I sang along with the CDs Fred had supplied.

Nearly every day now found Gene scheduled for some sort of doctor's appointment, his driver Ernie charged with getting Gene to and from their offices. As Gene spent more time away from Paramount, I began to notice that Ernie was assuming tasks that had been my responsibilities for nearly two decades. He was opening and sorting the mail directly from home, rather than bringing it to me. He occasionally answered some of Gene's correspondence too, and would call up Jana with appointments he had set. Eventually, this information would filter down to me. Sometimes, he would arrange meetings I knew Gene didn't want, but I was becoming powerless to handle everything with an absentee boss.

Although I resented this encroachment, I was at the same time pleased when Ernie was charged with seeing to Gene's medical needs. Not only did he take him to doctors, but he supervised his medication which, when left to his own devices, Gene always seemed to confuse. On a couple of occasions, Gene had taken the wrong prescriptions on the weekend when no one was paying any attention to his meds. Once Gene stumbled and fell in the Paramount commissary when he forgot his cane as he got up to greet a colleague. As he walked down the steps to the lower level, he lost his balance and landed on his side. There was a collective gasp, followed by a collective hush in the large dining room as a couple hundred executives looked on in horror. I was on my feet in an instant, racing to Gene's side, as were the rest of us at Gene's table — Richard, Ernie and some guests. As quickly as the fall happened, Gene was assisted back to his feet, and shrugged it off by insisting that he was fine. I think he was more embarrassed than hurt, although it had to have hurt quite a bit as his two-hundred-fifty pound bulk crashed to the unyielding Mexican tile floor.

On another occasion, he stumbled trying to walk down the three steps at the entrance to the Hart Building. Ernie rushed him to the doctor, who said it was nothing to fear, just a mix-up in the prescription, which he felt Gene had accidentally taken twice. Ernie went to the drug store and bought one of those little pillboxes that has a compartment for each day clearly indicated on the lids to each section, to aid to Gene in taking just the right pills. It was foolproof and seemed to do the trick.

In mid-October, Richard, Ernie and Gene flew to London, where Gene, wheelchair bound, received an award from the British video industry. I longed to go with them, but of

course, it was out of the question. Majel flew in for the event, then immediately home again, thus dashing my hopes for a chance to be with him for this honor. While he was over there, he hired a driver to take them all down to the Hampshire home of his old friend Rupert Evans, whom he had known since the days of filming *Spectre*. Later, Rupert confided in me his shock at seeing Gene in a wheelchair. He also mentioned that Gene hadn't been his old, talkative self, and that Ernie seemed to be guiding the conversation as well as directing Gene in everything he did.

The difficulty I had in trying to elicit interviews for our book was nothing compared to the difficulty Gene had in reading a one-page script on camera in early December. Several months before, Fred Bronson and I had been hired to write a script for the new Universal Studios-Florida *Star Trek* presentation. As one of its theme park attractions, the studio planned the video equivalent of the old "four poses for a quarter" photo booth, only this would be a video, with the paying guest interacting with *Star Trek* characters in a private, personal recording session. When Gene saw the studio's proposed script, he rejected it as too gung-ho-kill-the-evil-aliens, and urged that it be rewritten. He wasn't up for it, but he recommended my partner and me. Fred and I then held several meetings with the executives from Universal and devised a story that had Kirk, Spock and some of the other regulars in a scenario with the guests. It was approved, and sets were constructed, but at the last minute, Leonard Nimoy and William Shatner insisted that although they had con-

Gene taped the introduction to the Universal Studios Florida interactive video in December, 1990. He wasn't well, as can be seen in this photo, as he prepares to read his lines from a TelePrompTer.

tracts, they would not play the Kirk and Spock characters. The feeling was that they were tired of being these characters and wanted to do something different. They would do the video as long as they could appear as themselves. Our carefully thought-out script was quickly scrubbed and a new one hurriedly written in-house. Shatner and Nimoy now appeared as co-directors of a video starring the tour guest, and new scenes with the other cast were also included. Gene was to record an introduction that would be incorporated into the tapes.

A dressing room trailer had been set up for Gene's use, where he studied his lines while someone applied makeup, and I combed and straightened his hair. By the time he got to the stage, where he stood with the aid of his cane, he was already beginning to show signs of exhaustion. He was led to the blue screen and seemed impressed when he was shown the process that would matte his image into a shot of a cityscape. Then he began to record his lines. There was a TelePrompTer and only a few paragraphs of dialogue, but he just couldn't get through the bit. Poor Gene, I thought as trickles of perspiration streamed down his face from the frustration I knew he was experiencing. I felt that familiar sinking feeling and mentally cringed whenever he blew a line. Tape was stopped, restarted, stopped and started anew many times. You could hear the assembled crew inhaling simultaneously, waiting anxiously each time to see if he would make it through the lines. Finally, there was a collective exhalation. He had not quite made it through the entire reading, but the editors were certain they had enough footage to piece together a coherent whole.

That December was the first time since our involvement that we didn't celebrate my birthday. Gene simply wasn't up to going out to dinner. There was no excuse he could use to get away for an evening, and he just wasn't strong enough to drive over to the Valley to be with me. I was more concerned with his health than disappointed about not having our annual dinner. He was definitely no longer the robust, energetic man I had known, but my love for him was undiminished. Seeing him deteriorate was breaking my heart, and while only four months before I had graduated from the Experience Weekend feeling oh-so-empowered, I continued to deny that anything was seriously wrong.

Surely, all those doctors he was seeing would somehow make him all better.

LOG ENTRY 50 :

Mom had flown in from Florida to stay with me over the 1990-91 holiday season, and I was grateful for her company. With Gene's health declining, it was good to have an energetic eighty-five-year-old to help me through these difficult days. Thoughtful as always, Gene was able to swing reservations for my mother and me to have lunch Christmas Day at the Hotel Bel-Air — no mean feat, since the dining room had been booked solid for months. And despite his health problems, Gene gave me a wonderful Christmas gift. That fall, my sixteen-year-old Shepherd/Husky, Heidi, had died. I knew her days were numbered; the poor thing could no longer stand on her hind legs, and I had to euthanize her. I grieved for several days, which Gene didn't seem to understand. He had given me one day off to mourn, but I was still sad nearly a week later, and he chastised me for it. This seemed strange behavior, since he had been so sympathetic when Phaser had died in 1986. His impatience hurt; only later did I realize it was a symptom of his rapidly progressing illness. So it came as a total surprise when, a couple of months later, I told him I was thinking about getting a new puppy, and he insisted this be a gift from him.

Two days after Christmas, Mom and I drove out to Lynne's Kennel in Acton, a high-desert community about forty-five minutes north of Los Angeles (near the famous *Star Trek* location known as Vasquez Rocks). Lynne had two litters of Golden Retriever puppies, and from this pile of sandy-white fluff in perpetual motion, we picked out my new treasure. I named the seven-week-old puppy Tasha, actually a nickname for her American Kennel Club-registered moniker "Lynne's Natasha Yar." I had decided to give her the name in honor of the blonde character who had been in the first season on *TNG*, since

Gene, Richard and me on the set of Next Generation.

this pup was more taffy blonde than golden. This was one of the best presents Gene had ever given me, and Tasha was a well-loved member of my household for many years. (Sadly, Tasha died in December, 1998, of a brain tumor. I miss her to this day.)

Gene was not well during the Christmas holidays. He told me he had taken a couple of falls in his home. A well-meaning friend tried to give him a walker for a present, but the proud man disdained it. After the holidays, he was really under the weather, and more medical tests were ordered. On February 12, Gene checked into UCLA Medical Center as an outpatient for tests to check on a damaged heart valve. Ernie drove him, but I asked Gene if he would like me to be with him. He practically begged me to come along, seeming a bit nervous about the procedure. The tests were not pleasant. After being sedated, he was required to swallow some sort of internal viewing device. I sat on the edge of his bed and held his hand throughout.

The video monitor gave us a true glimpse into the wonders of modern medical science. The improperly closing valve appeared on a TV monitor, the star of its own series, which seemed stranger than fiction. Despite his discomfort, Gene was impressed by the video image flickering by his bedside. As soon as the novelty wore off, we began concentrating on what the doctors were seeing. The news was not good, and I was alarmed to discover yet another flaw in Gene's body which by now even I was forced to admit had none of its old resiliency. My own thoughts were that the damage to his heart valve might possibly be related to his abuse of cocaine, although I never presumed to mention this to the doctors. Two years before, my housecleaner's twenty-one-year-old son, in the prime of his life, had died due to a faulty heart valve. His doctors attributed the damage to heavy cocaine abuse. I knew Gene was still using, although not anywhere near as excessively as this unfortunate young man. I had gently mentioned this to Gene at the time and continued to slip newspaper and magazine clippings relating to drug abuse in with his personal mail. But Gene's denial always led him to think that these things happened to other people, never to himself, so he dismissed it with his usual, "Stop bawling me out."

Two days after the heart valve test, Gene had another MRI in Santa Monica. According to Gene, the doctors were aware that there was something going on in his brain, but after more than two years, they had yet to pinpoint the cause or devise any effective treatment. I was to learn later that Gene spared me the truth of what was really wrong; when I asked about his tests, he simply told me, "They haven't figured it out." One of the things he told me they suspected was multiple sclerosis. I told Gene that seemed highly improbable, since this disease strikes mainly people forty and under. Sure enough, they ruled out MS, along with a number of other neurological diseases.

Meanwhile, the list of Gene's doctors was growing so large that it was hard to keep track of them all. The various medical personnel poking and prodding him included his internist, a psychiatrist, neurologist, neurosurgeon, cardiologist, opthamologist (for the beginning of vision difficulties most likely attributable to his diabetes), dermatologist, audiologist (for his hearing loss) and more.

Gene's involvement in the show was now limited to attending the screenings of rough cuts of the episodes in Rick Berman's offices. A long flight of stairs led up to Rick's suite in the production offices on the second floor of the Gary Cooper Building. It took every ounce of strength for Gene to mount this staircase, assisted by Ernie, and at times, several others. On days when he came in for a screening, I always feared he would tumble down the stairs and was greatly relieved after every session.

Jeri Taylor was then supervising producer, which meant that not only did she participate in pitch meetings, but she was involved in the rewriting of most scripts as well as creating some of her own. I found Jeri to be the most personable producer on staff, warm and friendly. The executive producer, Rick Berman, reminded me of a high school principal — an authority figure whose path you dreaded crossing. This probably wasn't intentional on his part; I think this was just my reaction to anyone with that much power. The co-executive producer, Michael Piller, I found to be a brilliant man who knew his job and was highly effective at it, but he never exhibited much warmth, keeping pleasantries to a minimum. Jeri, on the other hand, was charged with less of the top-level decision making, which may have had something to do with her more relaxed attitude. I was also delighted that we had a woman producer on the show.

I got to know Jeri better after she ran a "Name the Episode" contest in early 1991, during the fourth season. She had written a show about a symbiotic creature called a "Trill" who shared a body with another, living in the stomach of the host organism. (This species eventually was incorporated with the "Dax" character in the spin-off series, *Star Trek: Deep Space Nine*.) The contest winner was promised a lunch in the "good" side of the commissary, i.e., the executive dining room, not the cafeteria where we grunts usually ate. I sent Jeri the following memo:

TO: JERI TAYLOR

DATE: 2/27/91

FROM: SUSAN SACKETT

COPIES: ABSOLUTELY NO ONE

SUBJECT: NAMES, NEW

Here are some possible names. Most are meant to amuse.
(Can you tell which ones?)

INTERNAL AFFAIRS

SKIN DEEP

THE JOINING

HOST (featuring Whoopi oldberg — no 'g')

I'VE GUT A SECRET

MAY I JOIN YOU?

THE TRILL IS GONE

THE HOST WITH THE MOST

The title she decided to go with was "The Host." Since I came closest, I was pronounced the winner, and we became acquainted over lunch in the executive dining room.
The least political of the producers on the series, Jeri continued to be receptive to pitches
from Fred Bronson and me long after all my ties with *Star Trek* had been severed.

The week before the show wrapped for the fourth season, producer A.C. Lyles
requested permission to bring a special guest on stage. A.C., as everyone called him, was
Paramount's "producer-at-large." He had been around Hollywood longer than most people on the lot had been alive. His ties went back to the early days of film, and he was
regarded as one of the true gentlemen in Hollywood, always dapper in a suit and tie. He
hobnobbed with celebrities of the old school (read: Republicans) like Charlton Heston and
Jimmy Stewart. During the Bush (Senior) administration, A.C. invited Vice President Dan
Quayle's boys onto the lot. I was sitting with Gene on the Commissary patio, where
power lunches usually took place, when A.C. brought the boys over to meet the creator
of *Star Trek*. I was impressed with how charming they were, in a preppy sort of way. They
couldn't have been more polite, and I could tell they were big fans of the show.

Among A.C.'s closest friends was ex-President Ronald Reagan. A.C. was included in
all the big Reagan events, like fund-raising dinners, the dedication of his Presidential
Library, and so forth. On the 15th of April, A.C. brought Reagan and his entourage onto
the set of *Star Trek*. Gene was never a fan of the Republicans and, in fact, he had very little use for the party or their adherents. Nevertheless, he was pressed into service for that
great Hollywood (and Washington) tradition, the photo op. Ernie whisked Gene to the set
to pose dutifully with the ex-president and some studio executives. I was told by several
people that Gene managed to rise out of his director's chair and stand unaided long
enough to be photographed with the bewildered Reagan, who had probably never seen
Star Trek and hadn't a clue who Gene was. That's Hollywood.

LOG ENTRY 51 :

That spring, Gene and I attended what would be our last wrap party on April 21, 1991, in Santa Monica at the Sand and Sea Club. The invitation stated it was the celebration for the completion of Season Four and the One Hundredth Episode. A huge tent set up in the cloth-covered sand displayed festive decorations, food stations and a bandstand. Fred accompanied me, as usual. I enjoyed being with him, and although he wasn't an official member of the crew, he knew everybody and was graciously received by them all. Gene arrived in a wheelchair, the first time I was aware of him appearing so openly immobile at an event. He had previously taken great pains to conceal his use of the wheelchair in front of the cast and crew, but there was no way he was going to be able to walk on that lumpy surface. Ernie and someone he introduced to me as "the nurse" accompanied Gene. (Majel was out of town.) I was startled to learn that this attractive black woman had recently been hired to care for Gene on weekends at his home, since the regular household staff were off.

He had never mentioned a nurse; more denial on his part, I assumed. I think he felt it would only upset me. Indeed, I hadn't realized his health had deteriorated that much. I had seen less and less of him lately. He had been avoiding the office and working out of his house, since the strain of a daily trip to Paramount was clearly taking its toll.

The wrap party held at the beach. Gene, Fred Bronson, and me.

After the wrap party buffet lunch, there were some musical performances, including a very suggestive dance by a black woman. Gene, ever the joker, looked around and quipped, "Is that my nurse?" He smiled broadly, but there was a hint of confusion in his voice, and I got the impression he was actually a bit confused and wasn't really certain if it was the nurse or not.

In May, Gene and Ernie flew to Washington, D.C. for an event that Gene insisted on attending. The National Space Society, on whose board Gene had been an honorary director for many years, held a special affair that would be attended by the whole cast. Gene wanted to keep up appearances and insisted on being present for the festivities. At the end of the five-day stay, the pair flew on to Chicago, where I was to meet Gene for the annual awards gathering of the American Humanist Association. David Alexander, whom Gene had met at the Ted Turner award banquet the previous year, had kept his promise and arranged for the membership to give its Humanist Arts Award to Gene. So rather than this being a chance for us simply to convene with our like-minded fellow Humanists, the Chicago meeting was an important event. Which meant that Majel and Rod would be flying in for the awards ceremony the following evening.

I corralled Fred Bronson to fly to Chicago with me, so I would have someone for moral support. I knew that being around Majel would make me uneasy and I wanted Fred by my side. Our flight arrived in time for us to join Ernie and Gene for dinner at Chicago's famous Pump Room. Later that evening, when we returned to the hotel, Fred went to his room, and Gene insisted that I join him in his. Naturally, I welcomed the chance to be alone with him.

We cuddled and smooched, petted and caressed each other, and I let him know that this was much more important to me than anything else. Indeed it was. There is nothing like being held in the arms of the person who loves you and accepts you. And I was always so happy to be able to give this man the love I knew he so desperately needed.

I was shocked, however, when I looked down at his feet. His ankles were horribly swollen from edema, the first time I'd ever noticed this. I feared this might be a symptom of heart or kidney failure, and I flashed back to the final days of my father's illness when he had suffered the same symptoms of water retention after his kidneys had begun shutting down. I tried to control my panic, and casually questioned him about the swelling. Had he noticed this himself? He admitted he had not paid much attention to it, and I remarked that he ought to have another physical check up when he returned to L.A. He agreed, and we continued to hold each other until he drifted off to sleep and I quietly left for my own room. It was our last happy time together. By now, he was no longer able to climb the fifteen stairs to my house, nor would I let him. I didn't want to see him take a tumble right in front of my home.

The next morning, Gene hired a driver to show us around Chicago. I had never been there before, and I enjoyed the tour of the suburbs, the drive along Lake Michigan and the campus of Northwestern University. We returned to town in time to have lunch at Images, on the ninety-sixth floor of the John Hancock Center. From our aerie high above the street, we watched Chicago's celebration of the recent Gulf War victory. Our altitude

was even greater than the small airplanes, which flew in formation below us!

After lunch, Majel and Rod arrived amid much confusion about their ride from the airport. Somehow the driver of the limo sent to meet them had missed them, despite much paging and sign waving, and this aggravated Gene no end. I was sorry to see him under stress, as this was supposed to be a stress-free weekend.

Eventually, they reached the hotel. I had an immediate feeling of loss from the moment of their arrival, since I could no longer spend time with Gene. At the dinner that night, I wore one of my specially purchased outfits. Not surprisingly, Fred and I were not seated with the family but, rather, two tables away from Gene and his entourage. When his name was called, he struggled to his feet and, using Rod as a crutch, somehow made it to the podium only a few yards from the table. I crossed my fingers, hoping that he wouldn't fall. But the only stumbling he did was with words. It was expected that he would make a speech, but he was only able to manage a few remarks lasting about six or seven minutes. "Louder! We can't hear you!" some rude person in the back complained, and I cringed in embarrassment for Gene. I wanted to rush to the podium and tell them, "Leave him alone. Can't you see he's not well?" Worse, I knew the event was being taped and that copies of the video would later be sold in the lobby, a routine for all Humanist award events.

Gene and Majel headed for the hotel bar after dinner, while Rod wandered aimlessly through the lobby, looking lost, admitting he was bored. His parents had given him a hundred dollars and told him to have a good time. Fred and I were stunned that this seven-

Fred Bronson, Gene and I are high above Chicago having drinks in the John Hancock building. We were in town for the American Humanist Association's convention in 1991, one of Gene's last public appearances.

teen-year old was given the freedom to wander the unfamiliar streets of Chicago alone at night. Rod seemed eager for company, and we asked him to join us. The three of us piled into a taxi and headed for McDonald's. It turned out to be an historic McD's, one of the oldest still operating in the country. It was also packed. We had some sodas, then caught a cab for a Chicago-by-night drive. Rod told us of his ambitions to become an astronomer someday, so we had the driver take us to the planetarium. We drove past what I call the "Love and Marriage" fountain[14] from the *Married...with Children* TV series, and we observed the twinkling Chicago skyline from a distance.

When we returned to the hotel, Gene and Majel were still in the bar, so Fred and I dropped off Rod and headed for our rooms.

I saw Gene the next day at breakfast, with Ernie and David taking turns pushing Gene's wheelchair, which he used full-time now. I was shocked when he even used it to go across the hall that first evening, from his room to the rest of the suite. I pleaded with him to at least try to walk the ten or so steps, which he had been able to do until now, but this time he wouldn't — or couldn't.

Gene didn't attend any of the Humanist festivities that day, nor did he go to the special banquet that evening. He put in a hasty appearance, then was rolled out of the room to places unknown. The next morning, Gene and Majel flew back as separately as they had arrived. Since Majel had an earlier flight, that left the coast clear for Fred and me to hitch a ride to the airport with Gene in his limo. This, too, became a problem. When the limo didn't show up on time, Gene bristled and fumed. He seemed to be flying off the handle much too easily these days. Whenever he had these volatile moods, Fred would patiently remind me that Gene was not well. This wasn't a great comfort, but at least I was able to understand the personality changes he was undergoing. Gene eventually calmed down, and we reached the airport in plenty of time, but I was glad to be returning to L.A. after what would become our last trip together.

[14] The actual name, I learned later, is Buckingham Fountain.

LOG ENTRY 52 :

Later that month, McDonnell Douglas arranged for the staff and crew of *TNG* to visit their facility in Orange County and tour the space station they were building under government contract. About twenty of us were able to get away and attend. Gene went too, but was confined to his wheelchair, unable to tour the inside of the station, the highlight of the visit. Inside the mock-up we got to see where the astronauts would work, sleep, exercise and so on. Afterwards a small group of us went to lunch at a Thai place nearby, and although Gene didn't say much, he smiled a lot and seemed to be having a good time.

A few days later, Gene, Ernie and Majel went on the annual "Sea Trek" cruise out of Miami. Photos of a grinning Gene in his wheelchair told me that he was still sadly immobile but bravely determined to put up a good front. Before he left, I pleaded with him not to drink on the trip, since this would only further hasten his deterioration. Of course, he paid me no mind and indulged himself with happy abandon on his Caribbean voyage.

All of Gene's doctors had reiterated the need for him to lay off the booze; one even attempted to stave off his drinking by prescribing a medication that would make him feel sick if he drank. He ignored the medication as well as the advice of everyone while continuing to deny his addiction.

I tried to do whatever I could to help him. Having seen what drinking was doing to him, I set a good example whenever I was around him, like ordering iced tea at lunch, hoping he would do the same, but he insisted on his two glasses of wine. In the office, I discovered fifths of vodka hidden in the center drawer of his desk. He had been doing this for years, but I was dismayed that he continued secreting these flasks despite the edicts of his physicians. Whenever I could, I would pour half the vodka down the bathroom sink and replace it with an equal amount of tap water. If he noticed the difference, he never mentioned it.

During the early months of 1991, I worked closely with the editors at Pocket Books on the simple polishes they felt necessary to improve the manuscript for our book, *Star Trek: The First 25 Years*. Requests were for a word or two here or there for clarity, a paragraph either added or deleted for space requirements — nothing I was not used to from my many years of non-fiction writing. Gene's attorney, Leonard Maizlish, however, also oversaw my rewrite. He scrutinized every paragraph for any implication that *Star Trek: The Next Generation* might somehow be related to the original *Star Trek* series. It didn't matter if I was directly quoting someone whom I had interviewed; if they said *Star Trek* when they really meant to say *Star Trek: The Next Generation*, I was obligated to spell it all out. The reason for this was a lawsuit in which Gene's first wife, Eileen, was claiming royalties she felt she was due from the new series. In her original divorce decree from 1969, the judge had awarded her community property rights that included a share in profit participation in *Star Trek*, which at that time was limited to a television series, and a failed one at that.

Gene once told me that when *Star Trek* went off the air in 1969, he could have bought the rights for around a hundred thousand dollars, but he didn't have that kind of money in those days, so they reverted to Paramount. However, his corporation, Norway Productions, was entitled to profit participation from reruns, should they ever occur. Gene and Eileen divorced in that same year. When the judge began divvying up the community property, Eileen was offered shares in Gene's royalties from *The Virginian*. She turned them down. *The Lieutenant*? No. *Have Gun, Will Travel*? No. What then? *Star Trek*, she insisted. Everyone laughed — it was a failed TV series with little or no future. "Done!"

For years, Paramount had shown no profit on its books for the series, but eventually there was a financial reckoning, which Gene had requested for his own benefit as well. A distribution was made, and Gene felt Eileen had received her due, but her attorneys disagreed, saying that *"Star Trek is Star Trek,"* and she was entitled to her share of the profits for the new series.

I could see her point. But I also didn't want to do anything that might harm Gene. I loved him and didn't like to see him having to fight for everything he ever did in his life. So I agreed to the requested changes in the book even though I thought it compromised and weakened my narrative. Gene, however, loved the book and told me he was extremely proud of it. I knew how tough he could be, so I felt great joy when he told me he thought I had done an excellent job of writing.

LOG ENTRY 53 : By spring, everything was in place for the book to be published to coincide with the twenty-fifth anniversary on September 8, 1991. Galleys (a proof of the typeset pages) had been printed, and a classy cover jacket was created. The coffee-table book would sell for close to fifty dollars, and advanced orders began to pour in to Pocket Books from booksellers around the country. Even though my royalties would be minimal (Gene received five times the advance I did), it was an assured best-seller. But I didn't care about that. I wanted this book! I wanted it on my coffee table. It was packed with trivia, anecdotes and commentary from all the important people associated with *Star Trek* over the years. It also contained some of the finest quality photographs ever compiled, thanks to the efforts of Richard Arnold, who pulled out all the stops in selecting and acquiring hundreds of beautiful stills and slides. I wanted to own this book as any collector might.

But it was not to be. With the final text approved and literally on the presses ready to roll, the project screeched to a halt. There have been many rumors about what happened, but here are the facts I observed: Richard Arnold was charged by the publisher with securing releases from everyone whose likeness was to appear in the book. As the presses were about to roll, it was realized that Leonard Nimoy had not yet signed off on his photos, and he was politely requested to do so with some haste due to the publisher's urgent deadline. My impression was that he was not happy about being rushed into signing. He said he needed more time. The publishers pushed for less time. Leonard then said he could not sign off on the photos. The book would have to be delayed. The publishers knew there was nothing they could do and agreed to try to work things out with him. Leonard, meanwhile, had asked to see a copy of the manuscript in which his photo would be appearing. Following this, he decided he would not sign off on the photos because there were some editorial changes he would first like made to the copy.

Leonard held all the cards, and he knew it. No *Star Trek* book could be published without pictures of Spock — although this idea was considered and discarded. It wasn't just a question of airbrushing him out. The fans would feel cheated at this obvious omission.

A meeting was held in Gene's office at Paramount. Gene, his attorney Leonard Maizlish, Leonard Nimoy and his attorney huddled behind Gene's closed door. I, the author, was not allowed to attend this meeting. When they emerged, Maizlish told me that the book was on hold because Leonard Nimoy didn't think the prose "lofty enough," as Maizlish put it, and wanted it more in the style of someone like Bill Moyers. I was baffled. Was this really what was on Nimoy's mind? Surely someone would work with him, perhaps let him write an introduction or expand the information about him and his character and fix whatever it was that was at the heart of the problem. Gene's attorney told me to butt out, that it would be worked out between him and Nimoy and the editor at Pocket Books.

The book never happened. For several years, they tried to work things out, hoping it might be green-lighted in time for the thirtieth anniversary. Leonard Nimoy never once spoke to me about this, nor was I ever contacted by the publisher to do any rewrites. Many times when this was in active discussions I asked why I couldn't simply pick up a telephone and call Nimoy and ask what the problem was and how I could work with him to solve it. After all, I had poured over eighteen months of my life into this project and I was willing to do anything to see it to fruition. But each time I asked, I was told to stay out of it. My anger and disappointment continued to mount, as did my feelings of frustration.

My biggest disappointment, however, was the hurt this caused Gene. I knew he would never write anything else, that this would be his last book. This, too, was pointed out by Gene's attorney to Nimoy, but he stubbornly held his ground. I wish I knew why.

In 1994, Paramount/Pocket Books published an oversized book called *Star Trek: Where No One Has Gone Before – A History in Pictures.* The text is credited to J.M. Dillard, but an extensive amount of the copy was taken from my manuscript (which Paramount owned outright, since I was paid as a writer for hire). When I learned of the proposed book, I contacted Pocket Books, and they hastily cut me a small check and added my name on the front page in the first space under "Additional Material by."

There were few celebrations for the twenty-fifth anniversary that year. Much of what was discussed never got off the drawing board. There was talk of a *Star Trek* opera (yes, opera!) on Broadway. Nothing was ever on the drawing board, however, and that idea quickly evaporated. There were tentative plans for a large studio party, like the one for the twentieth anniversary five years earlier, but Paramount did not want to spend very much money on it, proposing instead some sort of *Trek*-themed party for local underprivileged kids. It, too, never got off the ground. And they planned a celebration around the dedication of a new building named after Gene.

When the studio first broke ground for a TV department building the previous year, I began petitioning the studio executives through memos and in person to name this new structure after Gene Roddenberry. This was not some wild idea, since many of the buildings around Paramount had been named for people who had made important contributions to the studio — an eclectic group of show biz movers and shakers like Lucille Ball, Ernst Lubitsch, Cecil B. DeMille and Bing Crosby. A few structures, like the A.C. Lyles Building, had been named after the living, so it was certainly within the realm of possibility that Gene Roddenberry, creator of a phenomenon that had made billions for the studio, should have a building named in his honor.

The studio succumbed to the requests from myself and many others who apparently felt the same way I did, and on June 6, 1991, the dedication ceremonies for the Gene Roddenberry Building were held as part of the year-long celebration of *Star Trek's* twenty-fifth anniversary. There was an outdoor breakfast for the press and invited guests, which included the entire roster of Paramount employees. Gene, who was very self-conscious about being wheelchair-bound, was brought around to the back of the platform in order to hobble the few steps to his seat on the platform without being seen this way by his many fans and especially the press. Called to the mike, he rose unsteadily, physically supported by members of the *Star Trek* cast. Somewhere in his inner reserves he found that great determination that had always been part of his being, and he managed to deliver a few brief, humorous remarks to the crowd. Nothing profound, just the same sort of things he had said for years, but it lifted his spirits immensely. Later, he mustered even more strength as he posed for pictures while leaning on friends and his cane.

That night, Leonard Maizlish threw a party for Gene and a select group of his friends and family at the classy Four Oaks restaurant in Beverly Glen. I was invited, but knowing how awkward I would feel to be within a few feet of Majel, I brought Fred Bronson as my escort. Fortunately, Majel and I were assigned to opposite ends of the table. I was seated next to Gene's daughter Darleen, who spent the evening telling me how distressed she was over her father's health. Maizlish 's invitation did not include Gene's other daughter, Dawn, due to the ill feelings Maizlish harbored toward her because of her mother Eileen's lawsuit for a share of *Star Trek* profits. Although Dawn was not involved, Maizlish refused to extend any courtesies toward her.

On June 25, A couple of weeks later, Gene was lauded at a *Star Trek* twenty-fifth anniversary convention at Los Angeles' Shrine Auditorium. This time he opted to remain in his wheelchair even though the estimated seven thousand fans would now see just how frail he appeared. If the fans were shocked, they didn't show it, and roared appreciation with a standing ovation for their hero.

Throughout all this, Gene never relented in a search for the source of his problems. Ever hopeful of a precise diagnosis and confident of a complete cure (his doctors had never indicated otherwise), he submitted to yet another barrage of tests when, on June 17, his doctor admitted him to UCLA for two days of poking and probing. He had been diagnosed with something called "normal pressure hydrocephalus," which meant that he had too much fluid on the brain. The doctors wanted to see what effect draining this fluid would have on his unsteady gait and impaired reasoning abilities, which were Gene's main symptoms. I visited Gene in the hospital — the first time I had seen him hooked up to IVs and tubes since his "spider bite" hospitalization many years before. He was delighted to see me and claimed he was walking with less difficulty. I wondered if this was really true. I noticed he still needed help from a nurse to get to the bathroom. He appeared optimistic however, and I was cheered by his upbeat attitude. His only complaint was a pounding headache, a side-effect of the testing, he had been told.

Things were looking up. Maybe now at last, I thought, he'll get the help he needs.

Gene is surrounded by members of both casts for the dedication of Paramount's Gene Roddenberry Building, June 6, 1991. Left to right: Jimmy Doohan, DeForest Kelley, Walter Koenig, Nichelle Nichols, Gene, Bill Shatner, George Takei, Patrick Stewart, a very pregnant Gates McFadden, Marina Sirtis, Jonathan Frakes and Wil Wheaton.

LOG ENTRY 54 :

There was no change in Gene's health after he left the UCLA Medical Center, except for residual pounding headaches. He complained about these frequently, unusual behavior from a man who seldom complained and to my knowledge had not suffered from chronic headaches before. The pain eventually grew so strong that Gene phoned his doctor and asked for codeine, a morphine derivative. He claimed nothing was helping him, so the doctor prescribed the requested painkillers. I was baffled; I had never heard of codeine for a mere headache. But Gene had a way with his medical practitioners. What he wanted, he usually got.

Gene began having physical therapy sessions at UCLA three times a week to strengthen his muscles, supplemented with exercise sessions at home. I was relieved that he was finally getting some professional therapy.

Meanwhile, I sought solace in my writing projects. While awaiting word about the on again/off again status of the twenty-fifth anniversary coffee table book, I began pursuing another project. During my research for the anniversary book, I had dusted off Gene's partially completed manuscript for *The God Thing*, the novelization of his rejected movie script. I remembered how much work Gene had put into it, and asked him if he would allow me to bring it to the attention of David Stern, our editor at Pocket Books. Although it was originally contracted with Bantam, nearly fourteen years had passed since that time and perhaps a new publisher would be interested. At first, Gene wasn't wild about this idea.

"It needs work," he said.

"Not much. I've read it over and it's not bad. It just needs fleshing out. At least, let me send it to Pocket. They might just go for it. Think of it as possible money for Rod's college education."

Gene relented when I said this, and I shipped the rough copy off to New York. David Stern seemed quite taken with the manuscript, agreeing, however, that it needed expanding and updating. Would Fred Bronson and I (by now our names were interlinked as a team) be interested in completing this project for Gene? I gave Gene the good news, and he was enthusiastic about giving us the opportunity to do this for him. "You certainly know my style better than anyone," he admitted.

Everyone was enthusiastic about the potential of this book. That spring I had my assistant, Jana, prepare a retyping of the manuscript, since it had last been worked on in 1977 by Gene's secretary in England while shooting *Spectre*. The type was barely legible and it needed to be put on computer disk. As she progressed, I began working on pages, changing typos, editing awkward sentences, finding areas I wanted to expand. David, too, began making a series of notes and was eager for our deal to be formalized so that work could begin in earnest.

The delay in getting our contracts for this book seemed endless. Negotiations had begun in April, 1991; in July, Fred and I met with Gene and Maizlish to discuss how much money would be involved and how the cover credits would appear. We had had a verbal agreement for months, but still no contract. Maizlish blamed the delay on Paramount, which needed to reach an agreement with Pocket Books. I could never understand why these two entities — one of which (Paramount Communications) owned the other (Pocket Books/Simon & Schuster) — had so much trouble communicating. Weren't they all one big happy family?

Despite these meetings and the pressure from our editor in New York, the deal was still not nailed down, and Fred and I continued to play the waiting game.

On July 25, Ernie, Gene's driver, left for vacation, so I drove Gene to a doctor's appointment with his regular internist's associate. He was given some mental acuity tests, and I asked Gene afterwards how he did. He said he thought he tested okay, since he was so quick that if he showed just average intelligence, it made him look normal! As I puzzled over this, he waited while I had his prescription filled — more codeine tablets for the headaches he said he was still having. This worried me. He had been experiencing these headaches since the UCLA tests more than a month earlier. I wondered if there was a connection, since Gene had seldom complained of headaches before.

A couple of months before all this, a woman from Northern California named Yvonne Fern had contacted Gene about writing a short monograph about him for Berkeley Press' series on geniuses of the twentieth century. Gene was naturally flattered and agreed to participate. Yvonne flew down from the Bay area a couple of times to interview him, but although she was scheduled for several hour-long blocks of Gene's time, and even guested overnight at Gene's home a couple of times, she told me that she was very frustrated because she wasn't getting to spend the time with him she needed, and when she did, he wasn't feeling well enough to be interviewed.

On July 31, Yvonne flew down to attempt another interview with Gene. He and Yvonne were driven to the office by someone from Gene's household, leaving Gene without a car. He then took her to lunch at the Paramount Commissary dining room. Coincidentally that same day, I had planned a surprise birthday party for our secretary, Jana. It was a huge success, but Gene seemed either bored or tired and quite edgy, so we hurried the revelers out of his office as quickly as possible.

Gene seemed frantic to pick up Rod at the Beverly Hills Budget Rent-A-Car, where the seventeen-year-old had been trying to rent a car. Gene phoned Budget several times from the office, arguing with clerks, who simply couldn't bend the rules and rent to anyone under twenty-five. Frustrated and extremely agitated, Gene told Rod to wait there and he'd come pick him up and take him home and asked if I'd mind driving him there.

Part of the personality change Gene had undergone in the past few years had manifested itself in his impatience as a passenger. He would ridicule me if I didn't drive fast enough or if I waited until oncoming traffic was completely clear before making a left turn. He would become especially annoyed if I deviated from the exact route he was expecting me to take to his destination. Driving with him was not the pleasure it used to be. He had become impatient and controlling. Yet I knew how ill Gene was, so I tended to be forgiving. That hot July afternoon, however, I finally reached a breaking point.

Regardless of the hassle of putting up with Gene's back seat driving, I still enjoyed doing things for him. "Of course I don't mind," I told him. "I'm always glad to spend a few minutes with you." Yvonne, who was staying at the Roddenberry's home at Majel's invitation, left the studio with us and settled into the back seat of my Isuzu Trooper, while

Gene sat in the passenger's seat next to me.

All went well until we got close to the Budget office on Santa Monica Boulevard. I had never been that familiar with the area and deliberately avoided driving in Beverly Hills whenever possible, since the traffic congestion, on a par with New York City, always made me uneasy. Because I was unfamiliar with the streets, I tended to be extremely cautious. As we drove through town that day, we passed by some new buildings I'd never seen, and Gene mentioned that they were part of the new City Hall complex. Long before we neared the corner of Wilshire and Santa Monica, I asked where Budget was. "Up ahead" was all I was told. Suddenly, we were upon it, and I was in the center lane, unable to pull over to the Budget office, which was on the far right. Gene became upset and said, "I'll get out here!" "No!" I pleaded, scared that this man who could hardly walk would stumble in the middle of Santa Monica Blvd. And the traffic was moving too fast for him to walk across the two lanes to the curb. So I said, "Don't worry, I'll turn left and circle the block and we'll be back in no time." I was trying to stay calm, to be cheerful, and yet I could sense his anger, bordering on panic.

I glanced over and saw a wild look in his eyes, and then his voice rose and he began really yelling at me. I was embarrassed because we had a guest in the car, and I tried to ignore him as I made my left turn. Once on Wilshire, I found myself again in the left turn lane, with no choice other than to make another left, taking us farther and farther away from our destination. As I signaled for a left, his face became red and blotchy with anger as he suddenly screamed at me, "No, turn right, turn right!" He was indicating one direction, but saying another; he seemed totally confused and even more frustrated because of his own confusion. I was tense and nervous at the whole traffic situation, doing my very best to get us all safely to Budget, knowing that it might take us an extra five minutes or so and that there really was nothing else I could do. Gene's last outburst pushed me beyond my tolerance, and for the first time, I defended myself. "It's my car and I'm doing the best I can!" I said, my voice raised from my own anxiety. "So just let me do the driving!"

That was the only time I had ever snapped in all his years of back-seat driving. After this one and only attempt at self-defense, he seemed to back off. When he didn't say anything, I figured he was really mad at me. I tried to calm him with a joke: "Oh, look, here we are at that pretty City Hall again. I didn't think we'd get to see it twice in one day!" Still, Gene said nothing, sitting with his arms folded over his chest in a huff. Once more around the same block, this time I knew to get into the right-hand lane and managed to find the entrance to Budget, which was not clearly marked. I'd barely pulled up and stopped the motion of the car when Gene, cane in hand, hobbled off to find Rod. As I sat waiting for them with the motor running, Yvonne remarked, "You can't argue with him. He has to be in control. He has to win. I've seen this at his home." She could see my distress, as I was now close to tears. I said nothing. Gene returned with Rod, and the ride continued in silence the two miles or so to his house, where I off-loaded my three passengers. Gene said nothing, but Yvonne said good-bye.

That was the last I heard until the following morning.

LOG ENTRY 55 :

Gene had been scheduled to do a phone interview with *The New York Times* the next morning. I arrived at Paramount by 9:15, the phone already ringing as I walked through my office door. It was John Wentworth, the Paramount publicity executive who had arranged the interview. He told me he had just phoned Gene's house and spoken with Richard Arnold, who was over there on business. Richard had informed John that Gene was ill and was being taken to the hospital. John wanted more information from *me*, but I had no idea what he was talking about. As we spoke, I felt a creeping uneasiness. "I'll call you back," I told him.

I immediately phoned the house and learned from Richard that Gene had been having difficulty communicating and had been rushed to the emergency room at UCLA for an examination. I thanked him, hung up the phone and waited for further word, all the while experiencing helpless feelings of anticipation and dread. I heard nothing until noon, when Gene himself, now back home, phoned me.

"Hi." That was all he said at first, but I knew immediately he was in trouble. I tried to remain calm.

"Hi yourself. I hear you're not feeling well."

"I'm okay. I just can't . . . can't . . ."

"Can't find the right words?" I was good at finishing his sentences for him. Our minds had always been in synch, and I knew he was struggling for words. It was beginning to

On June 6, 1991, the Gene Roddenberry Building on the Paramount lot was dedicated. Afterwards, I posed for this shot with Gene. I love it because we are holding hands in public, framing the name sign for the building! It was our last photograph together.

sound serious, and I was frantic. What should I do next? Make a joke? Ask if I could be helpful? Let him know I care? Oh God, this was horrible.

"I have to go back, to have . . . to have . . . surgery," he said through great effort.

All I could think was, had our spat in the car caused this? "This isn't because of what happened in the car yesterday, is it?" I asked weakly.

"No, no, no. No." He was very forceful now, and I knew he meant it. "I have to go. I . . . love you, darling." I repeated his words back to him, assuring him of my love, yet so frightened for him.

I paced the office most of the afternoon, awaiting some word. Eventually Maizlish phoned me. Gene had undergone surgery for a large blood clot on the brain, a subdural hematoma. It was not a stroke, but had a similar effect. And it was not caused by any argument, that was definite. This had been coming on for quite some time; his argumentativeness was simply a precursor, a warning sign that he was not well. Later, I was led to understand that this may have also been related to the fluid draining procedure in June and the subsequent headaches he experienced.

Maizlish told me Gene was in intensive care, and — and this was the point of his call — *I was not allowed to see him!* I couldn't believe my ears. The man I loved most in the world was lying wired up to machines in a strange room somewhere, possibly dying, and his attorney was telling me not to go to him. What kind of cruelty was this? "If Majel were to see you there, any confrontation might have an adverse effect on Gene." So that's what this was all about. I thanked him for the information and asked what the prognosis was. He hesitated but said the doctors expected him to make a full recovery. He also ordered me not to telephone Gene's daughter Dawn. We certainly didn't want to worry her needlessly, he said.

Brain surgery! Worry his daughter needlessly? How could a child worry needlessly about a parent she loved? One thing was clear — Maizlish was taking control of the situation now. He reminded me of Alexander Haig who rushed to the fore when President Reagan had been shot, sweeping up the reins of office before they had hardly touched the ground. Some people just seem to thrive on power.

Only a few names were on the visiting list, I was told. Majel, of course. Maizlish. Ernie, who was still out of town. Yvonne Fern was on the list, a guest of Majel's who had remained in town at her request, according to Maizlish. And Rick Berman. I phoned Rick in his office, frantic for more information, tearfully pleading with him to tell me everything he knew. He, too, cautioned me not to go up there and upset things. (What had he been told about me, I wondered. Was nothing secret anymore?) I begged him to give Gene my love if he was conscious and to keep me posted. I now trusted him a lot more than I did Maizlish.

I had just fallen asleep that night when my phone rang. "Susan . . . (long pause) . . . Leonard," he said in the familiar sing-song voice he always used to announced himself. It was after 11:00 p.m. The reason for his call? He was upset because someone had notified Dawn! Gene was in intensive care, fighting for his life, and he was worried about who told whom. I assured Maizlish that I had respected his wishes, which I had. (I later learned that Dawn had found out about her dad from her sister's business partner. Darleen was already in Los Angeles at her father's bedside when Dawn finally heard the news.) Maizlish sounded very upset, saying that Dawn had walked in to see Gene, and it had caused him to have a seizure. I knew Maizlish disliked Dawn because it was her husband Richard who had advised Eileen that she was entitled to profits from *Star Trek: The Next Generation*. He saw Rick as the instigator and Dawn as a co-conspirator, although Dawn had always maintained neutrality. It seemed obvious to me that Maizlish didn't want Dawn to know about her father's illness as a way of getting even with her. I learned later that Gene had suffered several seizures that night and over the next few nights, a common side effect of brain surgery, not the fault of anyone.

The following week Ernie returned from his vacation. I still was not allowed into the ICU to see Gene, although by then he was awake and speaking. Ernie phoned me from the hospital his first morning back and told me Gene was asking, "Where's Susan?" I burst out crying. I longed to go to him. This was a living hell; my loved one was asking for me and I couldn't be there for him. The nightmare just kept worsening. "Please tell him I'm waiting until he's stronger before I see him," I said, after I had explained to Ernie the real reason I couldn't be there.

A few days later Gene was well enough to have his own room, with round-the-clock nurses and sitters. Although Maizlish tried to play the hero by calling me to tell me when the coast was clear so I could visit, it was Dawn who really kept me informed. She didn't know of my relationship with her father, but she knew he cared for me deeply and that I had always shown concern for his health. I didn't think it was right to take her into my confidence, since I knew this would violate Gene's wishes, so I just let her know that, yes, I really did care a great deal about her father.

Dawn and I began to form a bond throughout this ordeal — two outcasts who loved this man with all our hearts, relegated to the sidelines. No one was going to keep her away from her dad at this critical time, and she was at his side frequently throughout each day. I got most of my reports on his progress from Dawn, since no one else was giving me the details. She would call me from the hospital and say, "Majel's just left. Come on up." And I'd break all speed records driving across town to be there.

The first time I saw him, nearly a week after the surgery, I was prepared for a shock. He looked better than I had hoped. His head had been shaved and you could see the stitches, but by the time I was allowed up there, any bandages had been removed. He couldn't talk much, just simple things. I joked with him, and he always brightened at my visits. I was optimistic that he was on the road to recovery.

LOG ENTRY 56 :

Gene was released from the hospital after two weeks, to begin the long road to recovery at home. He was depressed and weak. Dawn told me the doctors said his heart was strong and that a full recovery was possible. He had home nurses and sitters and therapists for walking and speaking. He was either bedridden or wheelchair-bound all the time.

There was no talk of his returning to work, although I insisted on maintaining an atmosphere of business-as-usual at the office. Again, this was partly denial on my part, but I also needed to do this out of respect for my employer, who, I was constantly reassured, was expected to make a full recovery. So I was stunned when Leonard Maizlish called me into Gene's office one day — he was using Gene's desk more and more as if it were his own — and told me I would have to fire my secretary, Jana! She had been with us for over three years, and I desperately needed her to help with the huge mountain of *Star Trek* fan mail, not to mention Gene's considerable amount of mail. I had had a secretary since 1976, and I couldn't see how I would function without one. Maizlish was adamant. He insisted we had to "show good faith" to Paramount (I had no idea what he meant) by reducing the size of the office staff and letting Jana go. Reluctantly, I told her she had a month, and that I'd do everything in my power to see that she was relocated within the *Star Trek* family. She took it very well, and I began trying to secure her the show's script typist position. Fortunately for her, the person doing that job was leaving. By the time her secretarial job was phased out a month later, the typist position was hers.

Next Maizlish told me I would have to take a salary cut. I had just fought for and won a raise that January, my first in two years, and I didn't see why I needed to take home less money. I was doing even more work now without Jana. I told him that I still needed Jana's assistance and was planning to pay her out of my own pocket, so I certainly couldn't handle a pay cut. But again, those words "good faith" came up, and I told him that I would offer to pay my own health insurance premiums and drop a few other perks. I failed to see how the savings of perhaps two thousand dollars per year could be of any value or political importance to a company worth millions. But this seemed to satisfy Gene's accountants and Maizlish, and I was able to retain my position.

I visited Gene in his home as frequently as possible. Both Dawn and I were *personae non gratae* in the Bel-Air home, so our visits had to be timed with Majel's golf, shopping or other ventures away from the house. Ernie and Dawn kept me posted as to the best times to visit, and I'd drive right over to see him.

The bedroom had been converted into a sickroom. There was a hired sitter with him at all times, although this distressed Dawn immensely since she felt (and I agreed) that he should have had an RN with him. He was very frail, having frequent bad days, and did not seem to be making great progress.

Majel had gone to La Costa the weekend before Gene's birthday. It was a break for me, as Fred and I went by the house briefly on August 18 to deliver a birthday present and cards. He was not well, however, so we quickly left. Over the weekend, Gene developed a high fever, and on August 19, the day of his seventieth birthday, he was not feeling at all well. His fever was up, and I was unable to visit him. The next day, he was brought to Century City Hospital to determine what could be done. According to Dawn, who spoke with his doctor, Gene was suffering from malnutrition, but she felt the doctor was withholding the full story.

I was unable to visit Gene at Century City, since by now it was impossible to predict when Majel might appear, and no information was forthcoming from either Ernie or Maizlish. They simply didn't care if I visited. Maizlish also did his best to exclude Dawn from knowing how her father was doing. Dawn called me as much as possible to report on his condition, giving me news of any difficulties he was having.

Gene returned home on August 24, and I managed to sneak in a visit as soon as it was safe. He brightened immediately. A couple of times he sent his sitter into the kitchen, then had me close the door and stretch out on the bed next to him and hold him. He seemed so sad and lonely, existing in some sort of twilight world of the half alive. I tried to act upbeat, hoping he would feel this way, too. Knowing of his love for the Horatio Hornblower books, I asked if he would like me to read to him, since he couldn't sit up or concentrate well enough to do this for himself. He was overjoyed, and I began reading *Beat to Quarters*, his favorite in the series. I tried to involve him in the story, asking him questions about the naval terminology he knew so well. "What does 'larboard' mean?" I inquired, but he could only shake his head and say, "I don't know." This brilliant mind now lay in fragments before me. I hoped it could be put together again.

I read to him on a few more occasions, and he appeared to be following the story, nodding as I tried to be as dramatic as possible with words I knew he had long ago committed to memory. More than once he dozed off in the middle of the half-hour readings, a pleasant smile on his face, no doubt dreaming of his hero, the naval captain who had been the blueprint for James T. Kirk.

We were about halfway through the book, and I was really enjoying sharing these moments with Gene. Then one Monday, as I prepared to continue the story, Ernie informed me that he had finished reading it to Gene over the weekend. I had a tough time containing my disappointment, but I didn't want Gene to see me upset. At first, I was furious with Ernie, as I felt he was extremely insensitive to the importance of my sharing these moments with Gene. But then I realized that this was not out of character for Ernie. After all, he had taken it upon himself to assume many of my duties. During the year and a half since Gene had hired him simply as a driver, he had begun opening and answering Gene's home mail, handling calls to the house and even setting up meetings for Gene, all without properly consulting with me. I guess it probably never occurred to him how much pleasure reading to Gene gave me. But in the end, I was glad Gene had a chance to hear his favorite story, which was what really counted.

While Gene was convalescing at home, plans were under way for a back-to-school celebration for Rod on August 31 — a hundred and fifty teenagers and three rock and roll bands would be blasting away within yards of Gene's sickbed! I asked Maizlish if he couldn't talk them out of it, but he was unable to. The party went on as planned, and Gene was checked into a nearby hotel for the night, along with his nurse.

Early in September, our friend from Scotland, Janet Quarton arrived. She had had a standing invitation to visit Gene and me for over a year, since back then we had thought there would be a twenty-fifth anniversary celebration. Gene had known Janet nearly as long as I had, having corresponded with her since the mid-'70s. Janet was very active in British fandom and we had enjoyed visiting with her and her family on separate occasions during various trips to Britain. This was her first trip to the U.S., and I invited Janet to stay in my guest room, but because of Gene's poor health, it was not the happy visit she'd been awaiting all these years. I drove her over to his house several times when Majel was out, and Gene acted pleased to see Janet, even though they weren't able to converse much. Janet wanted to bring him a gift, so we went to the supermarket and bought all sorts of sugar-free chocolates and sweets for diabetics, which delighted Gene.

Star Trek's twenty-fifth anniversary fell on a Sunday evening, and nothing was planned by the studio. I couldn't bear to let the day pass without some sort of recognition, so I set up a dinner at the Old Spaghetti Factory in Hollywood for about twenty fans and friends, including Janet. The high point of the evening was a planned telephone call to Gene at his home. When Gene came to the phone, we all gathered around the receiver and shouted, "Happy Anniversary, Gene!" After that we all went back to our pasta and garlic bread. I never had a chance to speak with him personally.

No sooner had Janet returned to Scotland than I had to leave for New York. I hated being out of town for even a minute while Gene was so ill, but I had no choice. I had won this trip earlier in the year in a raffle, and I had invited my secretary, Jana, as my guest. It was an all-expenses-paid deluxe vacation including accommodations at the Ritz Carlton and tickets on MGM Grand, the plushest planes in the sky at that time. From New York, I checked with the office daily, hoping for any word from Ernie or Richard on Gene's condition, which remained status quo. I relaxed for the moment as we saw the sights of the city. I even treated Jana to a daytime ride through Central Park in a horse-drawn carriage, which jolted my memory of a happier time when Gene and I had driven through the park one romantic evening so long ago.

I was more anxious than ever about Gene's condition when I returned to town. Dawn had gone by the house for a visit on the morning of October 11. She called me later and said she was worried that her father didn't seem to be having a very good day and that his speech seemed incoherent, but that she had been asked to leave when the therapist arrived. Around noon, I got a call from Maizlish, telling me that Gene had been taken back to Century City Hospital. He apparently had suffered another stroke. *And under no circumstances was I to tell Dawn*. That game again! I no longer cared. Gene was gravely ill and I refused to play any more games. Still, I knew Maizlish held most of the cards, and I felt intimidated. I compromised. I immediately phoned Dawn and told her that there was something I was not supposed to tell her, but she ought to phone the house at once and inquire about her father. When she got nowhere with the maid, she took the step of phoning his doctor, whose receptionist gave her all the details.

Gene was sent home two days later, his right side now even weaker than before. I was unwavering in my optimism, but Maizlish had been telling people that Gene had less than three months, at best. I refused to listen. I had never allowed myself to use the "d" word. I loved Gene so much, surely he would bounce back. He always did.

But I was beginning to wonder just when that might be.

LOG ENTRY 57 : "Phillippe's? Where is that?" I asked when Ernie called.

It was Monday, October 21, 1991 — the first day of the new workweek — and he was asking if I wanted to join Gene and him for lunch at Phillippe's. I had never heard of this restaurant, a downtown Los Angeles institution credited with inventing the French dip sandwich. I didn't eat red meat, but who cared? I was going to have a chance to see Gene, away from the house, without the worry of a close encounter with Majel.

Ernie had been taking Gene for drives these last couple of weeks, and although I worried about his strength in attempting to do too much, I was at the same time pleased, thinking that he must be strong enough for these outings.

Ernie pulled Gene's Rolls up to the Paramount main gate, and I jumped in the back seat where his nurse's aide/sitter was already buckled in. From the front passenger seat, Gene grinned and said only, "Hi!" but it was enough to raise my spirits. He said little else on the six-mile drive along the Hollywood Freeway. We exited on Alameda Street, and I was reminded of happier days when I would take the same off-ramp to Union Station to greet Gene after his train rides up from La Costa. Phillippe's was on Alameda, not far from the station, and had a convenient parking lot behind the restaurant, a rarity for downtown L.A. The nurse helped Gene from his front seat into the wheelchair, which had been stowed in the car's trunk. I was surprised at the amount of difficulty she had getting him into the chair. This strapping six-foot woman virtually lifted him while Ernie rolled the chair into position. It had to have been humiliating for Gene, although he didn't complain. In fact, he didn't say much of anything.

Phillippe's had sawdust on the floor and rows of long tables and benches, one of which had to be removed from one side of a table to accommodate Gene's wheelchair. With Gene and the nurse properly ensconced, Ernie and I stood on line for the food. I was terribly depressed by Gene's appearance, and for the first time I feared the worst. He did not look like a man who was on the road to recovery.

"Ernie," I ventured gently, "what will you do if something happens to Gene? Do you think you'll stay on with Majel?" I was surprised at my own ability to sound so nonchalant. His answer surprised me even more. He told me he would, if the deal was right. I didn't perceive any regrets or sadness as he spoke, just a matter-of-fact, business-as-usual attitude. The whole conversation was eerie, and I too felt a detachedness I didn't think myself capable of.

We returned to the table with trays laden with food — Ernie with beef sandwiches for Gene, the nurse and himself, and me with a salad. Throughout the meal, Gene was silent. His right arm hung uselessly by his side as he used the fingers of his left hand to convey the morsels of juicy meat and bread dripping with gravy into his mouth. It wasn't pleasant, but I overlooked this as I smiled cheerily up at Gene's eyes, hoping he might gain some strength from the fortitude I was attempting to convey.

After a struggle into the car at the end of the meal, we drove back to Paramount. Gene seemed exhausted from the whole ordeal. As I rose to exit from the car, I leaned over into the front seat, kissed him lightly on the lips and whispered, "I love you."

I never saw him again.

< < <   > > >

The next day, Tuesday, Gene was driven to a screening of the newly completed film *Star Trek VI: The Undiscovered Country*. I begged Leonard Maizlish to allow me to attend, but again I was reminded of the possibility of a Majel confrontation that might alarm Gene. Ernie Over, Richard Arnold, Majel, Maizlish and a handful of production executives were the only people in the 400-seat Paramount Studio Theater. Gene was on the Paramount lot for the first time since the end of July, but he didn't come anywhere near the office. He was whisked in and out for the screening. I was told by one of the people attending that he seemed frail and disoriented, and his only comment on the film was a constant repetition of the word "no." What he meant by that can only be guessed. Before his illness, he had expressed his dissatisfaction with the script. From his reiteration of the word "no," it was apparent that he disliked the movie as well.

Two days later, Thursday, would be the saddest day of my life.

On October 24, a tape of the completed *ST:TNG* episode of "The Game" had finally arrived in our office, and Fred Bronson came over to watch it with me. It was our third sale (our second show to be filmed), and even though we received a story (but not teleplay) credit, we had been very close to this production from its inception to completion. We eagerly looked forward to seeing it all put together. Watching the tape, we were pleased for the most part with the results. Then Fred and I had a pleasant early bird lunch at the Commissary. We returned to the office around a quarter to one, and while Fred sat on Gene's office couch making business phone calls, I began finalizing some story pitches we planned to share with producer Jeri Taylor that afternoon. About an hour later, Jeri poked her head into my office to say she wouldn't be able to meet with us, as there was a big production meeting, and she would have to postpone our session. No problem, as this would give us additional time to prepare. I continued working at my keyboard, occasionally calling out to Fred, who was still seated on the nearby sofa.

Around three o'clock in the afternoon, I became aware of a number of people suddenly filing down the hallway. They seemed to be hurrying to a meeting. I could hear one of the writers saying something about "Michael Piller wants everyone in his office right away." It must be an important script meeting, I thought. But then I noticed not just writers, but secretaries and typists and production assistants heading off toward Michael's office, which was diagonally across the hall from mine. One of the secretaries called out to me that this meeting was indeed for everyone, meaning me, so I saved what I'd been working on at my computer and joined the throng now assembled in Michael's room.

What was going on here? Had someone done something really terrible on the set for which we were about to be chewed out? An assembly like this was unprecedented. Michael's eyes darted anxiously around the room. Richard Arnold walked up to him and whispered something in his ear, and Michael just shook his head.

"Is everyone here?" Michael asked. Total silence.

My thoughts raced ahead of his words. *Please don't say it. Say it's a problem on stage. Say someone did something terrible and now they're fired. Say anything else.* I waited, I dreaded, I knew. Before he had uttered a single syllable, I knew.

My eyes were aimed directly at Michael's as he cleared his throat and began to speak.

"I have the sad duty to inform you . . ."

That the stage has been destroyed? That the show has been canceled? I knew I was thinking frantic, foolish thoughts, but my mind's defenses kept at it.

". . . that Gene Roddenberry died this afternoon."

"No!" I screamed, burying my face in my hands. Someone's arms were around me, perhaps those of several someones. I was too numb to see. Escorted by this sea of gently comforting arms, I was helped to my feet and out of the room. I raced to Fred, still chatting away on the phone.

"Hang up the phone!" I cried. Taking a look at my face, he unquestioningly set down the receiver. "Gene's dead," I sobbed, and buried my head into Fred's chest.

It seemed only a few moments later when I looked up to see a studio security guard. "I'm sorry, but we're going to have to lock up these offices."

"No!" I wailed. "You can't be serious!"

"I'm sorry. I have my orders."

Who was this Nazi, I thought, telling me he had "orders?" This was *Gene's* office, these were *his* things; *I* was responsible for all this, just as I had been for 17 years, and now some stranger was telling *me* to get out?

I rose slowly to my feet, still holding onto Fred. The guard, meanwhile, began dialing his headquarters, presumably for backup, since this hysterical, weeping person was not being cooperative.

At that moment, Dawn Roddenberry materialized at my office door. How? When? Questions rushed through my mind, but all I could do was throw my arms about her as we held on to each other, crying and sharing our mutual loss. She had heard the news only thirty minutes ago and had phoned Richard Arnold to tell him that she wanted to break it to me in person. Unfortunately, Michael Piller didn't know this, and by the time Richard had tried to clue him in, I had already been summoned to his office with the others.

Between crying jags, I was still arguing with the guards (there were several now), who were patiently trying to get me to leave. Dawn's mother's attorney, Nona McPherson, had driven Gene's distraught daughter there, and she tried to get me to calm down. The guards would not allow me to remove even my own personal possessions from my office, insisting that everything had to be sealed. What were they afraid of? All I wanted were my many years of photos and books and souvenirs and knickknacks that I had used to decorate my walls and desk. Dawn, too, was hoping to retrieve some keepsake, a memory of her father — perhaps some item he had loved or a favorite picture. I offered her the framed *Time* magazine inside cover from Gene's office. I had personally done the framing and had hung it just inside his office, behind my own wall, which had no more room. The guard wrested it from my hand, telling me that nothing could leave the room. Ms. MacPherson, who was a calming influence on both of us, spoke with the chief of security, who promised I could return in a day or two to retrieve what was rightfully mine. While I was pondering this, a studio locksmith arrived and began replacing all the door locks with new ones. Then two workers with dollies showed up to remove our filing cabinets from Jana's office across the hall. These were wheeled into Gene's office and the door behind them was locked.

Moving the cabinets drove it home. In less than an hour I had gone from panic, to grief, to anger, to frustration, and back to grief again. My world, so serene just a few hours earlier, was a maelstrom of confusion and disorganization.

I was aware of someone telling me it was time to leave. I took a sad last look around, then all of us — Fred, Dawn, Ms. MacPherson and myself, were ushered out. Behind us, the door, now with a new lock, was firmly bolted shut.

In the hallway, everyone was telling me how sorry they were that I had lost my boss. My boss! Of course — what did they know? Rick Berman came over and hugged me and asked me if there was anything he could do. "I need a job," I said, half-joking, half-serious. Even as I said it, I suddenly realized it was true. My future was a blank.

I was helped to my car and cautioned to drive carefully. This wasn't easily accomplished, since everything was blurry from the tears I couldn't stop shedding. As I headed home, I turned on the radio, hoping it would help me escape, but the wire services had already picked up the news. Not even my own car was a place of refuge. I switched to an all-music station, and Bette Midler's hit, "Wind Beneath My Wings" was playing. It touched a nerve. I had never listened closely to the words before, but as she sang the line, "Did you ever know that you're my hero?" I completely lost it and had to pull over. It seemed she was singing about me, about Gene. Did he know he was the wind beneath my wings? I hoped he did. I had never told him he was my hero.

Now, I never could.

LOG ENTRY 58 :

Fred had to catch a plane to London later that afternoon, and I didn't want to be alone in the evening. Richard Arnold and his mother Denny offered to come by, and I jumped at the chance. They stayed for a while and even helped me field phone calls from the press, which had somehow gotten hold of my home phone number. Once, I picked up my telephone and to my own horror said, "Gene Roddenberry's office." I was running on automatic, which was fortunate, since the reporter who was phoning had actually thought he was dialing Gene's office. After that, Richard fielded my calls, and I avoided the phone for most of the evening.

Later that night, my phone rang constantly with comforting friends. One call, though, was from Maizlish, who was all business. He wanted to discuss my future, and would I mind coming in tomorrow to go over things and to discuss severance? I told him indeed I would mind. "I'm taking off a day to mourn," I said with determination. His attitude puzzled me. He had just lost his supposed best friend, and all he wanted to do was discuss business!

Saturday, October 26, two days after Gene died, a party was held at the Roddenberrys' house. Majel had been planning a Halloween party for several weeks, despite Gene's weakened condition. Even Leonard Maizlish's pleadings couldn't get her to cancel it. Tents had been ordered, caterers had been arranged, food had been planned, guests had been invited. I was appalled.

The party went ahead as scheduled. I was informed by a friend that the party would now be considered a wake for Gene (a custom he once told me he detested). Some of the guests (mourners hardly seems an appropriate term) even had the chutzpah to show up in costume, not having gotten the word that out of respect for the deceased, costume wearing was a no-no. Live bands played; there was food, music, and much merrymaking — including magic tricks performed by a strolling amateur magician.

Although grief-stricken, I managed to get through the weekend before the inevitable confrontation with Majel at the studio on Monday. Leonard Maizlish phoned me several times to set things up. One minute I was going to be allowed to continue working for several weeks, the next I was not. He brought up the question of severance pay, and I was in too much shock to think clearly. I asked for two months' worth. I was offered four weeks, plus pay for my two remaining weeks of vacation. I agreed. I was later told by several friends that I had been too quick to settle, that I had not realized this was a cheap way of writing me off. After seventeen years of continued loyal service with hardly a sick day, standard procedure dictated that I should have received anywhere from six months' to a year's worth of salary as severance.

"Gene, what will happen to me if anything happens to you?" I had asked him many years before, when he was healthy and this seemed a distant impossibility.

"Leonard Maizlish will see that you are taken care of," he promised. And Gene frequently reassured my concerned mother that there would always be work for me if anything ever happened to him. He told my mom and me that there were years worth of manuscripts to be sorted through and updated, perhaps published posthumously, and I would be the best one to do this. So I always believed that my life's work would be cataloging and preserving the archives of Gene Roddenberry to safeguard his legacy.

It soon became clear to me that the only one Leonard Maizlish was taking care of was Leonard Maizlish.

I arrived at the appointed hour on Monday. The others were already there. Majel, however, was over in Rick Berman's office, so we had to wait. I was told that she, not a guard, was going to control what I would be allowed to take home. Along with Leonard Maizlish, she had brought David Alexander, now firmly entrenched as "Gene's biographer," and her loyal friend. I had no one there as my own advocate, although Richard Arnold volunteered to act as an impartial observer.

Majel entered my office, and while I was terribly nervous, I had been brought up to show respect for people in grief.

"My condolences to you, Majel," I offered, my quavering vocal chords not doing much to hide the trepidation I was feeling at having to speak with her after so many years of non-communication.

"Thank you," came the unemotional reply. If she was suffering any grief, I didn't see any signs of this.

Empty boxes had been brought in for my use, and I felt like some sort of criminal, scrutinized like a prisoner as I sorted through my things. Anything that wasn't obviously mine — that didn't have my own name on it or a personal label — was not to be removed. All my *Star Trek* books, the product of many years of collecting, were carefully checked to see if I had written my name inside, or if they were autographed. If they were one-of-a-kind and unmarked, they had to remain "for our files," I was informed. This was simply nonsense. Every book on my shelf had been given to me by Paramount, duplicates of the ones Gene had received and had taken home. Every item of merchandise on my shelves was also given to me by the studio in their kindness and gratitude for my helping with *Star Trek* continuity. My home was small, without much storage space, so I had long ago chosen to keep my collection at the office. It also brightened up the place as well as being handy for reference. Many of these were books I had approved for Bantam during the days when I'd assisted their editor. I was told that unless copies were found at the Roddenberry house, I could not have them. Fine, I agreed. I just wanted this nightmare to be over.

I pulled Leonard Maizlish aside. I was sure he would understand. He knew of my special relationship with Gene and how this behavior would have shocked and hurt his late friend. Surely, I had an ally in Maizlish. But he told me it would be best if I just went along with it. My heart sank.

In the hallway, Majel and Maizlish were arguing loudly over my severance pay. He seemed to be sticking up for me on that point. She left finally, and Maizlish told me to get out a clean sheet of typing paper. He stood behind my chair and began to dictate a letter, which I typed with shaking hands. I had no idea what this was all about, and I certainly hadn't planned to do any work that day. But he hovered close behind me and I felt confined. I was still grief-stricken and not thinking clearly, so I did as he demanded.

The letter was from me to him, releasing Gene's production company from all claims and accepting the severance pay. "Shouldn't I have an attorney of my own to look this over?" I asked. He told me I could trust him, to just sign it. Gene's words from so many years ago still echoed in my head: "Leonard will look out for you." I felt like the room was closing in on me. "Sign it!" he insisted again. In my haste to break away from this situation, I did as he commanded. I signed, and by doing so I had, in effect, just signed off on any possible wrongful termination suit I might ever consider, although at that moment I didn't know such a thing even existed. I had never had much contact with lawyers.

That, like so many things these past few days, was about to change.

Forest Lawn Memorial-Park

❀❀❀❀❀❀❀❀❀❀❀❀❀❀❀❀❀❀❀❀❀❀❀❀❀❀❀

Memorial Service

GENE RODDENBERRY

Service held
November 1, 1991 - 2:00 p.m.

at the
Hall of Liberty

❀❀❀❀❀❀❀❀❀❀❀❀❀❀❀❀❀❀❀❀❀❀❀❀❀❀❀

Vocalist
Ms. Nichelle Nichols

Pianist
Mr. Nathan Wong

Speakers
Mr. Ray Bradbury - Ms. Whoopi Goldberg
Mr. Christopher Knopf - Mr. E. Jack Neuman
Mr. Patrick Stewart

Scottish Pipers
Mr. Eric Rigler - Mr. Scott Ruscoe

Service conducted by
Forest Lawn Mortuary, Hollywood Hills

LOG ENTRY 59 : I had been excommunicated.

Not in the religious sense, unless *Star Trek* was considered a religion. (Fans had often tried to make that comparison, but Gene hated such references.) No, the attitude was more like I was an extra appendage, now extricated from the body, removed as quickly as possible. I had been so closely tied to Gene, that with him gone, it was clear to those in charge that I would no longer be needed. Perhaps it was because my being around would be like having Gene looking over their shoulder. So I was treated as an outsider.

I knew this was true the first Monday after Gene had died, as I said good-bye to my old office and to my co-workers. Rick Berman wanted to see me. I went to his office in the Cooper Building, trudging up the steep stairs for what would be the last time, the same steps I used to fret about whenever Gene made the climb. I was seated in Rick's office, and we talked privately. I thanked him for the tapes of our episode, "The Game," which he had given Fred and me. I told him how sad I was that Gene had never even had a chance to see it. Everything seemed so unreal, this meeting, these good-byes.

"I'd really like to continue working on the show," I said, hopeful that my many, many years of experience could be put to good use.

"I'm afraid there is nothing now. Perhaps in a month or two . . ."

"What about reading scripts? There are about two hundred piled up in Eric's office. I know *Trek*. I know good writing. Why not put me to use as a reader?" I knew there was a solid six months' worth of concentrated reading, which would keep me busy until something else might open up.

"Sorry. That's a union position. I've tried to get others into the readers' union, but unsuccessfully."

That was it, then. Rick was telling me he had nothing for me, no work, no ideas, and from his lack of enthusiasm, no interest in pursuing this any further. We parted friends; I still hoped that Fred and I could sell scripts to the show, and I had begun to feel more relaxed around Rick.

But I was on a road to nowhere.

I went to Michael Piller's office, also to say good-bye and to let him know I forgave him. I doubt he thought he needed forgiving; he probably didn't realize that his bad tidings the previous Thursday had put me in a shoot-the-messenger mood all weekend. I apologized for my thoughts and felt better after that. I don't know if Michael felt anything. He was, as usual, inscrutable.

A good part of the remainder of the week was spent thinking about my future. I had a friend, Michael Grusd, who owned a travel agency and who once had invited me to work with him. He knew of my interest in the field; in addition to having visited virtually each of the United States, I had traveled to nearly fifty countries over the last twenty-five years. Perhaps this experience could be turned into a new career. I thought about whom I might line up as clients.

The reality of my excommunication from *Star Trek* hit me at Gene's memorial service on November 1, eight days after his death. I assumed I would be seated with my colleagues from the office. Leonard Maizlish, who had planned the event, had asked me where I wanted to be, and I told him, "With my friends from work." Instead, I was seated off to the far left with the only familiar faces being Gene's son-in-law — a family outcast who was not allowed to sit with his wife, Dawn — and Nichelle Nichols, in the row in front of me. Nichelle soon left, however, as she went to take her place on the stage so she could sing her song, "Gene."

I was really too dulled by grief to care where I sat. I was so glad when the whole thing was over. I had invited a few close friends to be with me back at my house. I wasn't the grieving widow, but I still felt like one. I needed to have the company of people I liked. Later, a few of us went down to the corner Thai restaurant for supper. My friends have told me of this; I don't recall the dinner at all, my mind having gone on hiatus most of the day as a defense mechanism.

I felt sad, not only at my loss of Gene, but at the loss of people I had once called friend. I had received a lot of support from my family and close friends, and many wonderful cards from *Star Trek* fans, but surprisingly, none of the *TNG* cast wrote or phoned, although I did have a good cry on Marina Sirtis' shoulder. She seemed a lot like her character at that moment when I ran into her on my last day on the Paramount lot. Perhaps she was becoming an empath like Deanna Troi. I sensed a genuine concern for my feelings. I was very touched. Only one other cast member expressed sympathy to me — I received a thoughtful card from Ann and Mark Lenard (the late actor who played "Sarek," Spock's father). I was very moved that they took the time to remember me. I was also delighted with the cards from hundreds of fans who didn't know me personally but wrote to express their condolences "upon the death of my friend and associate," as one put it. It was very touching to know these people cared and were sensitive enough to share these feelings. Gene had always had such a fondness for the fans.

People continued to write to me for months afterwards with their comments about the show, assuming I would always be a part of *Star Trek*. It seemed so natural after all those years, with our names linked together as a team. So much mail was arriving that I rented a post office box. One of the production assistants from the studio was kind enough to forward my mail. Then, six months later, this mail abruptly stopped. It didn't trickle off — there just ceased to be any more letters coming from the studio. I think the Paramount mailroom returned it to the senders, or maybe they just tossed it. Who knows? I still correspond with a number of fans who became good friends over the years, but I miss the chance to interact with new ones through our letters.

My abrupt eviction from *Star Trek* left me shell-shocked. I hadn't envisioned myself in a world without Gene and without continuing to do the work I so loved. After more than seventeen years, it was tough to be a civilian again. I hadn't just lost my job — I'd lost the central focus of my life. I never thought of what I did as my *work*. It defined me as a person. It was simply who I was and what I did.

When I realized I was truly on my own, one of my first concerns was to ensure I was emotionally centered. I didn't want to go into the clinical depression I had endured when my father died back in 1982. I had a couple of sessions with my former therapist, who assured me that I was definitely grieving properly; no doubt the entire box of Kleenex I used during each session was his first hint. I was on the road to recovery. I just had to watch out for the potholes.

I began having dreams. I would dream Gene wasn't really dead and that it was all a mistake. There were dreams of meeting Gene in a mysterious far off place that was also near. In one such dream, I told him I was unhappy without him and asked why couldn't I just stay there, where he was? He said it was not my time, I was not allowed to be there. It seemed so very real, I almost felt as if he was trying to communicate with me from some other plane of existence. He probably would have been the first to laugh at this silly superstition. Sometimes when I'd be in that shadowland of half-awake, half-asleep, I felt as if he were in the room with me. I would try so hard to see him, always just beyond my limited human vision. I realized these events were just my mind's way of helping me cope with death, but at the time, some of these experiences felt very real.

Once, about a year later, I had a strong impression that he was guiding me. I was on a weeklong scuba diving trip, trying to cope with the trepidation I felt as I was about to make my first night dive. I donned my gear and got into the rough seas along with the more experienced divers. A few yards from the boat, I suddenly chickened out and aborted the dive. I was terrified as the crew hauled me back aboard. The sky was inky black, the sea even blacker. It didn't matter that we had underwater lights. I wasn't going down. The next night, we were anchored in a peaceful cove in only twenty feet of water, and I was determined to try again. I was still pumping massive amounts of adrenaline as I began gearing up. Then the most peaceful feeling suddenly passed through me, and I felt a strong, almost familiar presence. It was not like anything I'd ever experienced before. If I had to give it a name, I would have called it "Gene." As a skeptic and rationalist, I know it was only my imagination, perhaps remembering the story of Gene's bravery when he had gone diving in Bimini so many years before. Whatever it was, I spoke out loud, "Okay, I'll do it." I felt calm and safe as I entered the water, convinced that nothing would go wrong. And, of course, nothing did.

LOG ENTRY 60 :

Before Gene died, I had been involved in several *Trek* projects that were now left dangling. *Star Trek: The First 25 Years*, the long-awaited coffee table book, was still in limbo, and I began to seriously doubt the promises of "Oh, we still hope to publish that."

Fred Bronson and I had been faithfully pursuing *The God Thing*. I had had it retyped, had begun a detailed pencil edit, and had noted several places where we were planning on expanding the manuscript. It had been Gene's fervent wish that we complete this project for him, and we had had lengthy talks about it with editor David Stern at Pocket Books. We had waited patiently for six months for our contracts, which Leonard Maizlish had been negotiating with Paramount and their licensee, Pocket Books. Two days after Gene died, Leonard telephoned me to say that Fred and I would no longer be working on the project. It wasn't hard to guess why.

Another project that had been pending was an animated series Fred and I had been developing for over a year, with Gene's blessing, for the Fox Children's Network. My good friend Margaret Loesch, whom I had known for over twenty years since the days when we were both rookies in the entertainment business, was now president of Fox Kids, and she was very interested in our proposal for *Starfleet Academy: The Animated Adventures of Wesley Crusher*. Early in October 1991, Margaret had finally been able to arrange a lunch to pitch this to John Pike, then-president of network television for Paramount. Unfortunately, the pitch meeting was the same week that Gene died. Prior to the lunch, Pike had indicated to her that the studio was willing to entertain her ideas for an animated series, but at the lunch Margaret learned that Paramount was no longer interested. The studio had just approved a new live-action *Star Trek: The Next Generation* spin-off and had no wish to pursue any other incarnation of the *Star Trek* franchise. Thus died our animated project.

What new spin-off? Certainly not the one Gene had nixed two years before, during the third season, when Michael Piller and Rick Berman had proposed a new series to Gene. I had asked him about it immediately after his meeting with Piller, and Gene said he wasn't interested in their proposal. He told me had turned them down flat, saying he didn't want a spin-off, and that he did not care for this one. I never heard another thing mentioned about it until the week after Gene's death. That same week Margaret was told about this new series, Piller and Berman received a go on something called *Star Trek: Deep Space Nine*. Talk about timing. I wondered if it was just a coincidence that Paramount decided to go with a new *Star Trek* project less than one week after Gene's death.

To my knowledge, Gene had never given his blessing to the spin-off. Nevertheless, under the guidance of Rick Berman and Michael Piller, the series proved successful. Yet another new spin-off, *Star Trek: Voyager*, later served as the flagship for the Paramount-owned network, UPN. Its last episode aired in 2001. After that, another new series, a prequel set a hundred years before Kirk and Spock, called *Enterprise* (minus the *Star Trek* moniker for the first time) premiered in the fall of 2001. Nothing would have pleased Gene more than to have grandfathered a whole new universe.

< < <   > > >

After a couple of weeks without work, I phoned my travel agent friend Michael and told him I had decided to take him up on his offer. He informed me that he couldn't pay me a salary, a situation I hadn't anticipated. If I were to make any money, I would have to supply my own clients, drum up business on my own, and work in outside sales. Any money I'd be earning would come through commissions only. I sent out hundreds of fly-ers announcing my new career. I printed up business cards. I took classes in my newly chosen profession. Then I waited for the phone to ring. And waited. And waited. Eventu-ally, I did get a couple of clients. Jana, my former assistant, then still working on *Star Trek* as the script typist, proved to be a loyal client. She phoned me whenever she needed to fly up to visit her mom in San Jose. At about a hundred dollars a ticket, my commission came to roughly four dollars and fifty cents, after taxes. She flew there about once a month. I also booked a couple of tickets to New York — a few here, a few there. But most of my friends and family said they felt awkward about "bothering me." At least I was signed up for unemployment benefits, which netted me about two hundred ten dollars a week (before taxes).

Fortunately, I had my writing. Thank you, Gene, for putting me on the writing path, back when I wrote my first magazine articles; you really were my mentor. The other day I found a note Gene wrote to me in 1975, when I had sold one of my first articles describ-ing a day at Paramount. On his personalized notepaper, he handwrote the following:

S   ,

<u>Very</u> good column. Nice personal touch to what would otherwise come off as a fairly tedious day. Have no fear. You <u>are</u> a good writer. Now, can you also be a good (and when necessary ruthless) editor & critic of your own work? In months to come, we'll see.

G (over)

P.S. I think you'll learn to handle that fine, too.

But even as I was beginning to work on various writing projects, it took a long time for it to sink in that my *Star Trek* days were behind me.

I think the first time it really hit me that my excommunication was final, and I was no longer in the loop, was at Deforest Kelley's Hollywood Walk of Fame star ceremony, held on my birthday, December 18, 1991. It was already a depressing birthday without Gene to celebrate with me. Then, at the ceremony on Hollywood Boulevard, I stood outside the VIP area with a group of fans. Sue Keenan, president of De's fan club, managed to get me into her roped off area, but I was no longer in with the cast and crew who had always seemed like an extension of my own family. I felt confused and alone.

I was a civilian again, and I'd better get used to it.

LOG ENTRY 61 :

Within a short time following Gene's death, I became aware of a controversy surrounding his will. I had known for many years that Gene had included me in the will. For one thing, when I had presented him with the original art that had graced the cover of the *Philadelphia Inquirer* Sunday Magazine back in 1980, I had attached a piece of red tape to my gift: I asked him to promise to will it back to me when he died. I loved this interpretation of him, not merely because it portrayed him handsomely, but also because it seemed to capture the soul of his intelligence. He readily agreed, and not long afterward told me that his will had been completed and I was remembered in it, not only with the picture, but monetarily as well. I told him I didn't want to hear of such things, that they depressed me, and anyway, this wouldn't happen for years and years. However, I did see that draft of the will when it crossed his desk in the early '80s, and sure enough, I had been mentioned for a generous gift of cash as well as the portrait.

Shortly after Gene's death, his daughter Dawn filed a will contest. This was not a question of greed. Dawn's husband had just won a multi-million dollar lawsuit against the City of Los Angeles, so she was not doing this for the money. She believed that her father was ill and had not clearly understood the terms of the most recent draft of his will when he signed it on August 24, 1990. She insisted that her dad had told her many times in the past that he loved all his children equally and intended to provide equally for them, one-third of the residual estate to each child. Instead, the will left a cash amount to each child, and one-half of the residual estate to Rod, with the remaining half split between the two daughters. In filing her contest, Dawn risked losing everything, as the will had a "no contest" clause, but Dawn, urged on by her husband, Rick, felt there was a principle at stake and proceeded with her case.

At the same time, preparations were under way for Eileen's civil trial. During their divorce proceedings in 1969, Eileen had dismissed the opportunity to share in any profits from Gene's television properties, with the exception of *Star Trek*. Why had she felt so strongly about this show? For one thing, when the kids were little, the family would go camping and lie out under the canopy of nighttime stars. Gene would make up stories for his kids, and Eileen suggested, "Someday, why don't you write a show about the stars?" When he finally began working on his pilot script in the early '60s, she was thrilled to have been a partial influence. She believed in the project from the start. When they divorced after twenty-seven years of marriage, she still believed in it, although no one could have predicted its huge success.

Now she was staking her claim to what she was convinced the court had granted to her in her community property settlement, i.e., fifty percent of Gene's share of *Star Trek*'s profits. When Gene had been alive, I had only heard about this from his point of view, and naturally I felt the way he did. But now I began to rethink the situation, trying to be more objective.

I was called in for depositions, a terrifying experience for someone who had never been involved in such a heavy-duty case before. Depositions are really fishing expeditions — both sides of a case trying to learn just what you know and how helpful or harmful that testimony might be.

I was, for example, asked outright if I had had a romantic, sexual relationship with

Gene. Who were these people to be asking me such things? I was not on trial. I felt it was none of their business.

At first, I refused to answer the question. However, there was a retired judge present to mediate the deposition, and he insisted I respond. I reluctantly agreed. I had never broken Gene's sacred trust by discussing our love with anyone other than my closest friends and family. But now I was being asked to spill my guts to a room full of strangers who kept pounding at me with a barrage of personal questions.

Later, I asked Eileen's attorneys what possible bearing this could have on their case. Didn't I get it? When the case went to trial, they would try to discredit me as a scorned woman. What? Gene never scorned me! I never had any marriage designs on him. How ridiculous, I thought. After viewing the evidence, I believed that Eileen's claims were legitimate — and I awaited the date when I could give my truthful testimony in court, regardless of how the opposition tried to paint me.

The week before I was to testify, I thought of a way to help clarify things for the judge — a visual presentation that would show the commonality between the two series, *Star Trek* and *Star Trek: The Next Generation*. Dawn's husband Rick Compton rented time at a video facility that catered to the legal profession, and I searched through hours of my own videotapes to find the proper footage. We prepared a tape which, we felt, showed that these shows were two peas in the same space-pod. The two captains recited virtually identical opening narrations; people used the transporters and beamed their molecules through space; *Enterprise*s labeled NCC-1701 and NCC-1701-D both plowed through the galactic void; both captains expounded on the Prime Directive and recorded their Captain's Logs; both shows had Vulcans, Klingons and Romulans, and so on.

I was called to the stand on May 14, 1992, one of the first witnesses to testify. This was my first experience of being in a courtroom, and it was much smaller than I had thought it would be. Perry Mason's court always looked as if it could hold a small city — judge, jury, lawyers, witnesses, visitors and a gaggle of reporters. Fortunately, this room had almost none of that — no jury was present, as the judge alone would hear this phase of the case. There were one or two spectators, but there hadn't been much publicity before the date of the actual trial, so the gawkers were kept to a minimum. Majel, Ernie Over, Richard Arnold, Yvonne Fern and a couple of others were seated in one row. Eileen, Dawn, her husband Richard Compton and I were seated directly behind them. This first-ever visit to a court gave me the jitters and made me think back to the terrible stage fright I'd experienced in my early days of appearing at conventions.

Once I settled into my seat in the witness box and answered some preliminary questions from Eileen's attorney, I got over my nervousness. The room was darkened and the videotape unreeled before the mystified judge, who until that moment, *had never seen Star Trek!* Yes, there were still a few people left on this planet who were *Trek* virgins. But I knew I had won over this justice, eighty-year-old Judge Macklin Fleming, when the tape ended, the lights came back up, and he asked, "How do they land the ship?" I promptly launched into a technical, convincing description of how the transporter worked as if we were discussing some extant reality instead of fiction. As I watched the judge nodding his comprehension, I stifled an impulse to laugh at the seriousness being afforded this fantasy television series.

Cross-examination wasn't as much fun. Majel's attorney as well as Leonard Maizlish (a defendant in this lawsuit, representing himself) both tried to trip me up and embarrass me, but Judge Fleming was having none of it as I sailed confidently through their questioning.

Judge Fleming decided in Eileen's favor, agreeing that both series were indelibly intertwined. A second phase of the trial was later held, having to do with the financial aspects of the franchise and how much she should be awarded. She won that suit as well. However, when the jury did not award Eileen any participation profits from the animated series, the movies and merchandising, she eventually appealed to the California Supreme Court, which refused to hear the appeal. This left intact a state appeals court ruling in favor of Gene's estate. Also, the estate appealed the lower court's decision and had Judge Fleming's judgement overturned as well, ruling that Eileen was entitled to a share of the profits from the original series, but nothing else.

During this time, I still had not completely severed the umbilical that connected me to the *Star Trek* universe. Although I was no longer involved in the production of the show, people continued to associate me with it. Most of the fans just assumed that my involvement was eternal, never realizing that *Star Trek* was, when all was said and done, just a well-paying job and not my birthright. It felt very odd, since my own self-image for so many years had been *Trek*-connected, too. I still can't watch an episode of *TNG* without wondering how it might have been improved, or what Gene would have felt about it. For example, a year or so after Gene's death, I began to notice that there was an increasing tendency on the part of the writers to masculinize the series. Obviously, this was because most of the writers and producers were male and were concerned less with the political correctness of content and more with the quality of the stories in general. During the early seasons of *TNG*, I was constantly on the lookout for gender-discriminating terminology, and when I was able to put a few words into Gene's ear, he would always agree that such things were important. Apart from the previously mentioned switch to "Where no *one* has gone before," I monitored scripts for things like "crewman," which would always be changed to "crew member," and sentences like "My men are working on it," which could easily be changed to "my staff (or crew) are working on it." These were subtle but (I felt) important contributions towards updating the '60s mentality of the original series. So I was startled to hear lines like "Take a four-man team" to do such-and-such, and seeing female officers being saluted crisply with "Yes, *sir!*" In semantic terms of equality of the sexes (which is an important reflection of a society's attitude), the show seemed to me to have taken a serious leap into the past, rather than the future.

In the year following Gene's death, I received invitations to several fan-run conventions, including one in Kansas City over the Fourth of July weekend and one that took me to Glasgow, Scotland, in mid-July. My biggest challenge was to come up with a talk that would be appropriate for these groups. I was no longer a cheerleader for *Trek*, as I had been for the past eighteen years. Instead, I decided to do a loving tribute to Gene through slides and music. Fred Bronson helped me prepare a tape of the three songs I felt were the most representative of my days with Gene and *Trek* (without giving away our private relationship): "The Way We Were," by Barbra Streisand, "The Wind Beneath My Wings," by Bette Midler, and "Imagine," by John Lennon. I selected slides from my personal collection of photos of Gene and myself, together and individually, on the sets and enjoying the adventure of life.

LOG ENTRY 62 : Gene's daughter Dawn continued to pursue her will contest throughout most of 1993, and I again found myself enmeshed in the litigation process. Since I was one of the heirs, the attorneys for both sides were obligated to furnish me with copies of all motions and briefs, declarations and statements, which crammed my mailbox unceasingly. Countless trees were sacrificed so that my overwhelmed letter carrier could keep his appointed round with my tiny mailbox; eventually, after much gnashing of teeth (his) and back-breaking hikes up long flights of stairs (mine) laden with the latest from attorneyland, I gifted said postal worker with an industrial-size mailbox.

As preparation for the case progressed, I began to grow weary of the paper chase fluttering past my doorstep, until one day late in 1993 a sworn declaration from Dr. P. Joseph Frawley arrived in the mail.

What he said gave me the shock of my life.

Dr. Frawley had never met Gene Roddenberry. At the time of his declaration, he held a medical degree from the University of Southern California, and was certified in Chemical Dependency by the California Society for the Treatment of Alcoholism and Other Drug Dependencies. He had authored numerous books and professional papers, and he was the Chief of Staff of the Schick-Shadel Hospital in Santa Barbara. Dawn selected him for his expertise in these areas, and in preparing his written declaration, he reviewed Gene's medical records. Here are some excerpts from that statement, filed with the Superior Court of the State of California, for the County of Los Angeles:

> From my review of Mr. Roddenberry's admission to Schick-Shadel Hospital in September of 1986, Mr. Roddenberry stated that he needed a drink upon awakening in the morning and consumed a half a bottle of wine or six cocktails per day over a period of fifteen years . . . in May, 1988, Mr. Roddenberry was drinking three times a week and sounded confused and intoxicated. He admitted . . . using Desyrel two to four times a day and he was placed on Trandate and Micronase . . . He began taking Ritalin sometime between 11/88 and 1/89 . . . In July, 1989 . . . he admits to two beers or scotches per night plus Dexamil or Ritalin, and that he has continued to use cocaine and it makes him nervous. He reports a bout of dizziness and a fall without any reported head injury . . . On July 31, 1989, he reports being out of it, confused and suffering from light-headedness . . . has been taking long naps in the afternoon, feels tired a lot and suffers from some confusion . . . he has doubled his dose of Prozac and that he has been very irritable with a change in his mood.

It got worse. The doctor described Gene's MRIs, the pictures taken of his brain, showing cortical atrophy and multiple strokes. He reported on dizziness, depression, gait difficulties, aphasia (groping for words) — all much more severe than I had ever realized. In an effort to spare me any worry, Gene had always denied that the doctors were able to determine what was wrong. It is also quite likely he denied this to himself. Dr. Frawley continued with a list of characteristics of dementia as exhibited by "this patient":

> Alcohol dependence, chronic over twenty years with impairment in memory and

accelerated brain aging with dilated ventricles and cerebral atrophy. . . . Mr. Rod-denberry also exhibited all the signs of sub-cortical dementia (Biswanger's Disease) and elements of normal pressure hydrocephalus . . . In reviewing all of the docu-mentation available, it is my opinion that the patient suffered a gradually recog-nized dementing condition or conditions which were exacerbated or accelerated by his use of both licit and illicit drugs and alcohol, as well as his underlying med-ical problems of hypertension and diabetes, and his depression . . . [It] is my opin-ion that the decedent had a dementing condition with associated exacerbating factors that could have impaired his ability to sufficiently concentrate, read and understand a forty-one-page complex legal document in August, 1990.

This key piece of evidence never had a chance to be heard in court. The trial was set for November 14, 1993, but at the last minute, Dawn withdrew her contest. Her hus-band, Richard Compton, had fallen gravely ill with lung cancer and was now living what the doctors predicted would be his final year. (He eventually lost his life to lung cancer in May, 1994.) During these final days, Rick needed her by his side to care for him and con-tinue to be the loving wife she had always been, and Dawn told me that she did not wish to waste any of her strength battling in the courts while her husband faced the biggest battle of his life. She chose to be by her husband's side, even though her attorneys said she had a strong case.

Dawn had another reason for withdrawing, in addition to her husband's precarious health. A few days before she was set to have her day in court, Dawn learned of a leak to the media that would have turned her father's life into a public spectacle. More than any-thing else, she did not want to see this become yet another Hollywood media circus with glaring lights and prying cameras carving up the raw flesh of her father's tragic life in a tabloid feeding frenzy. Several months earlier, one of the tabloids had printed a sleazy, misinformed story that claimed Gene's daughter was branding him a drunken sot. Dawn cried for weeks over this one-sided defamation of his character; she was determined not to let it happen again.

Although Dawn withdrew her case, the lawyers for the estate of her father convinced the judge that she had triggered the no contest clause, and Dawn did not receive any of the inheritance her dad had intended for her.

I can't help but wonder what Gene would have made of all this.

My conclusion: he never should have left us.

EPILOG :
Gene's been gone more than ten years. In that time, there have been three new *Star Trek* TV shows, several movies, a bazillion new items of merchandise and a theme ride in Las Vegas. No doubt there will be versions of Gene Roddenberry's creation for decades to come.

We've lost many beloved friends connected to *Star Trek*, including actors DeForest Kelley and Mark Lenard. Costume designer Bill Theiss died of AIDS, as did artist Mike Minor. Make-up artist Fred Phillips lived well into his eighties and is no longer with us. Others, too numerous to mention, are now gone.

Many of the people connected with *Star Trek* are still involved with various aspects and incarnations of the show. And there are the new, non-*Trek* series — the "Roddenberry franchise," as one source referred to it — based on scripts or ideas that Gene had once proposed, then moved on.

We all move on. Life is about change. In a way, it unreels like a long movie, with a beginning, middle and eventual "Fade Out, The End." Gene Roddenberry filled my Act II, the middle of my personal movie. It was a pivotal point in my life, a time when I learned to love and be loved.

And now it's on to Act III.

Star Trek fans frequently use Mr. Spock's Vulcan expression of parting, "Live long and prosper." But Gene Roddenberry seldom used that phrase. He almost always signed his photographs with "Live long, love long!"

Armed with this and other life lessons that Gene taught me, the love that he shared with me, and the passion for living that he instilled in me, I look forward to the richness that life in this universe promises.